Introduction to Area-Based Anti-Aliasing for CGI

Michel A Rohner

Gotham Books

30 N Gould St.
Ste. 20820, Sheridan, WY 82801
https://gothambooksinc.com/

Phone: 1 (307) 464-7800

© 2024 *Michel A Rohner*. All rights reserved.

No part of this book may be reproduced, stored in a retrieval system, or transmitted by any means without the written permission of the author.

Published by Gotham Books (June 1, 2024)

ISBN: 979-8-88775-974-6 (P)
ISBN: 979-8-88775-975-3 (E)

Because of the dynamic nature of the Internet, any web addresses or links contained in this book may have changed since publication and may no longer be valid.

The views expressed in this work are solely those of the author and do not necessarily reflect the views of the publisher, and the publisher hereby disclaims any responsibility for them.

Contents

Chapter 1 Introduction 1
   1.1 From TV to CGI 1
      1.1.1   TV Images and Displays 1
      1.1.2   TV Images and Movies 1
      1.1.3   Interlaced Display 3
      1.1.4   Progressive Displays 4
      1.1.5   Color Display Standards 4
      1.1.6   TV Images vs CGI 6
   1.2 CGI 6
      1.2.1   Early CGI Contributors 7
      1.2.2   Evolution of AA in RT CGI Systems 10
      1.2.3   Data Base Models 11
      1.2.4   2D Coordinate Systems 11
      1.2.5   Database Coordinate systems 12
   1.3 Geometry Transformations in 3D and 2D Spaces 15
      1.3.1   Objects in 3D Space 15
      1.3.2   Object Transformations of from 3D to 2D 15
   1.4 Image Rendering 20
      1.4.1   Image Plane and Image Size 20
      1.4.2   Image Coordinates 22
      1.4.3   Rendering Triangles 24
      1.4.4   Selecting the Pixel Sample Point 25
      1.4.5   Pixel Sampling with Jaggies 28
   1.5 Color Space 31
      1.5.1   RGB in Color Space 31
      1.5.2   *YCbCr* in Color Space 32
      1.5.3   Color Space and Conversion 33
   1.6 The Link DIG and the E&S CT-5 35
Chapter 2 Aliasing 37
   2.1 Aliasing and Anti-Aliasing 37

	2.1.1	Aliasing 37
	2.1.2	Anti-Aliasing and Edge Smoothing 37
	2.1.3	Digital Signal Processing 38

2.2 Simple Example of Signal Sampling 38

2.3 Anti-Aliasing in Real Time CGI Systems 40

	2.3.1	Definitions of AA for RT CGI with the 5 A's 40
	2.3.2	Spatial and Temporal Image Artifacts 41
	2.3.3	Double Imaging 50
	2.3.4	Definition of Aliasing in Broadcast TV 53
	2.3.5	Sine Function and Frequency 53
	2.3.6	Aliasing when Sampling a Sine Function 54
	2.3.7	Sampling Frequency and Nyquist Frequency 54
	2.3.8	Sampling of a Sine Function as Aliasing Example 56
	2.3.9	Aliasing when Sampling a Sine Function 57
	2.3.10	Sine and Cosine Functions after Sampling 61

2.4 Sampling of TV Signals 63

	2.4.1	Standard TV 63
	2.4.2	High-Definition TV (HDTV) 66

2.5 Aliasing with Digital Signals 66

	2.5.1	Point Sampling and Z-Buffer 67
	2.5.2	Sampling Frequency and Nyquist Frequency 67
	2.5.3	Checkerboard Pattern with 1 Sample per Pixel 68
	2.5.4	Box Filter and Frequency Response 75

Chapter 3 Anti-Aliasing 79

3.1 SSAA and MSAA 79

	3.1.1	Super Sampling AA (SSAA) 79
	3.1.2	Multi-Sample AA (MSAA) 80

3.2 Processing Subpixels as Bed of Nails 82

3.3 MSAA and the 8 Queens Puzzle 83

3.4 Introducing Area-Based Anti-Aliasing 90

	3.4.1	ABAA vs MSAA 90
	3.4.2	Comparison of MSAA vs ABAA with 4 or 8 Subpixels 92

3.5 Selecting Subpixels for AA 92
    3.5.1   Advantages of ABAA over MSAA 97

Chapter 4 Area of Trapezoid 99
4.1 Optimized Edge Definition for Area-Based Anti-Aliasing 99
4.2 Area of Trapezoid 100
4.3 Implementation of ABAA with Subpixel Areas 104
    4.3.1   ABAA with 4 Subpixel Areas 104
    4.3.2   ABAA with 8 Subpixel Areas 106

Chapter 5 Rendering Polygons and Triangles 109
5.1 Image Coordinates 109
    5.1.1   Fixed-Point and Floating-Point Image Coordinates 110
5.2 Projected Triangles into Image Coordinates 112
    5.2.1   Basic Triangle Edge Definition 112
    5.2.2   Edge Parameters Computation 113
    5.2.3   Edge Definition for Triangle Rendering 115
    5.2.4   Definition of Edge Directions and Types 116
    5.2.5   Rendering a Triangle Inside of Spans 119
    5.2.6   Edges Traversing Spans for Triangle Rendering 121

Chapter 6 ABAA with 4 Subpixel Areas 127
6.1 Solution with 4 Square Subpixel Areas 127
    6.1.1   ABAA vs MSAA Examples with 4 Subpixels 130
6.2 Example of ABAA4-X with Fans of Thin Triangles 132
    6.2.1   Comparison of ABAA vs MSAA with 4 Subpixels 132

Chapter 7 ABAA with 8 Subpixel Areas 137
7.1 ABAA8-X Solution with 8 Half-Square Subpixel Areas 137
7.2 Comparison of ABAA8 vs MSAA8 144
    7.2.1   Thin Triangles Processed with 8 Subpixels 144
    7.2.2   Four Examples of ABAA8 vs MSAA8 with Tri-Fans 144

Chapter 8 Inside the Binary World 147
8.1 Programmer and Computer Interaction 147
    8.1.1   Fixed Point vs Floating Point 147
    8.1.2   Inside each Computer there is a Binary World 148

  8.1.3 Pixel Colors and ARGB Color Components 149

 8.2 Decimal vs Binary Number 149

  8.2.1 Decimal Digit vs Binary Digit 150

 8.3 Binary Numbers 152

  8.3.1 Operations with Binary numbers 152

  8.3.2 Boolean Single-Bit Operator 154

  8.3.3 Integer Multiple-Bits Bitwise Operator 157

  8.3.4 Binary Coded Decimal Integers 157

 8.4 Comparison of Different Integer Types 158

  8.4.1 Integer Tables 158

References 161

About the Author 171

List of Figures

Figure 1-1 TV Image 2
Figure 1-2 TV Image with Interlaced Scanlines in Field0 and Field1 3
Figure 1-3 Progressive Display Image (Non-Interlaced SLs) 4
Figure 1-4 Triangle In 2D Coordinate System 12
Figure 1-5 Gaming Area and Coordinate Systems 14
Figure 1-6 Triangle, Strip and Fan 15
Figure 1-7 Vertex Translation 16
Figure 1-8 Vertex Vt Rotated into Window Coordinate 17
Figure 1-9 Window Clipping 18
Figure 1-10 Projection from 3D to 2D 19
Figure 1-11 Triangle In 2D Image Coordinates 20
Figure 1-12 Image Size of *PixMax* Pixels by *SLMax* Scanlines 21
Figure 1-13 *(Pix, SL)* and *(xi, yi)* Coordinates 22
Figure 1-14 Single Sample Point Selection 24
Figure 1-15 Sample Point Selection 25
Figure 1-16 Pixels Located Inside of *SL* and *Pix* Grid 28
Figure 1-17 Assign Color Using 1 Sample Point per Pixel 29
Figure 1-18 Mix Color of Half-Covered Pixels 30
Figure 1-19 Pixels along SL with *ARGB* or *RGB* Color Components 32
Figure 1-20 Pixels along SL with *YCbCr* Color Format for Television 33
Figure 1-21 *RGB* and *YCbCr* in Color Space 34
Figure 2-1 Sampling Example of Sprinter Running *100 meters* in *10 seconds* 39
Figure 2-2 Edge Stairstep and Edge Crawling 42
Figure 2-3 Examples of Narrow Face Breakup 43
Figure 2-4 Examples of Face Popping 44
Figure 2-5 Example of Moiré Pattern 45
Figure 2-6 Checkerboard with Squares Equal to Pixel Size 46
Figure 2-7 Checkerboard with Squares Greater than Pixel Size 47
Figure 2-8 Small Checkerboard Moving 1/4 Pixel to the Right 48
Figure 2-9 Displayed Squares from Shrinking Checkerboard 49
Figure 2-10 Example of Double Image 51
Figure 2-11 Double Imaging During Plane Roll 52
Figure 2-12 Sine and Cosine Functions 54
Figure 2-13 Signal to Sample and Signal after Sampling 56
Figure 2-14 Aliasing when Sampling Sine Function 59
Figure 2-15 Aliasing when Sampling Cos Function 60

Figure 2-16 Signal to Sample and Signal after Sampling 61
Figure 2-17 Cosine Function Sampled at Nyquist Frequency ($fN=2*fS$) 62
Figure 2-18 Sin and Cos Func Sampled at Twice the Nyquist Freq ($2fN=4*fS$) 62
Figure 2-19 Pixel Data Sampling and Transfer 65
Figure 2-20 Sampled Signal with 1 Sample per Pixel 70
Figure 2-21 Checkerboard with Squares Equal to the Pixel Size 71
Figure 2-22 Sampling when Sample Freq > Nyquist Freq 72
Figure 2-23 Checkerboard with Squares Close to the Pixel Size 74
Figure 2-24 Pixel Frequency Equal to 1/2 Nyquist Frequency 75
Figure 2-25 Two-Dimensional Box Filter in Spatial Domain 76
Figure 2-26 Box Filter in Spatial Domain and Frequency Domain 77
Figure 2-27 Box Frequency Response with sinc() Function 78
Figure 2-28 Signal to Sample and Signal after Sampling 78
Figure 3-1 Examples of Pixel Divided into Subpixels or Bed of Nails 80
Figure 3-2 Examples of Subpixels for MSAA 81
Figure 3-3 Edge to Subpixel Distance in (xi, yi) Coordinate System 83
Figure 3-4 Knights and Queens 85
Figure 3-5 Solution where no more than 2 Queens are aligned 87
Figure 3-6 Four Examples of 8 Queens Solutions 88
Figure 3-7 Identified ¼ Pixel Gaps in 8 Queens Solutions 89
Figure 3-8 Comparison of Subpixels with ABAA and MSAA 91
Figure 3-9 SSAA Examples of Triangles and 4x4 Subpixels 93
Figure 3-10 SSAA Examples of Triangles and 8x8 Subpixels 94
Figure 3-11 SSAA Examples of Triangles and 4x8 Subpixels 94
Figure 3-12 MSAA or BON: Examples of Triangles and 8 Sparse Subpixels 95
Figure 3-13 ABAA Examples of Triangles and 4 Subpixel Areas 96
Figure 3-14 ABAA Examples of Triangles and 8 Subpixel Areas 96
Figure 3-15 Number of Intensity steps for ABAA8 and MSAA8 98
Figure 4-1 Area Measurements when Intersection within 0.0 and 1.0 101
Figure 4-2 Pixel Covered Area Computation for *VE* 102
Figure 4-3 Pixel Covered Area Computation for *HE* 103
Figure 4-4 Four Subpixel Areas Intersected by *VE(BE)* and *HE(BE)* 105
Figure 4-5 Four Cases of Edge Crossing 4 Subpixel Areas 106
Figure 4-6 Expanding 4 Subpixels to 8 Subpixels 107
Figure 4-7 ABBA 8: 4 Cases of *BE* Edges Moving Across Pixels ($|Slp|<0.5$) 108
Figure 5-1 2D Orthogonal Coordinate Systems 109
Figure 5-2 (Pix, SL) and (xi, yi) Image Coordinates inside Square Canvas 111
Figure 5-3 Triangle Consisting of 3 Vertices or 3 Edges 113

Figure 5-4 Triangle in 2D Image Coordinates 114
Figure 5-5 Beginning and Ending Edge Types 116
Figure 5-6 Edge Parameters Decoding 117
Figure 5-7 Eight Cases of Edge Types 118
Figure 5-8 Triangle Rendering According to Edge Info 120
Figure 5-9 Span Traversing with 3 Triangle Edges 122
Figure 5-10 Processing of Edges E0 and E1 124
Figure 5-11 Processing of Edge E2 and Final Triangle 125
Figure 6-1 Pixel Covered Area Computation for Negative VE 127
Figure 6-2 Pixel Map with 4 Edge Cases for ABAA4-X 128
Figure 6-3 Flowchart to Decode Subpixel Mapping for ABAA4-X 129
Figure 6-4 ABAA4-X: Four Cases of Edge Crossing 4 Subpixel Areas 130
Figure 6-5 ABAA4-X vs MSAA4: Moving edge across 4 Subpixels 131
Figure 6-6 ABAA 4 vs MSAA 4 for Pos Edges A 133
Figure 6-7 Summary of Results for 4 Examples with 4 Subpixels 134
Figure 7-1 Example of Pixel Covered Area Computation for Negative VE 137
Figure 7-2 Pixel-Map with 8 Edge Cases for ABAA8-X 138
Figure 7-3 Subpixel Coverage Decoder for ABAA8-X 139
Figure 7-4 Example of Slope Transition from S0 to S1 for d=0.0 141
Figure 7-5 ABAA8-X: 4 Cases of Edge Moving Across 8 Subpixels (S0: |Slp|<0.5) 142
Figure 7-6 ABAA8-X: 4 Cases of Edge Moving Across 8 Subpixels (S1: |Slp|>0.5) 143
Figure 7-7 ABAA8 vs MSAA8 for Pos Edges A 145
Figure 7-8 Four Cases of Thin Triangles with 8 Subpixels 146
Figure 8-1 Interaction between Programmer and Computer 148
Figure 8-2 AND, NAND, OR and NOR Truth Tables and Gate Symbols 155
Figure 8-3 Exclusive OR and NOR Truth Tables and Gate Symbols 156

List of Tables

Table 1-1 TV Standards 5
Table 1-2 Graphics Display Resolution 5
Table 2-1 TV Digital Encoding 64
Table 2-2 Checkerboard Squares Near Pixel Size 73
Table 3-1 Intensity Jumps for Knights and Queens 85
Table 3-2 Comparison of Intensity Steps vs Edge Slopes 98
Table 8-1 Comparison between Decimal and Binary Numbers 150
Table 8-2 Numbers and Bases 151
Table 8-3 Decimal 1k vs Binary 1k 152
Table 8-4 Operations with Decimal and Binary Numbers 153
Table 8-5 Examples of Bitwise AND, OR, EX-OR and Invert 157
Table 8-6 Decimal Numbers vs EBCDIC 157
Table 8-7 Decimal vs Binary Positive Integer Numbers 159
Table 8-8 Decimal vs Binary Negative Integer Numbers 160

Preface

Anti-Aliasing (AA) is an important topic in Computer Generated Imagery (CGI). Several AA techniques have been developed for non-real time CGI applications. For real-time (RT) CGI applications, algorithms are limited to methods that can produce new images at rate of at least 50 images per second.

Multi-Sample or Multisampling AA (MSAA)

For RT CGI applications like computer games and flight simulators, the most widely used approach is Multi-Sample AA (MSAA). It consists of taking several samples within a Pixel and averaging the results. Also, see references [60] to [69].

Area-Based AA (ABAA)

In this book a new approach to AA is introduced, the Subpixel Area-Based AA (ABAA). Instead of sampling Subpixel points inside of a Pixel, ABAA computes the area that is partially covered by polygons within a Pixel. Then, it assigns this area to Subpixel Areas. Unlike MSAA, ABAA does not require multiple image computations.

My implementation of ABAA has evolved over the years. I have implemented and simulated several solutions to AA. In this book, I describe my latest ABAA implementations with 4 and 8 Subpixels. ABAA and MSAA approaches are compared, using many examples with analytic approaches as well as computer simulations. With half the number of Subpixels, ABAA can achieve an image quality comparable to MSAA, and at a significant lower cost.

The ABAA implementation described in this book is patent pending (Provisional Patent Application 63/549,290).

Three versions of the book

I have released 3 versions of this book about "Anti-Aliasing". The information provided in these 3 books is similar, but directed at different audiences.

The 'New Area-Based Anti-Aliasing for CGI' version contains more detailed analysis and descriptions of AA, for those interested in more technical depth. It also shows how the ABAA algorithm can be expanded from 4 and 8 Subpixels to 16 and 32 Subpixels.

The 'Anti-Aliasing with MSAA vs ABAA' version contains the same subjects but with less analysis details. This should make it more accessible for most readers.

The 'Introduction of Area-Based Anti-Aliasing for CGI' version is a brief introduction to ABAA.

Computer Generated Imagery (CGI)

Computer Generated Imagery [50] consists of computer applications for creating images in art, printed media, video games, simulators and computer animation. For CGI, the most generally used approach is to process models made of polygons (mostly triangles) in 3D coordinates, then project them onto a 2D image plane. The rendering consists of assigning the contribution of one or more triangles to each Pixel (abbreviation for Picture Element) of the computer-generated images.

There are other approaches like 'ray tracing' and 'voxel processing', that are even more computation intensive. But these implementations are not part of this book.

Non-RT CGI

At first, CGI consisted of static pictures, then movies that were produced in non-real-time.by general purpose computers. Because of the amounts of computations, most of the new algorithms for CGI were executed in non-real-time using the fastest computer systems. It took many hours (or even days) and many high-speed computers to produce beautiful 3D graphics static images and animated scenes for TV commercials and movies.

Triangles Forever

Because of my experience and emphasis on fast processing for 3D RT CGI systems, I am mostly interested in algorithms that use triangle processing. The algorithms described in this book assume triangle processing, at least, in the last step of rendering.

For curved surfaces, there are algorithms for creating models with curved surfaces using bicubic patches. They can produce more realistic images. But these models still have to be converted into triangle meshes [13][14][15] in 3D space before the projection onto the 2D image plane. Then the projected triangles can be rendered by the computer hardware.

As the RT CGI processing hardware has evolved with curved surfaces and 3D texture, the computer-generated images are becoming more realistic. But one thing has not changed: the last step in rendering still consists of mapping small triangles onto image Pixels. During rendering, the Pixels covered by the projected triangles are assigned colors samples derived from these triangles. When taking only one single sample per Pixel from the triangles, the sample color is assigned to the whole Pixel. The resulting image shows distracting effects, or artifacts. One approach is to take several samples per pixel, at the cost of increased processing time or more expensive hardware.

This book presents an efficient method for rendering triangles with minimum artifacts. Instead of taking sample points, the area that the triangle covers in a Pixel is assigned to a set of Subpixels with equivalent area.

Aliasing in CGI

For CGI, each image consists of 2 dimensional arrays of Pixels (picture elements), each having a single color. These arrays consist of *PixMax* Pixels horizontally by *SLMax* Scanlines vertically. VGA (Video Graphics Array) was an early standard from IBM for color display adapters in Personal Computers (PC). It has an image resolution of 640x480 Pixels. For HDTV, the image resolution can be 1920x1080, or even UHD at 3480x2160, which is common today.

When each Pixel is computed using a single sample, the resulting images show 'aliasing artifacts' such as stairsteps on feature edges, also referred to as jaggies. In dynamic scenes, 'aliasing artifacts' are more noticeable, resulting in edge crawling, line breaking and small features popping in-and-out of the scenes.

Aliasing artifacts can be minimized, if not eliminated by applying anti-aliasing (AA) techniques. There are several early articles from *Ed Catmull*, *F.C Crow* and *Jim Blinn* about AA for non-real-time solutions, such as Super-Sampling (SSAA). With SSAA, static images using one sample point per Pixel are computed at higher resolutions, then downscaled with filtering (2048x2048 to 512x512 for example). Because of the large amounts of computations, SSAA is not suitable for RT CGI applications. For RT CGI applications like computer games and flight simulators, a similar approach consists of Multi-Sample AA (MSAA). With MSAA, several images are generated by selecting a selection of sample points, or Subpixels, within Pixels. The anti-aliased image is produced by averaging these images. Because of the burden of generating several images, MSAA methods can be computation intensive and costly.

Designing Hardware for RT CGI

I have many years of experience designing several 3D RT CGI systems with innovative approaches to Subpixel Anti-Aliasing. I got involved into 3D computer graphics when there was a rapid development in 3D computer graphics algorithms. I was fortunate to get my first US job at the Advanced Product Operation (APO) of Link Flight Simulation in Sunnyvale, CA. The Link Company had a long history designing simulators and trainers for the Army, Navy, Air Force and NASA [90]. It has been the leader in Flight Simulators [81] since WWII, after Ed Link invented the Blue Box [98], the first Flight Simulator that was used to train around half a million pilots in WWII. Since then, the Link Company had delivered many Flight Simulator systems for the US Military and NASA. For airlines, there were flight simulators from other companies that produced lower cost systems.

Soon after joining Link Flight Simulation, I became one of the key designers and architects for the company's first Digital Image Generator (DIG). The Link DIG was a high-speed computer for producing RT CGI. Because of their cost (above $1M), only 4 companies could design and deliver such RT CGI systems at that time. Most of these RT CGI systems were used in flight simulators to train pilots for the US Military and NASA.

The DIG was a specialized computer generating 3D scenes in real-time to be used in aircraft simulators. The first DIG was delivered to NASA at the Houston Space Center, TX, for training astronauts in the Shuttle Mission Simulator (SMS) [96]. At the time of delivery, the Link DIG was the fastest RT CGI system in the world. It had edge smoothing and could produce out of the windows images made of 4000 projected triangles (12,000 edges) at a rate of 60 times per sec. With a price tag of $2M dollars, the DIG systems were not available to the general public. A total of four Link DIG systems were delivered to NASA in Houston for the SMS.

I continued working at Link for several years, making many improvements to the DIG. During a period of 10 years, Link sold around 70 flight simulators with 3 or 4 window displays driven by DIG systems, for use in helicopter and military aircrafts.

Anti-Aliasing in RT CGI

Besides the need for high-speed computations, edge smoothing was an important requirement for RT CGI systems to be delivered to the US Military and NASA. Distracting artifacts like jaggies, edge crawling and faces popping in-and-out of scenes were not allowed. It was considered as 'negative training'. So, I was involved with AA early on in my engineering career.

In the 1990s 3D RT CGI became feasible for implementation in the PC market. In 1996, while working at Oak Technology in Sunnyvale, I was one of the main designers of the Warp5, one of the first 3D graphics adapter/accelerator for the PC Market. Several members of the Warp 5 design team had experience designing RT CGI with AA for the Military and NASA. The Warp5 was the only PC graphics adapter with AA. There were many other 3D graphics adapters in the industry that were producing images using a Z-buffer with only one sample point per Pixel. Some were fast, but had jaggies. The Warp5 was the only adapter that could process anti-aliased images with 8 Subpixel samples, referred to as Bed of Nails (BON). A few years later, some manufacturers started to produce adapters with MSAA, but at the cost of reduced performances.

The AA solution adopted by most PC card manufacturer was Super-Sampling (SSAA) or Multi-Sample AA (MSAA) with reduced system performances. In the mean-time, I have experimented with various AA methods, including my own Area-Based AA (ABAA) algorithms. After several improvements, I have come up with the ultimate and best ABAA solution.

MSAA vs ABAA

There are several advantages of Subpixel processing with ABAA over MSAA. It will be shown with examples and simulation that ABAA is widely superior to MSAA.

For example, assume that each Pixel contains N Subpixels. Then consider a triangle edge moving over time from one end to the other end across a Pixel. For a good AA solution, is should be expected that when an edge moves across a Pixel, it should result in N equal color transitions, or increments. This is not true for MSAA

In the **MSAA** Implementation, the number of covered Subpixel is detected with point sampling.

1) Since MSAA uses Subpixel point samples, there are always pairs of Subpixels that are aligned with some edge orientations. For example, with 8 Subpixels there are at least 7+6+5+4+3+2+1=28 such pairs. Each time an edge moves across a Subpixel pair, it results in one double increment instead of 2 distinct increments.

2) The increments are not evenly spaced.

3) The quality of MSAA depends on edge orientation. It works fine for triangle edges that are near horizontal or near vertical. It produces the worst results for edges that are near 30 degrees.

4) The detection of covered Subpixels points is more computation intensive.

In the **ABAA** implementation, Pixels are subdivided into N Subpixel Areas of equal size. As an edge moves in any direction across the Pixel, the covered Subpixel Area corresponds to the Pixel covered area.

1) As an edge moves across a Pixel, the covered area gradually increases from 0.0 to 1.0, in N increments evenly spaced.

2) The quality with ABAA is independent of edge orientation.

3) There is no need for Multi Samples. For each edge position, the sampled area is detected in only one sampling, or measurement.

ABAA is the Green Solution to AA

When compared to ABAA, because of the duplication of circuitry, MSAA implementations require more HW and thus produce more heat.

Although the derivation of the ABAA algorithm may be harder to understand, its implementation with logic circuits is simpler than MSAA.

There are many advantages of ABAA.
- Better Image Quality, with less Subpixel samples when compared to MSAA.
- Proposed implementations are more accurate and can be scaled to 4 and 8 Subpixels.
- Simpler implementations resulting in lower system energy and cost.

Motivation to Write a Book

While designing high speed computer hardware, I developed several techniques of my own. I wanted to share my ideas with other engineers and scientists. So, I thought that by writing books, I could show with examples how these ideas lead to better logic designs [19]. I hope to get feedbacks from the readers about improving on some of my ideas and about other applications.

In my first book, 'New Fixed-Point Math for Logic Design' [6], I have showed how computations with Fixed Point binary numbers and *rounding* off partial results can lead to problems. I have introduced a new approach that avoid these problems. When fixed-point numbers need to be truncated, '*averaging*' should be used instead of '*rounding*'. There are examples of how math functions can be implemented efficiently with interpolation. The ABAA algorithm presented in this book is a result of applying these concepts to Subpixel computations.

This book, 'Introduction to Area-Based Anti-Aliasing for CGI', is the result of the many years of experience dealing with Anti-Aliasing. It is a brief introduction to a new solution that uses Area-Based Computations to solve aliasing problems. It is then compared with the widely used methods that rely on Multi-Point-Sampling.

Summary of the Chapters

Chapters 1 to 3 provide understanding about current algorithms for 3D graphics and antialiasing with SSAA, MSAA and BON.
Chapters 4 to 7 describe my new ABAA solution for AA.
Chapters 8 is a brief introduction to Binary Numbers and Boolean algebra.

Description of the Chapters

In Chapter 1, 'Introduction', there is a description of the evolution of TV, followed by early computer-generated images to the present real-time CGI systems. There is a description of 3D coordinate systems for data base objects, vector analysis and RGB color systems. There is a description of 2D coordinate systems and more specifically how they are used in the image coordinate system.

Chapter 1.6 has links to 'youtube.com' videos from early RT CGI systems, including the Link DIG and the E&S CT-5.

It is advisable to scan thru the last chapter (Binary Numbers) to get an idea about computation with binary numbers in computers.

In Chapter 2 there is a description of aliasing in CGI and the physical limitations that cause aliasing. Some of the analytic techniques in this chapter might be new and difficult to understand in the first reading. The reader can skip thru some sections and go back at a later time.

In Chapter 3, there is a description of anti-aliasing solutions.

In Chapter 4, the tools for the ABAA implementation are introduced.

In Chapter 5 describes the rendering operation.

In Chapter 6 and 7, ABAA with 4 and 8 subpixels is introduced.

Chapter 8, Computations with Binary Numbers

Chapter 8 does not follow a logical order in the book. For this reason, it has been inserted at the end as a general reference.

Because of the speed requirements of RT CGI, many computations in RT CGI systems are implemented with Binary Arithmetic. The chapter 'Inside the Binary World' provides basic information on different number representations such a decimal, binary, octal and hexadecimal. There is also information in the binary format for fixed-point and floating-point variables.

Intended Audience for this Book

When writing this book, I have consciously tried to make it available to a wide range of readers, from students interested in CGI to Graphics adapter manufacturers. These include:

- HW and SW students in computer and CGI.
- 3D game players interested in comparing AA techniques
- 3D CGI programmers, designers and managers
- 3D game artists and modelers
- Graphics adapter and card manufacturers
- Cell phone and laptop manufacturers

Forgive me when I try to explain some basic concepts that might seem obvious to you, like computing the area of a trapezoid.

Acknowledgements

Nowadays, Artificial Intelligence (AI) and Immigration are in the news.

I am often asked about why not using AI to find AA solutions. AI relies on large teams of contributors, large amount of investment and many technologies to develop new products. On the other hand, the AA algorithm described in this book relies on simple math and geometry like computing the area of a trapezoid. It also requires a good understanding and experience in 3D CGI and many iterations in the process.

I am a proud immigrant to the US from Switzerland. During my 20 years at Link Flight Simulation, I have been able to improve the image quality and density of digital visual systems in aircraft simulators. Because of the quality of aircraft simulators, they enhance the efficiency of training for aircraft pilots. I am proud to have saved lives of astronauts and military pilots, extended the life of military aircraft and saved fuel.

First, I am grateful to my parents, *Jakob and Jeanne Rohner*, who have given me the opportunity to learn accordion, piano and bass guitar, and who have supported me to study electrical engineering at the ETH, Zurich. I want to thank my aunt *Yvonne Morf* (my mom's sister) who strongly encouraged me to come to the US to get my Master Degree in EE (MSEE). She had spent many years in the US and she guided me applying for an emigrant VISA. I came to the US in the 1970s, when there was a rapid growth in 3D CGI.

I want to thank my distant relatives in the US who helped me settling in California. Among them, my Swiss born great aunt & uncle *Adele & Louis Panighetti-Aeshliman* in Connecticut, and my cousins *Richard & Michael Gagliasso* (and their family) in San Jose area (Silicon Valey), California. They were instrumental in making the transition easier. Without their help, there would be no book on AA, nor would I have been able to provide a new solution to the aliasing problem. We are all related to two *Panighetti* brothers from Northwest Italy (Piedmontese), who emigrated around 1885, one to Switzerland and one to the California.

I also want to mention *Jean Hoerni*, another Swiss scientist who immigrated to the US. He became an important contributor to the development of integrated circuits and microchips. *Jean Hoerni* first patented his 'planar process' in 1959, during his work at Fairchild Semiconductor. The planar process was critical in the invention of Silicon Integrated Circuit by *Robert Noyce*, who built on *Hoerni's* work with his conception of an integrated circuit (IC). *Noyce's* invention was the first monolithic IC chip. This invention is at the base of all the microchips built in the world. These scientists inspired me to come to Silicon Valley, CA. *Noyce and Gordon Moore* (Moore's law) left Fairchild Semiconductor to found Intel in 1968. [47]

My first manuscript of this book was ready a year ago. Since then, I have done many iterations and improvements. I thank Gotham books who supported me in the production of this book.

I thank *Dan Weaver* for reviewing my manuscript and for his many suggestions. *Dan* and I have worked together at several companies.

Chapter 1 Introduction

The field of images generated by computer is referred to as Computer Generated Imagery (CGI) [50]. CGI became feasible during the 1960s and many algorithms for generating 3D CGI were introduced.

During the 1970s, real-time 3D CGI systems (RT CGI) became available. This field has grown considerably over the years. Nowadays PC graphics adapters can produce 3D RT CGI for many types of applications.

In this chapter, several aspects of TV and CGI are considered.

- 3D CGI
- TV images vs 3D CGI
- Transformations from 3D objects to 2D images
- Pixel with 1 sample point
- Non-Real-Time 3D CGI vs Real-Time 3D CGI
- Introduction to Anti-Aliasing: MSAA vs ABAA

1.1 From TV to CGI

There are similarities between TV and CGI. TV is a ubiquitous medium used to broadcast dynamic scenes, TV programs, TV shows and movies. CGI uses digital computers to create synthetic images, simulations and movies.

1.1.1 TV Images and Displays

The early black and white (B&W) TVs were introduced in the 1950s. Color TVs appeared in the 1960s. Color TV technology was limited by the need to keep compatibility with black and white TVs. With the color TV standards, the same TV signals are used to transmit B&W or color TV images. The images were displayed with CRT (Cathode Ray Tube) display monitors. There were several TV standards [41]. In the US, TV images used the NTSC standard. The displayed images consist of 480 interlaced Scanlines (SL). Images are transferred and displayed one SL at a time to image displays [42][43]. In the US, TV images are updated 60 times per second, using alternated even and odd fields. In Europe TV images are updated 50 times per second. On two subsequent fields, even and odd SLs are interlaced to increase the apparent resolution and reduce flickering. In even fields SLs 0, 2, 4, ... are displayed. On odd fields SLs 1, 3, 4, ... are displayed. A pair of even and odd field forms a frame, displayed at 30 (or 50) frames per second.

1.1.2 TV Images and Movies

Image Flickering

On TVs, full images are updated at 30 frames per sec, but they are partially updated at 60 fields per sec, using interlacing. Besides providing more resolution, interlacing solves the problem of flickering.

In the movies, it is acceptable for the eye to capture and display images at 24 frames per sec. But

Introduction

when doing so, the eye perceives image flickering. When images are displayed at 48 times per second, the eye does not perceive image flickering.

The flickering problem in the movies is solved by introducing a shutter in front of the projector. The shutter modulates the light at the rate of 48 pulses per sec. Each image is repeated twice. This is not noticeable to the eye, even when movie images are only updated at 24 frames per sec. When there is movement in the scene, the moving scene elements in movies are recorded with 'motion blur'.

TV and Display Images

Although TV displayed images look like Photo or Movie images, they have a rigid structure. Each displayed image consists of a 2-dimensional array of sample points, or Pixels (Picture Elements). The size of this array of Pixels is *PixMax* Pixels Horizontally *and SLMax* Scanlines vertically.

Refer to Figure 1-1.

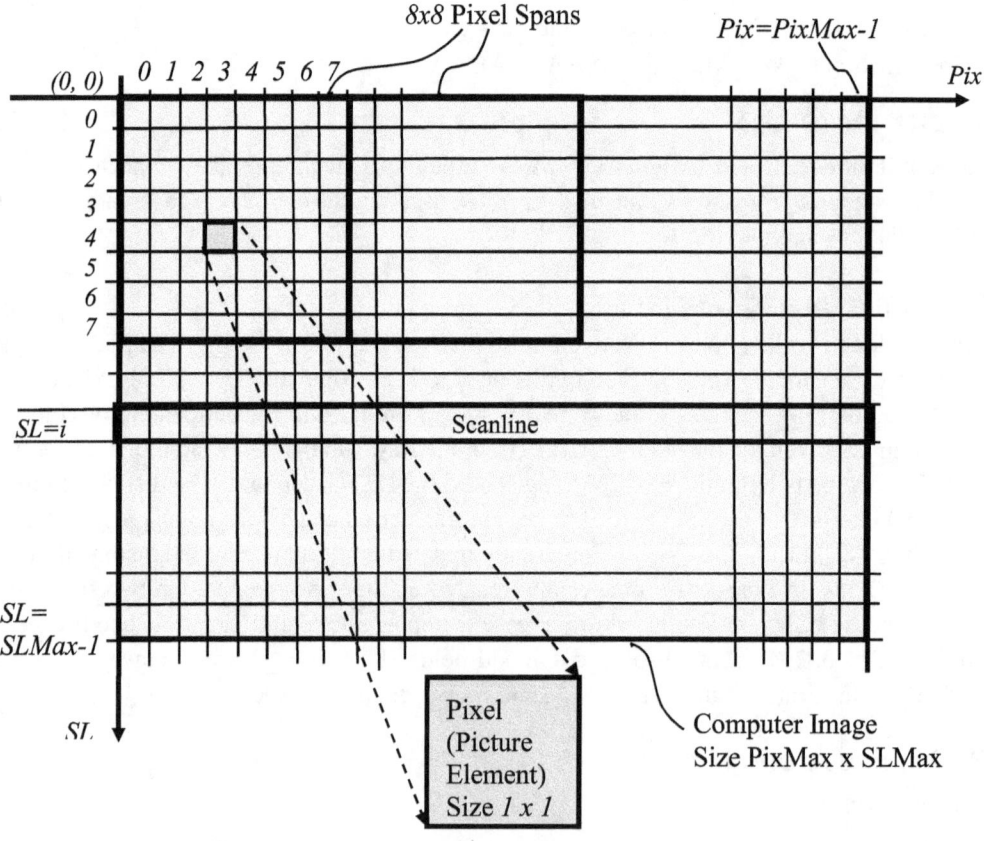

Figure 1-1 TV Image

A TV image is refreshed every 1/60 second. Pixels are painted one at a time from left to right in the horizontal direction. At the end of the line, the SL number is incremented, and the next line is painted from left to right., until the bottom of the image is reached.

In this book the description of Anti-Aliasing deals with images at the Pixel level. In order to have more visibility, the image is decomposed into Spans consisting of 8x8 Pixels only. These Spans are blown up representations of portions of the image They are partial images that will facilitate the descriptions of examples at the Pixel level.

1.1.3 Interlaced Display

In TV, the flickering problem is solved with SL interlacing. Half of the image is displayed at 60 fields per sec for NTSC (or 50 fields pre sec for PAL and SECAM TVs in Europe), using alternating even and odd fields. On even fields, only even SLs are displayed. On odd fields, only odd SLs are displayed. When TV images are recorded, the Video Camera records the image the same way as it is displayed, so there is no problem with moving components in the scenes.

Refer to Figure 1-2, 'Interlaced Scanlines in Field0 and Field1'

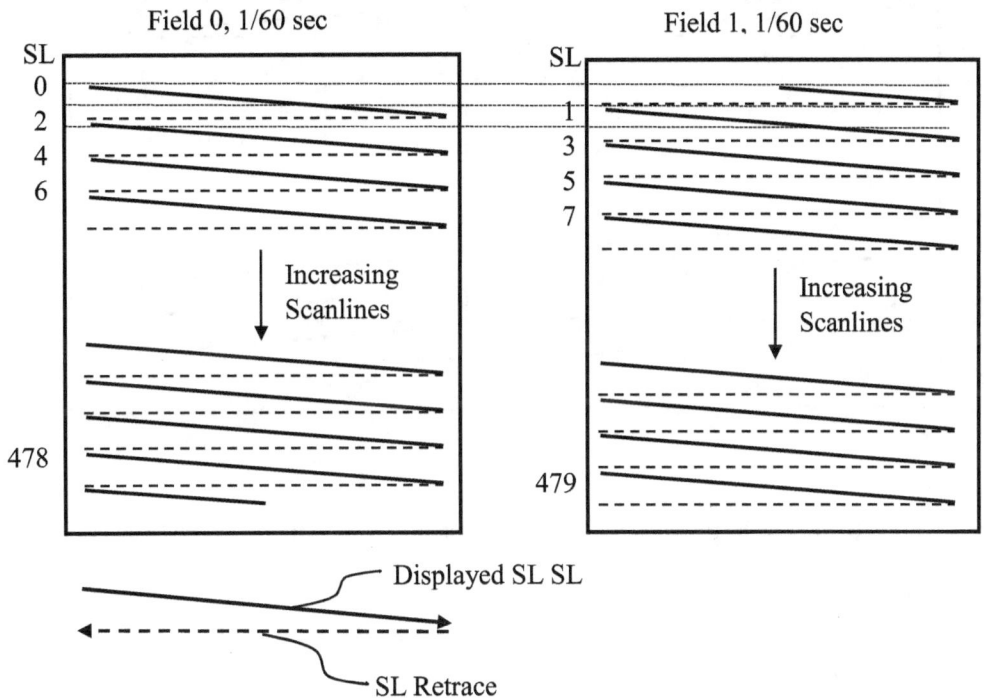

Figure 1-2 TV Image with Interlaced Scanlines in Field0 and Field1

For CGI, there is a problem when images are updated at 30 frames per second with interlacing. When the same image is displayed in both fields, the objects that move from field to field don't get updated with the correct position. This result in a visual effect referred to as Double Imaging. This can be solved by updating the image at field rate, that is 60 times per sec.

For CGI movies, some algorithms can simulate a 'motion blur' that look similar to the 'motion blur' in movies.

1.1.4 Progressive Displays

In Progressive displays, all SLs are displayed on every field, 60 times per sec. This requires twice the processing per image, when compared to interlacing.

Refer to Figure 1-3, "Progressive Display'.

With new technologies, most displays and TVs can display interlaced and progressive images as well.

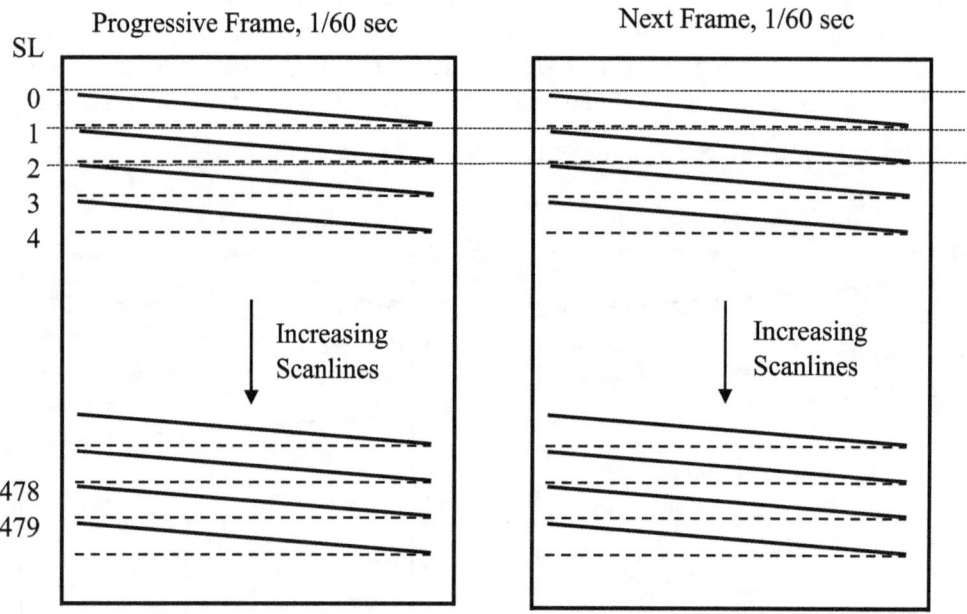

Figure 1-3 Progressive Display Image (Non-Interlaced SLs)

1.1.5 Color Display Standards

There are several standards for TV and CGI [40] [55]. Refer to Table 1-1, 'TV Standards'.
Refer to Wikipedia 'Standard-Definition Television' [41].
Refer to Wikipedia 'Graphics Display Resolution', 'Refresh Rate' and 'Interlaced Video' [42].

Standard Definition TV	Display Mode	Resolution PixMax x SLMax	Fields/sec
US: NTSC, 480i	interlaced	720 x 480	60/sec
France: SECAM, 576i	interlaced	720 x 576	50/sec
Germany: PAL, 576i	interlaced	720 x 576	50/sec

With the advent of HDTV, there were interlaced (i) and progressive (p: non-interlaced) standards.

High Definition TV	Display Mode	Resolution PixMax x SLMax
720i	interlaced	1,280 x 720
720p	progressive	1,280 x 720
1080i	interlaced	1,920x1,080
1080p	progressive	1,920x1,080
4k	progressive	3,840 x 2,160
8k	progressive	7,680 x 4,320

Table 1-1 TV Standards

For Graphics Display Standards, refer to examples in Table 1-2 for the Video Graphics Display resolution.

For CGI application, the display resolution can be between 720x576 and 1920x1080. UXGA (Ultra Extended Graphics Array), or UGA, is a display mode in which the resolution is 1600 Pixels by 1200 SLs

Video Graphics Array	Display Mode	Resolution PixMax x SLMax	Fields/sec
VGA	progressive	640 x 480	60/sec and up
SVGA	progressive	800 x 600	60/sec and up
XGA	progressive	1024 x 768	60/sec and up
UXGA	progressive	1600 x 1200	60/sec and up

Table 1-2 Graphics Display Resolution

With the advent of HDTV, the same standards can be used for PC monitors and TV displays. The most common are 720i, 720p, 1018i and 1080p.

Introduction

1.1.6 TV Images vs CGI

There are similarities between TV Images and CGI. The resolution of TV and CGI images are defined horizontally by *PixMax* Pixels (*Pix*) and vertically by *SLMax* Scanlines (*SL*). While in Standard Definition TV (SDTV) images use analog signals [41], CGI images are processed with digital signals.

With the advent of High-Definition TV (HDTV) since the 1990s, the TV broadcasts are transmitted with compressed digital signals [44]. The CRT displays have been replaced with larger size high resolution Liquid Cristal Displays (LCD) and Light Emitting Diodes (LED) displays.

In the US, the early TV images were encoded with the NTSC standard with a resolution of 720x480 Pixels. The refresh rate was 60 fields per second, using even and odd fields. NTSC produces 525 lines per frame, where only 480 are visible. The remaining lines are used for control. For CRT monitors, the extra time is used for line retrace, that is moving the display line control from the bottom-right to the top-left of the image. During retrace, the lines are not visible.

In Europe, the color images used the PAL or SECAM standards that have a slightly higher resolution of 720x576, but a lower refresh rate of 50 fields per second. PAL or SECAM produce 625 lines per frame, where only 576 are visible. The remaining *SL* time is used for control.

CGI first appeared in the seventies. Images were usually displayed with monitors similar to TV screen, often with higher resolution. In order to reduce flickering, the monitor also used interlaced images. Although Pixels were defined by the horizontal resolution of 720 Pixels, the TV output consisted of continuous analog signals. For CGI, the computed *SL* Pixels consist of digital signal that are usually stored in SL buffers with *PixMax* locations, each storing one color intensity in binary format. The SL buffer is then read and converted to analog signals with Digital to Analog Converters (DAC). In the SL buffer, each Pixel is defined by a unique color.

For interlaced monitors with *SLMax* Scanlines, even SLs are displayed on even field, and odd SLs are displayed on odd fields. Each field is displayed at 1/60 sec rate to prevent image flickering. By having interlaced (or interleaved) SL, the frame resolution of images at 1/30 sec appears to be double the field resolution at 1/60/sec.

For progressive monitors with *SLMax* Scanlines, all the SLs are displayed on each field. So, for progressive monitors, the image rendering has to be twice as fast as for interlaced monitors.

For more information about TV and Video, there is a good book from *Keith Jack:* "*Video Demystified*" [7].

1.2 CGI

CGI consists of computer applications for creating images in art, printed media, video games, simulators and computer animation. For CGI, the most generally used approach is to process polygons (mostly triangles) in 3D coordinates, then project them onto a 2D image plane. There are other approaches like 'ray tracing' and 'voxel processing', that are even more computation intensive.

As the processing hardware (HW) for RT CGI has evolved with curved surfaces and 3D texture, the last step in rendering still consists of mapping small triangles onto image Pixels. Because of my emphasis on fast processing for 3D RT CGI systems, I am mostly interested in algorithms using polygon (mainly triangle) processing. The algorithms described this book assume polygon processing.

1.2.1 Early CGI Contributors

CGI was pioneered in the late 1960s by *David C. Evans* and *Ivan Sutherland* (E&S) at the University of Utah [53]. Many of the early CGI contributors also came from the University of Utah. Among them were Jim Clark (founder of Silicon Graphics and co-founder of Netscape), *Ed Catmull* (co-founder of Pixar), *John Warnock* of Adobe, *Scott P. Hunter* of Oracle, *Franklin C. Crow* and *Jim Blinn*. In 1968, *Dave Evans* and *Ivan Sutherland* founded the first computer graphics HW company, Evans & Sutherland (E&S).

For curved surfaces, there were important developments in the French automobile industry at Citroën and Renault. In 1959, *Paul de Casteljau* (a French physicist and mathematician) developed an algorithm for evaluating calculations on a certain family of curves while working at Citroën. In the 1960s, *Pierre Bézier* at Renault used *Paul de Casteljau's* curves to develop 3D modeling techniques for Renault car bodies. These curves would form the foundation for much curve-modeling work in the field, as curves (unlike polygons) are mathematically complex entities to draw and create models as well. These curves are now called Bézier curves after *Bézier's* work in the field of automotive design. Refer to Wikipedia 'Bézier curves and Bicubic Patches' [13].

The curve algorithms are powerful tools for creating 3D representations with curved surfaces for CGI models. It is important to be aware that these models cannot be processed directly by CGI rendering HW. First, the 3D models with curved surfaces have to be converted by software (SW) applications into polygons (or triangle) meshes in 3D space [14][15]. Note that these conversions could also be implemented in HW using embedded programs in arrays of GPUs (Graphics Processing Units). Then the triangle meshes in 3D space can be projected onto the 2D image plane for rendering.

Non-Real-Time CGI

At first, CGI consisted of static pictures that were produced in non-real-time.by general purpose computers. Because of the amounts of computations, most of the new algorithms for CGI were executed in non-real-time using the fastest computer systems. These non-RT CGI computers were used to produce beautiful static images and animated scenes for TV commercials and movies.

Most of these implementations used the Z-Buffer approach for rendering. The coordinate Z is the depth coordinate the represents the distance from the viewpoint to sample points in the image. In this approach, the image was computed with 1 triangle sample per Pixel. The triangle sample that is the closest to the observer is selected. The Pixel Color and Z distance are stored into a frame buffer memory (Z-buffer).

Real-Time CGI Systems

In the early 1970s, for real-time (RT) CGI applications like virtual reality and flight simulators, fast and special purpose RT CGI systems became feasible. These systems were not available to the general public. They had to be developed from scratch by a few companies using proprietary special purpose computer HW and in-house developed SW. They were also expensive and cost above a million dollars.

At that time there was a separation between non-RT CGI using SW algorithms running on super computers, and a limited supply of fast RT CGI systems. The favorite computer for non-RT 3D algorithm development was the Cray-1 super computer [73]. Because of its high cost of $8M, it was limited to universities, research labs, animated scenes or special effects in movies.

For the general public, the state of the art in RT CGI were 2D graphics games like Pac-Man and Space Invaders running on PCs and play stations like Atari and Nintendo. The state of the art in PCs was the Apple II and DRDOS microcomputers, costing around $1k. Later on, there was the Microsoft Flight Simulator [75] with simple graphics for the IBM PC. The images consisted of flight instruments and simple out the window images.

In the 1970s, when RT CGI systems became feasible, only a few companies could manufacture these specialized systems [82] [83]. These RT CGI systems could produce nice CGI at 30 frames/sec, or even at 60 field/sec. They had good image quality and Anti-Aliasing (AA). They were the grandads of today's 3D graphics chips and graphics cards that are used in high-end PCs. Among them:

- Evans and Sutherland (E&S) in Salt Lake City, Utah [53][86],
  with CT-1 to CT-5 (Continuous Tone) CGI systems.
  There are several patents and publications from E&S about RT CGI in particular about Polygon Clipping [130] to [134].
- General Electric Ground System Division (GE GSD) in Daytona Beach, Florida,
  with CGI CompuScene systems [89].
  There are several patents and publications from GE about RT CGI, in particular about Edge Smoothing from *William M. Bunker and Richard G. Fadden* [120] to [127].
- A third company, the Advanced Product Operation (APO) of Link Flight Simulation in Sunnyvale, CA, was a late entrant with its DIG CGI Systems [90] to [99],. Link Flight Simulation had several patents and publications about RT CGI, in particular for High-Speed Sorter, Clipping and Texture from *Judit K Florence, Michel A Rohner, Johnson K Yan and Robert W. Lotz* [100] to [114].

Few people have heard about these RT CGI systems, or have experienced flying in these expensive flight simulators. They were designed under NASA or US military contracts and required security clearances to work on the projects. One of the biggest challenges was to eliminate (or at least reduce) distracting 'visual artifacts' like edge crawling (also referred to as jaggies) and small faces popping in-and-out of scenes.

For the early RT CGI systems designed in the 1970s, the low memory density available at that time prevented implementations with Color-Buffer or Z-Buffer. Instead, they were designed with Edge List and Scanline (SL) computers. In SL Computers, only a few SLs could be stored in local memory at a time. The edges had to be sorted along each SL before being displayed. In the 1980s, the increase in memory density made it feasible to design the rendering with frame buffers.

In 1977, four DIG-1 from Link Flight Simulation were delivered to NASA in Houston in preparation of the Shuttle space flights. At around that time, two other computers were announced:
- Cray-1 supercomputer
- Apple II microcomputer

The Cray-1 [73] supercomputer was designed by Cray Research. It was quite larger (Height: 77", Diam:104") than the Apple II and cost around $8M. When announced, the Cray-1 was the fastest general purpose super computer for 3D graphics and other non-real-time applications. This supercomputer had great 64-bit Floating Point performance and became in high demand all over the world. The first was delivered in the same year as when the first DIG-1 was delivered to NASA [96]. The DIG-1 was of a similar size and cost around $2M.

The Apple II [74] became the most famous microcomputer, until the first IBM PC was introduced four years later. These microcomputers were about the same size as a typewriter and cost around $1.5k. They could generate simple boxy 2D graphics images for games.

Comparison between DIG-1 and Cray-1 Super Computer

There are some similarities between the DIG-1 and Cray-1. These systems cost above $1M. They were the fastest at producing 3D Computer Generated Images, but they were designed for 2 different markets:

- Non-Real-Time Applications:
  The Cray-1 was the fastest for *general purpose* applications. For 3D Computer Generated Image rendering, many algorithms were developed in SW and executed on off the shelf super computers. Everybody in the 3D community knew about the Cray-1. The 1st Cray-1 Super-Computer was announced in 1976. That same year, 1st SMS DIG-1 was shipped to Houston. The non-real-time Cray-1, that was announced at the same time, can be compared with the real-time DIG-1.
- Real-Time Applications:
  The DIG-1 was the fastest RT CGI system in the world for generating 3D graphics scenes used in aircraft simulators, when it was delivered to NASA. It was at least 10 times faster than competitive RT CGI systems at that time. It was 5 years ahead of the competition. On the back page of the book cover, there is an example of image generated by the DIG. The DIG could process up to 12,000 triangle edges (4000 triangles) at the rate of 60 images/sec.
  Because of the limited market and the military applications, practically nobody in the 3D community were aware that RT CGI systems like the DIG-1 existed. Only 10 years later, other companies like Silicon Graphics started to produce such systems with wider distribution.

Although many SW algorithms were developed for both non-RT CGI and RT CGI, many of the RT CGI implementations were kind of proprietary. The 3D graphics algorithms for non-RT-CGI were developed using the faster Super Computers at that time. The Cray-1 was the favorite super computer [73] until workstation from Sun Microsystem and Silicon graphics appeared 10 years later.

1.2.2 Evolution of AA in RT CGI Systems

RT CGI with Edge Smoothing in the 1970s

During the 1970s, the limitation in memory density prevented RT CGI systems from implementing rendering with Color-Buffer or Z-Buffer. For this reason, the rendering was done one SL at a time in a Scanline Computer. Since the RT CGI systems were used for military and aerospace training, an important requirement was to eliminate visual artifact. In the DIG-1, the edge smoothing used analog circuitry with 4x4 Subpixel resolution implemented by *Robert (Bob) W. Lotz* [108]. For the DIG-2, I implemented a digital version of edge smoothing with 4x4 Subpixel resolution. I am not familiar with the edge smoothing approaches used by GE and E&S.

RT CGI with Face Buffer and BON in the 1980s

During the 1980s, the increase in memory density made implementation with Color-Double-Buffer feasible. This made feasible for companies like Silicon Graphics Inc (SGI) and Computervision Corp in Raleigh, NC, to enter the RT CGI market.

In most RT CGI systems anti-aliasing was handled using up to 16 sample points within a Pixel. The sample points are also referred to Bed of Nail (BON). Refer to Edge Smoothing patent from *Rick Fadden* (Reference [122], 16 sample points and [127], 8 sample points) and the Modular DIG patent from *J. K. Yan and J.K Florence* [111]. Some of these systems show a transition from standard logic circuit modules to ASIC (Application Specific Integrated Circuit).

First PC Graphic Adapters with RT CGI in the Mid-1990s

During the 1990s, there was a big development for ASIC design using RTL (Register Transfer Logic) programming with Verilog. This made implementation of RT CGI systems in a single ASIC chip feasible for the PC market. In the PC graphic adapters, ASIC chips were connected to the PC Bus and a few local memory chips. These 3D RT CGI implementations used a Double-Color-Buffer and a Z-Buffer.

Most of these graphic adapters used a single point per Pixel sampling and had no anti-aliasing. Soon after the introduction of these 3D RT graphics adapters in the PC market, consumers became aware of the artifacts, or jaggies, due to single point per Pixel sampling. One approach to minimize the jaggies was to increase screen resolution.

Using their background designing large RT CGI systems with anti-aliasing, a group of engineers from the leading RT CGI companies (*J. K. Yan, R. G. Fadden, M. A. Rohner*) decided to design a graphic adapter with AA for the PC market at Oak Technology. The result was the Warp5 that implemented AA with 8 Subpixels and was the 1st PC graphics adapter with AA. Prior to joining Oak Technology, I had worked on an early version of my algorithm using Area-Based Anti-Aliasing. Using an adaptation of ABAA, I was going to implement a better version of AA for the Warp5 follow-on, when the project got cancelled. Since then, I have made several improvements and the result is presented in this book.

At the beginning of 2000s, the PC graphic adapters started to implement AA using the Multi-Sample Anti-Aliasing approach (MSAA).

1.2.3 Data Base Models

Before CGI can be rendered, 3D models have to be created in a 3D Data Base. The models can consist of single objects or clusters of multiple objects. In most applications, the objects are described with connected triangles. There can be also lines and point lights. There are static models like terrain and buildings and moving objects like airplanes, tanks and living creatures. For moving objects like living creatures and tanks for examples, they can have articulated parts.

The 3D models are inserted into Gaming Areas, where these objects can be rendered by CGI systems in 3D before being projected into a 2D image plane. Depending on the distance between the observer and the models, the projection size of the rendered objects can vary greatly. For this reason, the same Data Base objects can be modeled with different 'Level of Details' (LOD). When the object is close to the observer, the models with higher LODs are processed. When the object is far away the models with lower LOD are processed. When the objects become too small in the scene, they are removed from processing. For example, when the distance to the object increases by a factor of 2, the number of triangles in the next lower LOD could be reduced by a factor of 4. The distances at which the models switch between LOD, are defined as 'Switching Distances'. In order to prevent object LOD to oscillate back and forth during transition, 'Hysteresis' should be applied to the Switching Distances. Distracting effects when objects transition between LODs should be avoided.

1.2.4 2D Coordinate Systems

For the CGI computations, a knowledge of geometry, coordinate systems and linear algebra is recommended [20].

Triangle In 2D Coordinate System

Given a 2D drawing area or geographic maps, any point insides of the area can be defined with *(X, X)* coordinates on two coordinate axis x and y. This 2D coordinate defines a 2D space.

For example, a triangle can be defined by 3 vertices *V1, V2* and *V3*.
The 3 vertices are connected by 3 edges: *E1, E2* and *E3*.

Refer to Figure 1-4.

Introduction

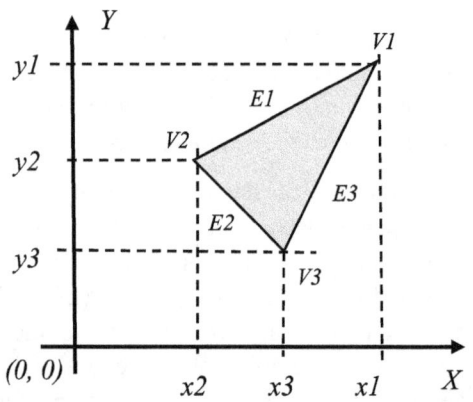

Triangle defined by 3 vertices:
Vertex $V1 = (x1, y1)$
Vertex $V2 = (x2, y2)$
Vertex $V3 = (x3, y3)$
Coordinate system origin:
Origin $= (0, 0)$

Triangle defined by 3 edges:
Edge $E1 = (V1, V2)$
Edge $E2 = (V2, V3)$
Edge $E3 = (V3, V1)$

Figure 1-4 Triangle In 2D Coordinate System

1.2.5 Database Coordinate systems

The image computations are performed in several coordinate systems:
- Database in 3D Coordinate system
- Image in 2D coordinate system

In Figure 1-5, there is a description of 3D coordinate systems in the Gaming Area.

In the three-dimensional coordinate system, the objects need to be rotated using vector and matrix computations. The vectors are defined by the three coordinate components: *(x, y, z)* [20]. The three rotation angles are defined as roll, pitch and yaw, or *(roll, pitch, yaw)*. The 3x3 rotation matrices (*Hr*) are computed from these three angles [23].

Several coordinate systems need to be defined.
The gaming area coordinate system, is the reference system *(Xref, Yref, Zref)*.
The coordinate origin for the gaming area, or data base (DB Origin), is at coordinate
   Vref = (0, 0, 0);

Since the first RT CGI were designed for aircraft simulation, the viewpoint position is also referred as pilot position. This also defines the plane, or aircraft, position. The viewpoint (or pilot position) is defined as:

   Vp = (xp, yp, zp);

The viewed object has a position *Vo* relative to the database origin:

   Vo = (xo, yo, zo);

The translated vector, *Vt*, for each object vertex is the difference between the vertex coordinate minus the viewpoint position:

   Vt = Vo - Vp = (xo, yo, zo) - (xp, yp, zp) = (xo-xp, yo-yp, zo-zp);

In this figure, the Viewpoint coordinate is defined in aircraft coordinate system, *(Xa, Ya, Za)*. In this system, the coordinate axes are defined as follows.

- the *Za* coordinate axis points downward,
- the *Ya* axis points in the direction of the right wing
- the *Xa* axis points in the forward direction.

Beside of the Viewpoint position *Vp*, the attitude of the flying aircraft and its coordinate system, *(Xa, Ya, Za)*, must be defined with 3 viewing angles with respect to the fixed data base orientation: such as *roll, pitch and yaw*.

Refer to [20] to [28].

The triangular faces defined by 3 coordinate vertices V_j = *(xj, yj, zj)* relative to the object position. For each face there is also a Face normal vectors *N*, that is used to eliminate back faces.

For each moving object, its attitude and coordinate system, *(Xm, Ym, Zm)*, is also defined with 3 angles (*roll, pitch, yaw*).

There can also be illumination sources defined by a Sun vector, *Vs* = *(xs, ys, zs)*, and Diffused Illumination, *Id*.

Introduction

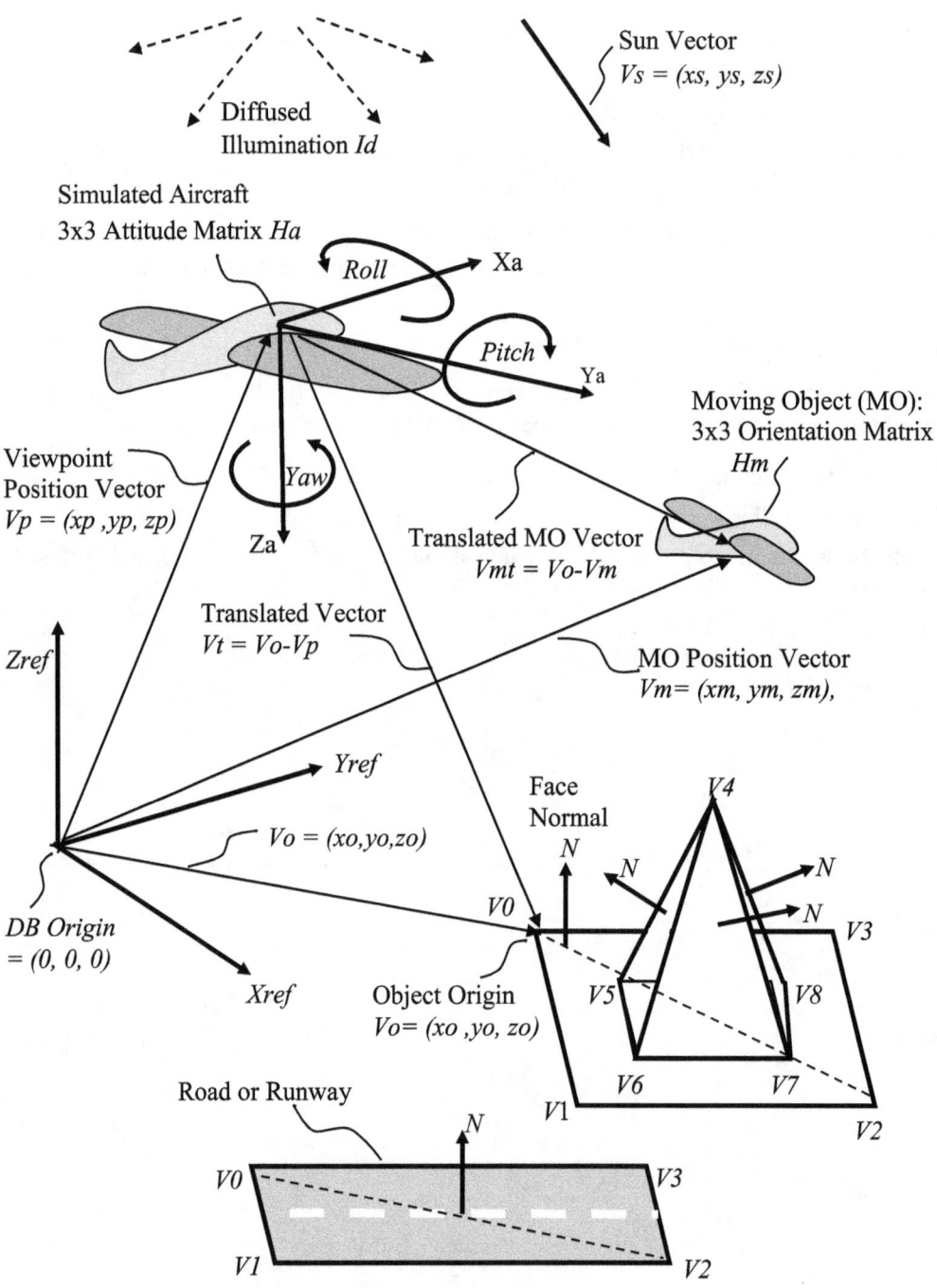

Figure 1-5 Gaming Area and Coordinate Systems

Introduction to Area-Based Anti-Aliasing for CGI

1.3 Geometry Transformations in 3D and 2D Spaces

1.3.1 Objects in 3D Space

The CGI processing deals with objects models defined in 3D space with surfaces made of adjacent triangles. The objects in the vicinity of the observer are stored in an Active Data base. Although general polygons can be processed, the most widely used models use triangles or meshes of triangles. Each object in the data base is defined with an object origin, a list of faces made of triangle and polygon vertices.

In this book, I deal exclusively with 3D images resulting from triangle processing. Each triangle is defined by a sequence of 3 vertices with (x, y, z) coordinates. Triangles can be single triangles or triangle meshes [15]. Triangle meshes can be organized as strips or fans [14]. Refer to Figure 1-6, Triangle, Strip and Fan.

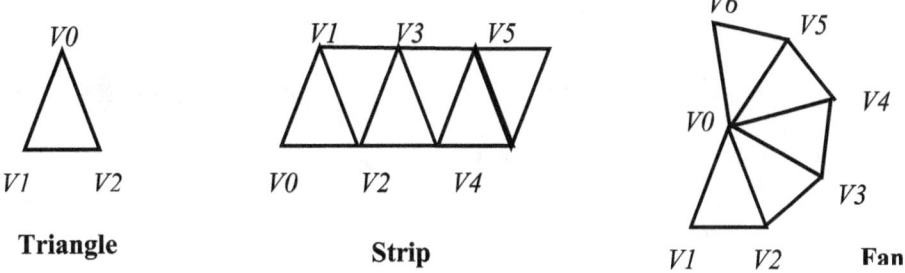

Figure 1-6 Triangle, Strip and Fan

1.3.2 Object Transformations of from 3D to 2D

The CGI systems consist of 3 main processing blocks:

- Geometric Processor (ex: Frame Calculator in Link DIG systems)
- Image Renderer (ex: Scanline Computer in Link DIG systems)
- Image Display System (ex: Video Generators in Link DIG systems)

The data base objects are defined in 3D space as surfaces made of adjacent triangles. The objects in the vicinity of the observer are stored in an Active Data base. The surfaces of these objects are made of many adjacent triangles. Each triangle is defined by a sequence of 3 vertices with (x, y, z) coordinates.

3D Geometric Processor

The first step in CGI is to access the triangle data from the Active Data Base. The data base consists of faces made of triangles in 3D space. Each triangle is defined by 3 vertices in 3D space. In the Geometric Processor, each triangle is defined by three vertices $V=(x, y, z)$ in the data base. These triangles are first processed with operations in 3D space, including Translations, Rotations and Clipping.

Refer to Figure 1-7, 'Vertex Translation'.

Introduction

Refer to Figure 1-8, 'Vertex Rotation'.

Refer to Figure 1-9, 'Polygon Clipping.

Also, refer to [23]: Rotations in Three-Dimensions, Rotation Matrix, and [24] to [28].

After the 3D operations, the triangles are projected onto a 2D image plane. The Clipping operation makes sure that all the projected vertices are inside of the 2D image.

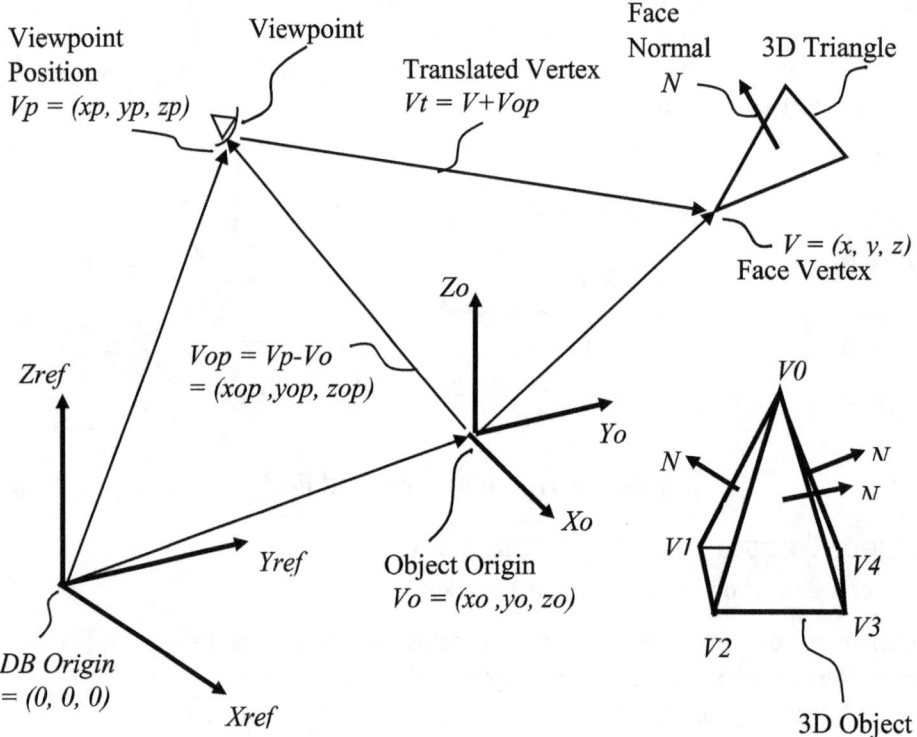

Figure 1-7 Vertex Translation

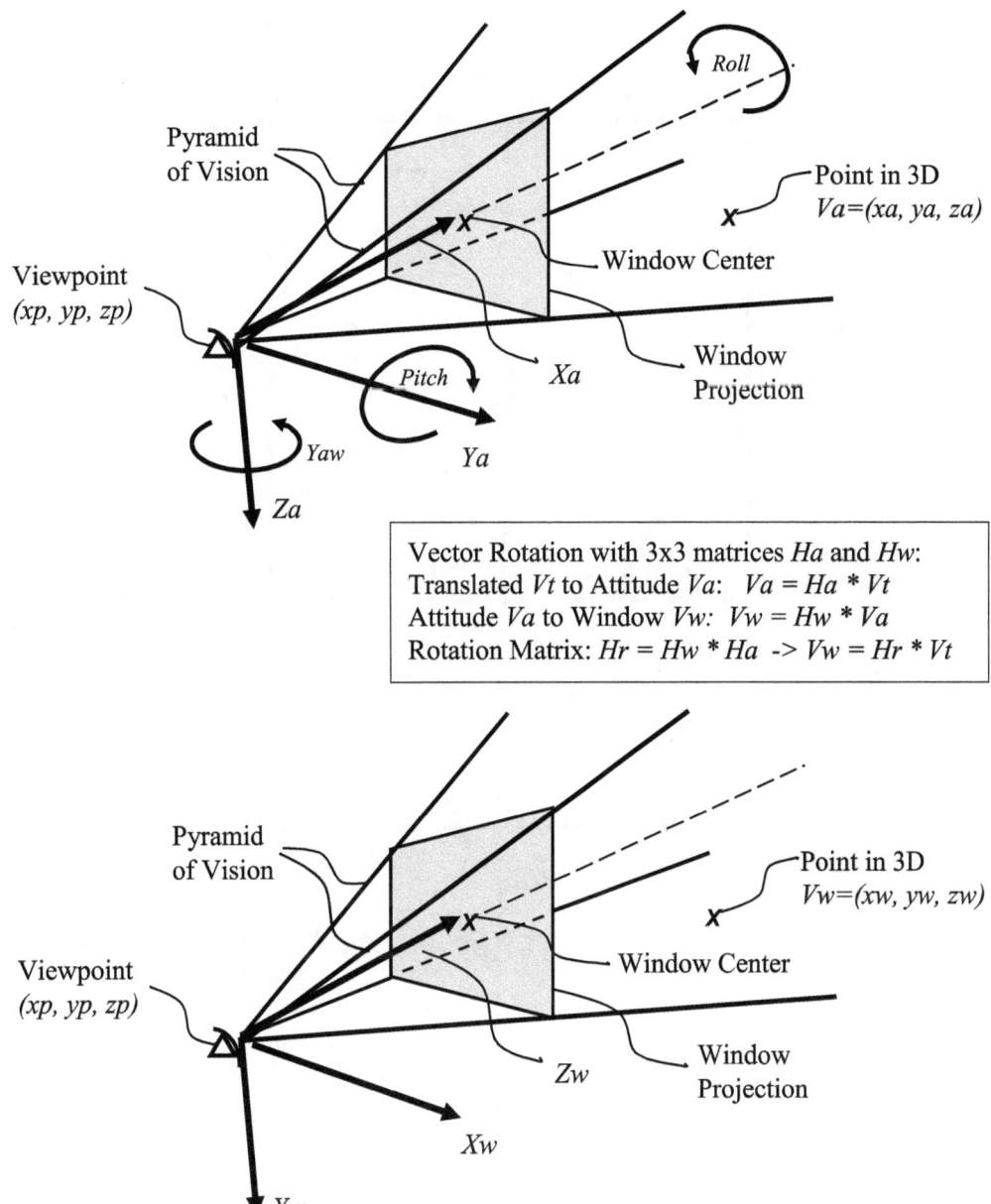

Figure 1-8 Vertex Vt Rotated into Window Coordinate

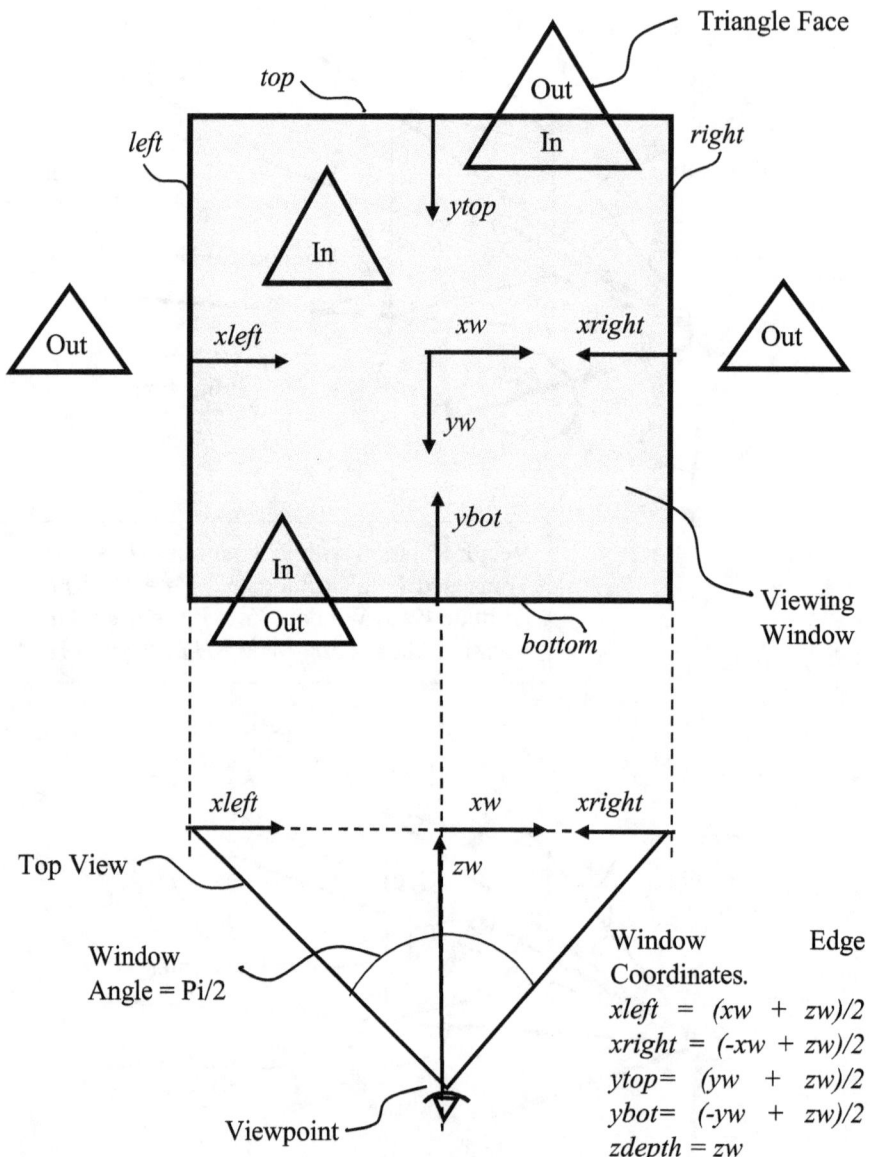

Figure 1-9 Window Clipping

Introduction

2D Geometric Processor

After several geometric transformations in 3D space, the triangle vertices are projected onto the 2D window space for triangle processing and image rendering. In the 2D image space, the computations are performed in *(Xi, Yi)* image coordinates. Each projected triangle is defined in 2D space with 3 vertices and 3 edges connecting the vertices. The 2D geometric Processor (Face Boundary Calculator in the DIG) generate edge slope and gradients for Image Rendering.

Refer to Figure 1-10, 'Projection from 3D to 2D'

Following the projection of vertices onto the window image plane, the triangle vertices are processed in 2D space. The parameters for the triangle edges are computed.

The projected triangles consist of 3 vertices and edges connecting theses vertices in *(xi, yi)* image coordinates. Each pair of vertices is connected by an edge with a slope *dx/dy* or *dy/dx*. The output of the Geometric Processor consists of 2D triangles defined by 3 vertices and 3 edges with color and other attributes.

Refer to Figure 1-11, 'Triangle In 2D Image Coordinate'.

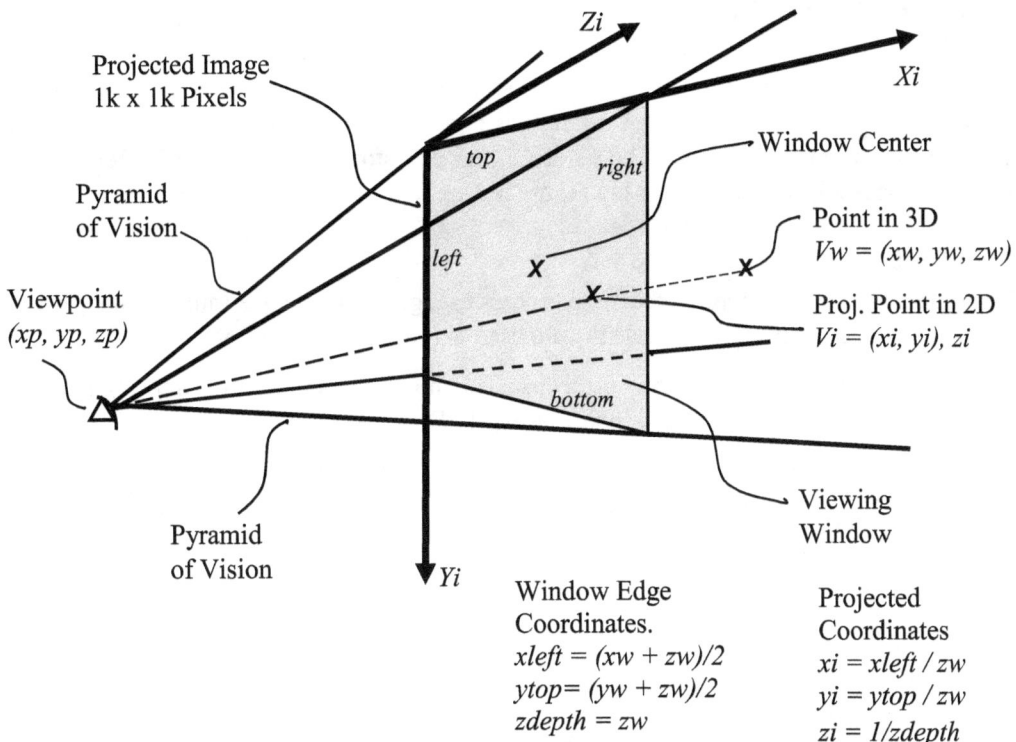

Figure 1-10 Projection from 3D to 2D

Introduction

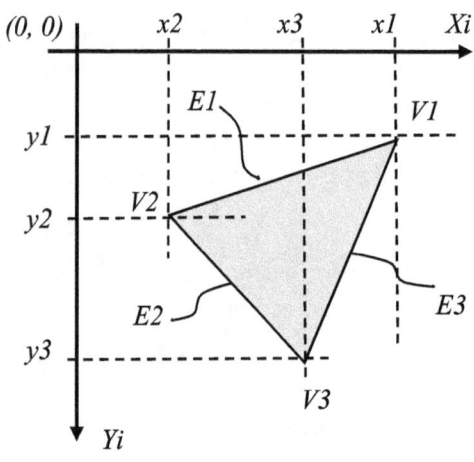

Triangle defined by 3 vertices:
Vertex $V1 = (x1, y1)$
Vertex $V2 = (x2, y2)$
Vertex $V3 = (x3, y3)$
Coordinate system origin:
Origin = $(0, 0)$

Triangle defined by 3 edges:
Edge $E1 = (V1, V2)$
Edge $E2 = (V2, V3)$
Edge $E3 = (V3, V1)$

Figure 1-11 Triangle In 2D Image Coordinates

1.4 Image Rendering

Following the geometric processing in 2D, triangles are processed by an Image Renderer. The task of the Image Renderer is to draw 2D triangles and maps them into Pixels. Implementation of the Image Renderer can differ. While each triangle is processed separately, all the triangles are put back together to form a 2D image. The rendered image is stored into a Frame Buffer. For each Pixel, there corresponds an address in the Frame Buffer.

1.4.1 Image Plane and Image Size

The early approach for CGI rendering was to process triangles with a single sample point per Pixel. Later on, multiple sample points per Pixel were used to reduce aliasing effects.

These 2D images consist of a 2D array of Pixels. The image size is determined by the horizontal and vertical resolution of the display monitor. Refer to Figure 1-12.

The 2D images consist of *PixMax* Pixels horizontally and by *SLMax* Scanlines vertically. Each image Pixel is of size 1x1 and has a uniform color defined by 3 color components, Red, Green and Blue (*R, G, B*).

Introduction

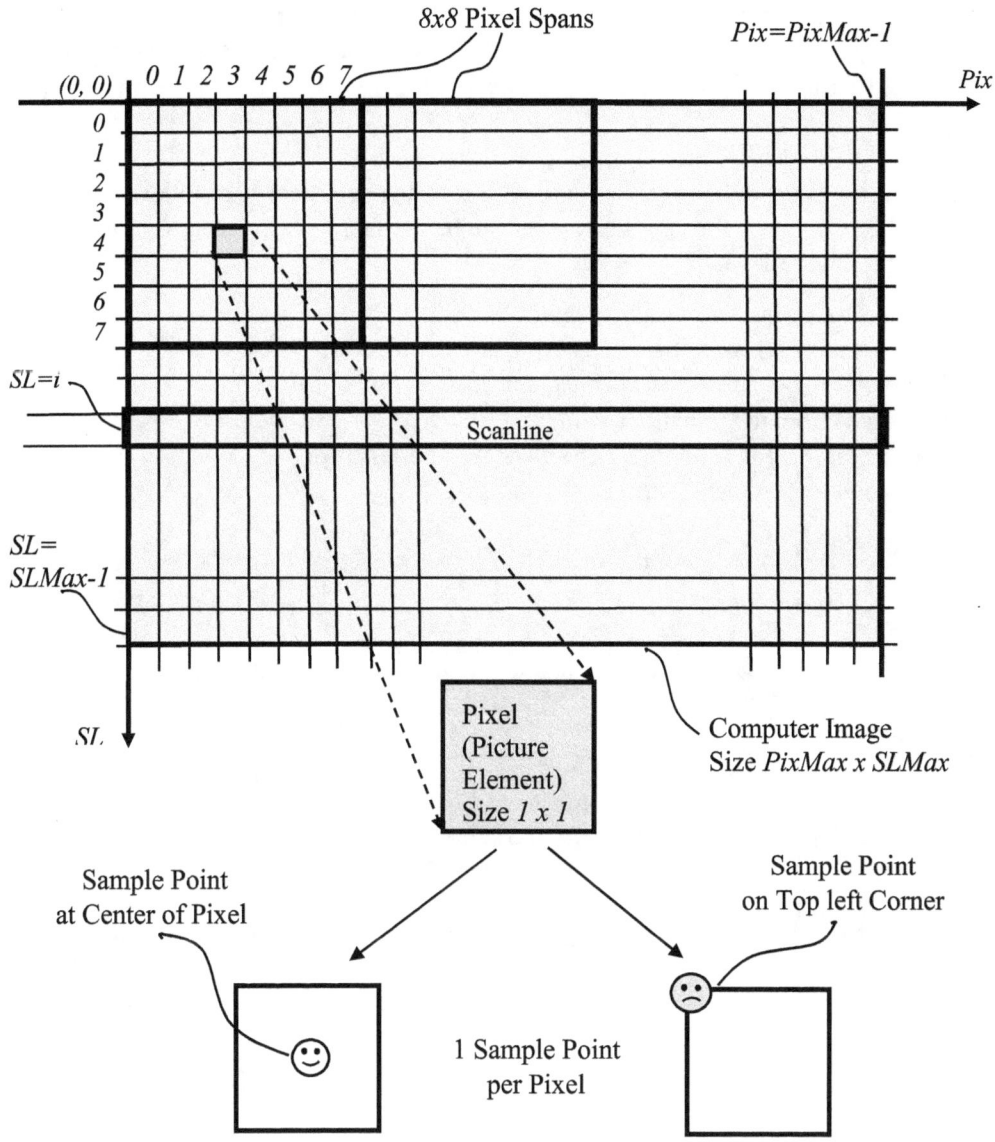

Figure 1-12 Image Size of *PixMax* Pixels by *SLMax* Scanlines

For the purpose of transferring the image data or accessing image data in memory, Pixels are organized horizontally from left to right into SLs. Each SL is a linear array of Pixels. SLs are organized vertically from top to bottom into a two-dimensional array that form the image. So, the image is a linear array of SLs.

Introduction

For the purpose of processing, the image is sometimes organized into small square areas of size 8x8 or 16x16 Pixels, referred to as Tiles or two-dimensional Spans. For image processing, such as image rendering in CGI or data compression for HDTV, there are advantages when the image is decomposed into Tiles.

1.4.2 Image Coordinates

The image coordinates are defined by two axes with *xi* and *yi* coordinates, as follows. Depending on the context, the values on the coordinate axes can be defined with fixed point or with integer numbers. Refer to Figure 1-13.

- Horizontal axis from left to right, using:
  - integer Pixel (*Pix*) coordinate (between *0* and *PixMax*) or
  - fixed-point *x* coordinate (between *0.0* and *1.0*).
- Vertical axis from top to bottom, using:
  - integer Scanline (*SL*) coordinate (between 0 and *SLMax*) or
  - fixed-point *y* coordinate (between *0.0* and *1.0*).

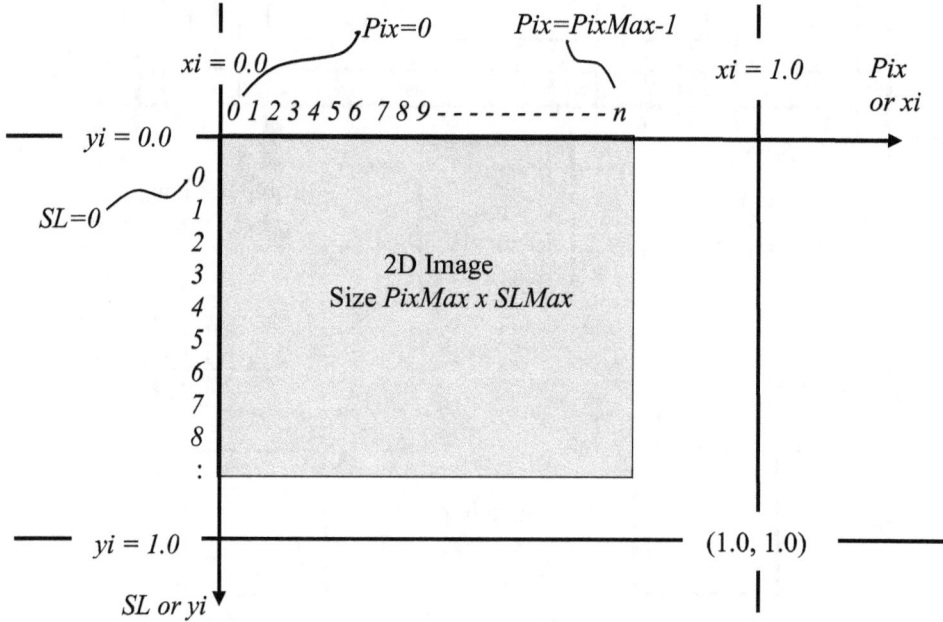

Figure 1-13 *(Pix, SL)* and *(xi, yi)* Coordinates

In the figure, the image is represented as a two-dimensional array of Pixels of integer size:
*PixMax * SLMax*

As can be seen in these figures, there are 2 coordinates units on each axis:

- integer (*Pix* or *SL*) coordinates and
- fixed-point (*xi* or *yi*) coordinates

In the Image Display system, the image is retrieved from the Frame Buffer using *(Pix, SL)* coordinates and converted from digital to analog. The image it then displayed on Video Monitors or other image display systems

Integer (Pix or SL) coordinates

Pix and *SL* are integer numbers that define Pixel positions in the 2D image.
The horizontal integer coordinate *Pix* ranges from *0* to *PixMax-1*.
The vertical integer coordinate *SL* ranges from *0* to *SLMax-1*.
Pix and *SL* Coordinates are used to access the Pixel data inside of the *Pix* and *SL* boundaries. They are also used to access the memory locations in the image buffer.

The range of Pix and SL variables depends on the horizontal and vertical range.

- For ranges up to *511*, they are 9-bit integers.
- For ranges up to *1023*, they are 10-bit integers.
- For ranges up to *2047*, they are 11-bit integers

Fixed-point (xi or yi) coordinates

The image coordinates *(xi, yi)* represent projection points in the image plane.

For example, for an *800x600* image, the fixed-point coordinates will fit within a *Pix* and *SL* range of *0* to *1024*. This corresponds to *1k x1k Pixels* and can be represented with 10-bit *(Pix, SL)* coordinates. For each point in the image, the *(Pix, SL)* coordinates are obtained by multiplying the *(xi, yi)* coordinates by *1024* then converted to integer values.

$$(Pix, SL) = (\,integer(1024*xi),\ integer(1024*yi)\,)$$

For the *(xi, yi)* image coordinates, a 16-bit fixed-point format is suitable for an image of *1kx1k Pixels* and an accuracy of 1/16Pixel.

This 16-bit signed fixed-point format is:

$sb.bbbbbbbbbb\text{'}bbbb$

where '*s*' represents the sign bit and '*b*' represent a bit. The last 4 characters '*bbbb*' represent a Pixel fraction with Subpixel resolution.

The fixed-point format for Pixel coordinates *(xp, yp)* is: $s.bbbb$

The integer format for Subpixel coordinates *(xs, ys)* is: $bbbb$

Conversion from Fixed Point (xi, yi) to Integer (Pix, SL)

The *(Pix, SL)* coordinates are obtained by shifting the point position of image coordinates *(xi, yi)* 10 places to the right and truncating the 4 bits of fraction.

The values of *xi* and *yi* fixed point numbers can be defined in a range from *-1.0* to *+2.0*. This range covers a 3x3 image area.

Only the values between *0.0 to 1.0* can be inside of the image.

Introduction

The values outside of the image are used for interpolation. The portions of triangles that reside outside of the displayed image need to be clipped. Refer to Clipping patents [105][132].

1.4.3 Rendering Triangles

During rendering, triangle surface defined by vertices and edges is mapped onto image Pixels. For a triangle to be displayed inside of a Pixel, at least one sample point has to be defined inside of that Pixel. In the simpler case, only one sample point is defined inside of each Pixel. Refer to Single Sample Point Selection in Figure 1-14.

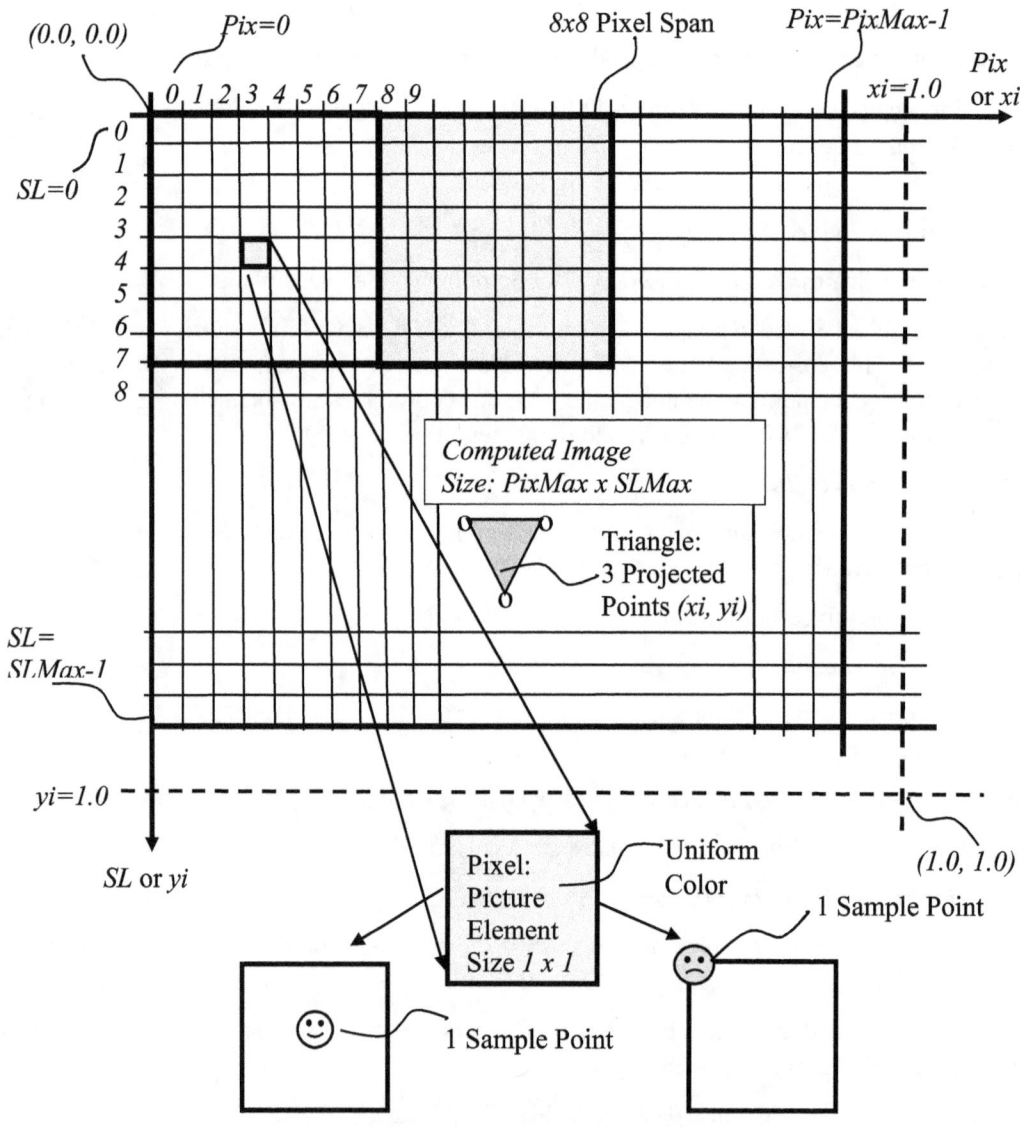

Figure 1-14 Single Sample Point Selection

When only one Sample Point is used to compute an image, this result into aliasing effects consisting of jaggies (jagged edges), edge crawling and face popping. In order to reduce aliasing effects, several Sample Points should be used inside of Pixels.

In this figure, there are 2 approaches for selecting a Pixel sample point:
- On the left side, Sample Point at the 'Center' of the Pixel.
- On the right side, Sample Point on the 'Top-Left Corner' of the Pixel.

1.4.4 Selecting the Pixel Sample Point

Most of the image rendering algorithms use only one sample point to select whether a triangle is displayed on each Pixel. For real time applications, there are 2 dominant Application Programming Interfaces [76]:

- OpenGL (originally from the proprietary 'Graphics Language' developed by Silicon Graphics)
- Direct3D (from Microsoft).

These application interfaces provide functions to process triangles in 3D and 2D space, and to render the polygon onto the 2D image. But these interfaces ignored antialiasing and decided to select the sample point on the 'Top Left Corner' of the Pixel element.

Single Sample Point Selection

There are two main definitions for selecting a single sample point inside of a Pixel.

Refer to Figure 1-15.

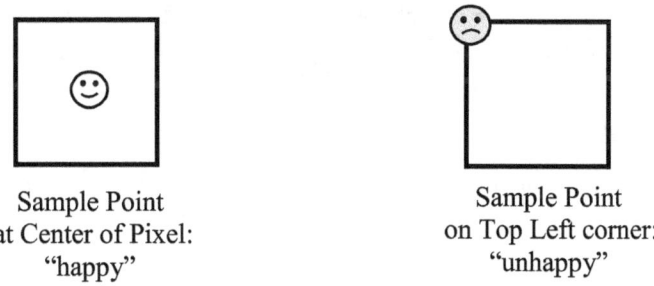

Sample Point
at Center of Pixel:
"happy"

Sample Point
on Top Left corner:
"unhappy"

Figure 1-15 Sample Point Selection

I strongly disagree with the Sample Point selection on the 'Top-Left Corner'. For me, the Sample Point should be at the 'Center of the Pixel', for the following reasons.

Introduction

Sample Point on top left corner

There are disadvantages when selecting the Top Left Corner. It is the result of arbitrary decisions according to the wrong reasons. This is why the selected point on the right side of the figure is unhappy.

I can think of three main reasons for selecting the top left corner of Pixels as reference point.

- One of the reasons for selecting the Sample Point on the top left corner is the results of Rounding or Truncating the results of the projection.
- Another reason is the legacy of 2D graphics. Early implementation of 3D graphics used the same approach as used in the 2D graphics games like Pack Man and other 2D graphics game consoles. For these 2D graphics images, the top left corner made sense because Pixels were mapped into memory locations with integer addresses.
- The top left corner is also a legacy of early 3D graphics images using Z-buffer. Because of the memory limitation and cost for Z-buffers, these images did not process Subpixels for antialiasing. The Pixels were only accessed with integer numbers. In the Z-buffer, they are mapped into the *(Pix, SL)* memory addresses used to access the Z-buffer.

Selecting the sample point on the Top Left Corner results in limitations for rendering in 3D graphics.

As I mention in my previous book, 'New Fixed-Point Math for Logic Design' [6], 'Rounding or Truncating' have been the cause of many problems when doing computations in 3D graphics. In this book there are several examples of problems that can be prevented by applying this 'New Fixed-Point Math' approach. Also, I have discovered the 'Area-Based AA' algorithm while applying these fixed-point math concepts.

Some techniques, like the 'Bed of Nail' (BON) approach, use sample points inside of the Pixel for Anti-Aliasing. In the 'BON' approach, 8 sample points (for example) arranged in a semi-random fashion inside of the Pixel are selected. It was used by the early designers of RT CGI since the 1980swith good results

Sample Point at Center of Pixel

In 3D graphics, the displayed information consists of real numbers, resulting from the projection of triangles from 3D space onto a 2D screen image. In the displayed image, there are Pixels, Scanlines and projected points. In the 2D image space, the Image Renderer maps the triangles onto Pixels defined in *Pix* and *SL* coordinates. After rendering, the Pixel data is stored in a temporary image buffer using Pixel *(Pix, SL)* coordinates before being sent to the Display system.

For the purpose of computations, the *(xi, yi)* image coordinates can be represented with fixed point numbers (instead of floating points). The edge data can be provided in fixed-point format *(xi, yi)*, so that the Pixel geometric information can be processed with Subpixel resolution.

The projected points reside inside of Pixels limited by *Pix* and *SL* boundaries. The xp and yp coordinates inside of Pixels can be expressed with 4 fractional bits. Inside of Pixels, the Subpixel positions can be defined with signed 5-bit Pixel coordinates *(xp, yp)=(0.bbbb, 0.bbbb)*, or unsigned 4-bit Subpixel coordinates *(xs, ys)=(bbbb, bbbb)*.

The displayed points from the computed image consists of **real numbers** that **cannot** be projected onto the **integer numbers** on the Pixel and Scanline grid. When several Sample Points per Pixel are used, the average of all the points within the Pixel boundary converge to a point at the center of the Pixel.

The sample point at the center of the Pixel represents the average of a large number of sample points inside of the Pixel. It is also the center of gravity of the Pixel. This is similar to computations in mechanic, where the motion equations apply to the center of gravity of objects.

The Pixel (*Pix*) and Scanlines (*SL*) integer numbers define a Display Grid on the 2D Image. Each Pixel on the image represents a *1.0x1.0* area inside of Grid Lines. The Grid Lines define thresholds that defined where the projected points transition from Pixel to Pixel. No point that is projected from 3D space onto the 2D image can result into a pure integer point on the Display screen.

There are many advantages for selecting the reference point at the center of the Pixel. This is why the happy Sample Point (on the left) in the previous figure is smiling.

Example of Mapping Image Pixels onto Display Screen.

As I have explained in my previous book, the center of the Pixel represents the average of all the points inside of the Pixel. Rounding or Truncation should not be considered. For more information, refer to my previous book [6]:

'New Fixed-Point Math for Logic Design'

On a Display Screen representation, the lines that represent Pixel and Scanline boundaries have no width. They have integer values and represent boundaries or threshold.

On the other hand, the Pixels that fill the area between these boundaries are the result of projection computations with fixed point numbers with fractions. In order for a fixed point to equate an integer value, it would have a fraction consisting of an infinite number of 0's, which is not practical.

On the image plane, the integer Scanlines and integer Pixels form a grid. The grid lines have no widths, because they represent boundaries (or transition thresholds). So, the Pixel areas cannot touch the integer threshold on the grid lines. Figure 1-16 shows a simplified view of a Pixel grid and Pixel area on a displayed image.

Introduction

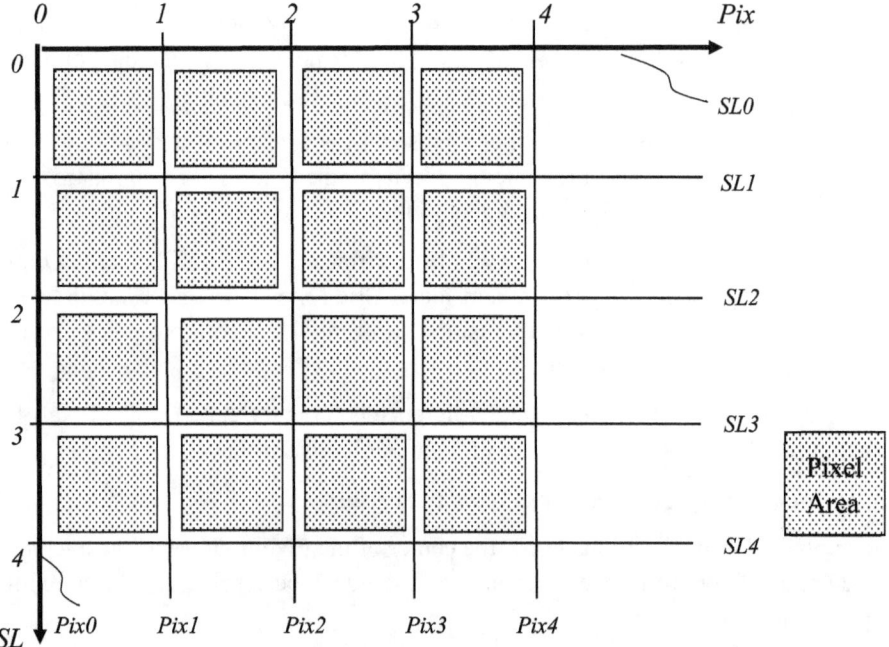

Figure 1-16 Pixels Located Inside of *SL* and *Pix* Grid

The Pixel areas form square Tiles surrounded by the grid lines. The Tiles do not touch the gridlines. When the polygon edges are traversing the Tiles, the rendering algorithm compute their intersections with Pixel boundaries and do the processing with fixed-point *averaged* numbers. The intersections of edges with Tile boundaries consist of fixed-point numbers.

When the image is rendered, the Pixels are filled with the computed color components. This simplified view of the image plane represents how the Pixels should be rendered when the edges are processed during the edge traversing phase. After rendering, each Pixel has only one uniform color.

Note that in this example, the grid lines represent static data, while the Pixel information represents dynamic data.

1.4.5 Pixel Sampling with Jaggies

Single Sample Point per Pixel

When rendering a triangle, the simple approach is to select a single Sample Point inside of Pixels. When the surface of the triangle covers the Sample Point, the color of that triangle is assigned to the whole Pixel. Although this approach can produce decent images, one of the drawbacks is that the assignment of only one triangular color to square Pixels results in aliasing artifacts (jaggies and crawling) in the computed image.

Refer to Figure 1-17 where the color of sample points is assigned to the uniform color of Pixels.

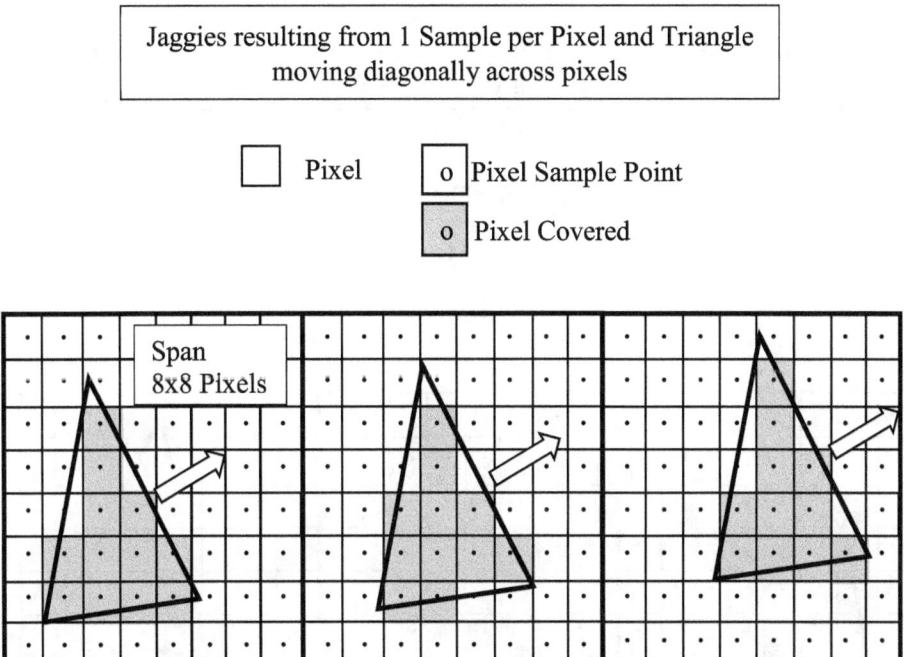

Figure 1-17 Assign Color Using 1 Sample Point per Pixel

In this figure, there are 3 identical triangles inside 8x8 Pixel area. From the left to the right triangle, each triangle is displaced by 1 Pixel horizontally and by 1/3 Pixel vertically. The shape of Pixel coverage from left to right shows the effect of crawling.

Reducing the Jaggies with Subpixels

The distracting effect of the jaggies and crawling can be reduced by mixing the colors of 2 adjacent triangles in Pixels. In the image in Figure 1-18, the partially covered Pixels are blended with the background when the triangle covers between 1/3 and 2/3 of the Pixel area. This image shows the improvement when Subpixel information is used to improve the image quality. The application of Subpixel coverage is referred to a 'edge smoothing', or 'anti-aliasing'.

As a polygon edge moves gradually across a Pixel, the mixed color will result in N incremental steps (N>1). In this document, the Pixel is divided into N Subpixel areas, where N can be 4 or 8. When using N steps, the color of the Pixel changes gradually in N steps increments. With N=4 steps, there is a good improvement over single point sampling. With N=8 steps, there is another noticeable improvement in image quality.

Introduction

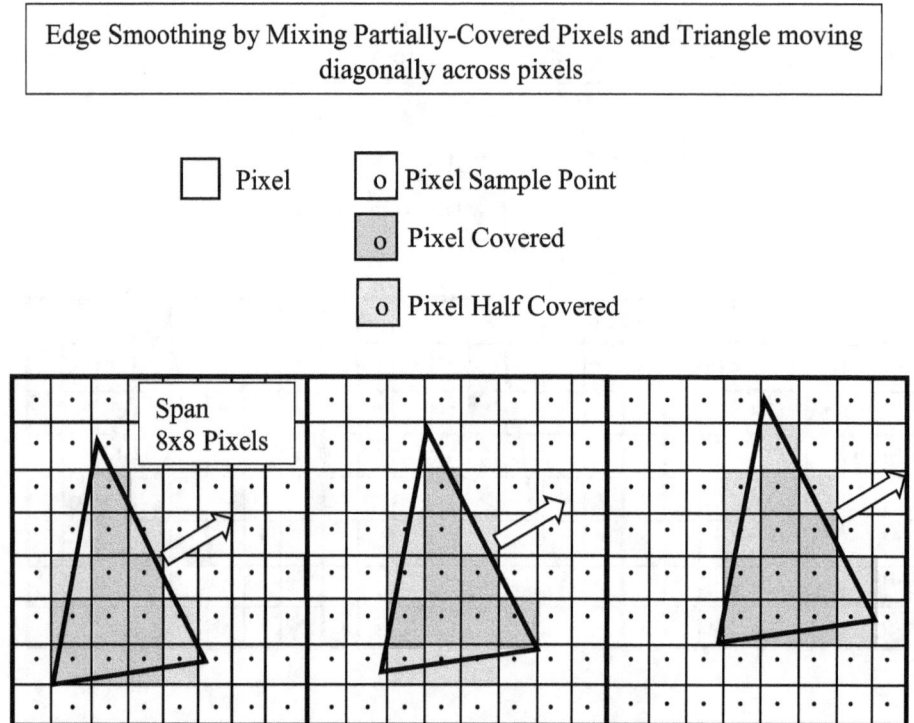

Figure 1-18 Mix Color of Half-Covered Pixels

1.5 Color Space

There are several formats for defining colors components in the Color Space. Refer to [45]. For CGI, the color computations are usually done in the *ARGB* format *(Alpha, Red, Green, Blue)*. *Alpha* is a 4th component that specifies transparency.

For Display Monitors, the PC VGA adapters use the *RGB* format.
For Television, for practical reasons, the colors are defined in the *YCbCr* format.

1.5.1 RGB in Color Space

For CGI, the color computations are usually done in the *ARGB* format *(Alpha, Red, Green, Blue)*. For Display Monitors, the PC VGA adapters use the *RGB* format. Color values are stored as binary numbers consisting of *0's and 1's*. For example, it takes 8 bits to store values between *0* and *255*.

ARGB Color Components

For processing, the *(A, R, G, B)* components can be defined with 16, 24 or 32 bits (binary digits):

- 32 bits with *(A[8], R[8], G[8], B[8])*, where *A* is the alpha transparency.
- 24 bits *(R[8], G[8], B[8])*
- 16 bits *(R[5], G[6], B[5])*

For 32-bit color, the components are defined by 8-bit integer values ranging from *0* to *255*.

```
31      28      24      20      16      12      8       4       0
+-------+-------+-------+-------+-------+-------+-------+-------+
|     A[8]      |     R[8]      |     G[8]      |     B[8]      |
+-------+-------+-------+-------+-------+-------+-------+-------+
```

For the 16-bit format:
- *R[5]* and *B[5]* range from 0 to 31.
- *G[6]* Ranges from 0 to 63.

```
15      12      8       4       0
+-------+-+-----+-----+-+-------+
|  R[5] |  G[6]  | B[5] |
+-------+-+-----+-----+-+-------+
```

In case of the 16 bits format, the *Green* component has an extra bit because the human eye is more sensitive to the *Green* than the *Red* or *Blue* colors.

When using *RGB*, each Pixel color is defined by four *ARGB* or three *RGB* components. Refer to Figure 1-19.

Introduction

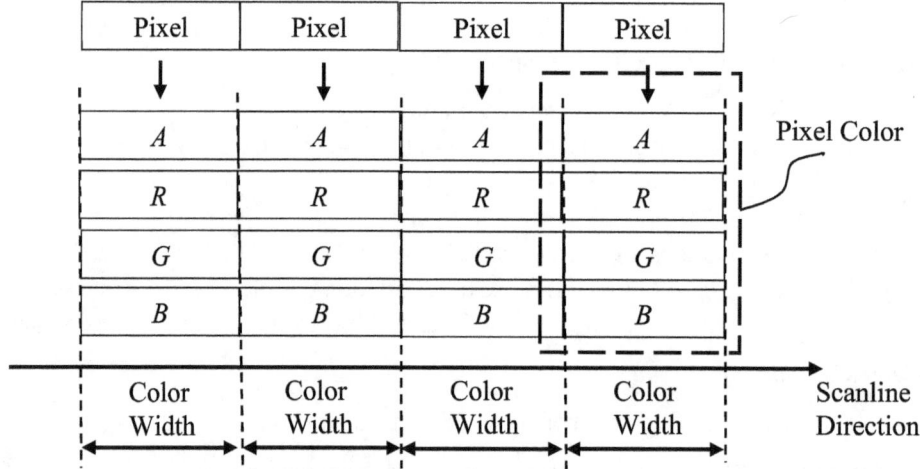

Figure 1-19 Pixels along SL with *ARGB* or *RGB* Color Components

1.5.2 *YCbCr* in Color Space

For Television, for practical reasons, the colors are defined in the *YCbCr* format.

YCbCr Color Components

Refer to Figure 1-20

In the YCbCR format, the *Y* component represents the *Gray* shade.
- The *Cb* represents the *Blue* contribution added to the *Gray* shade.
- The *Cr* represents the *Red* contribution added to the *Gray* shade.

There are advantages to use the *YCbCr* format for TV. In the *YCbCr* format, the *Y* component represents the Intensity or Gray shade. The *CbCr* components represent the color hue in the TV image. Because the eyes are more sensitive to color intensity *Y* than the color hue, the *CbCr* information can be shared between 2 adjacent Pixels.

Another advantage for TV is that the *YCbCr* format can be used for Black &White TV, as well as Color TV. For Black & White TV, the image can be displayed with the Y component only.

For a practical point of view, when you need to adjust the contrast and brightness in a TV set, you are modifying only the *Y* component. When you adjust the color, you are modifying the *Cb* and *Cr* components.

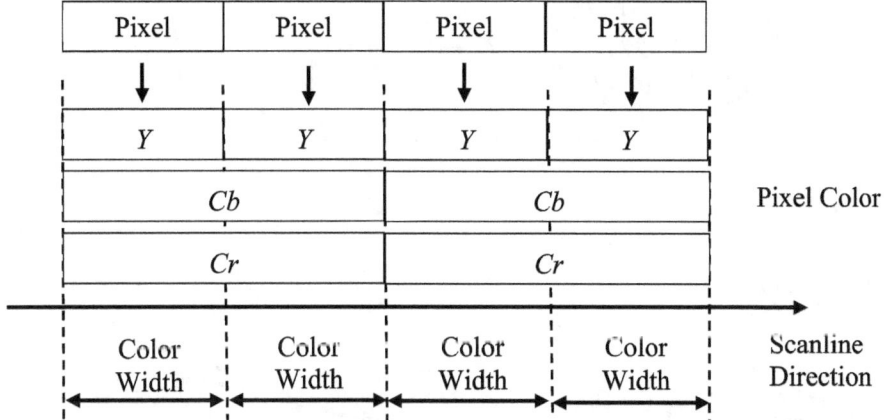

Figure 1-20 Pixels along SL with *YCbCr* Color Format for Television

1.5.3 Color Space and Conversion

The *RGB* and *YCbCr* components are related by the following equations. Depending on the application, these equations can vary slightly.

Refer to [45].

RGB to Gray Conversion

$Y = 0.299R + 0.587G + 0.114B$

RGB to YCbCr Color Conversion

$Y = 0.299 R + 0.587 G + 0.114B$
$Cb = (B-Y) * 0.564 = -0.168935 R - 0.331665G + 0.50059 B$
$Cr = (R-Y) * 0.713 = -0.499813 R - 0.418531 G + 0.081282 B$

YCbCr to RGB Color Conversion

$R = Y + 1.403 Cr$
$G = Y - 0.344 Cb - 0.714 Cr$
$B = Y + 1.773 Cb$

In the book 'Dirty Pixels' from *Jim Blinn* [3] (Chapter 8), there is a simpler set of equations for *RGB to YCbCr*. Refer to Figure 1-21.

Introduction

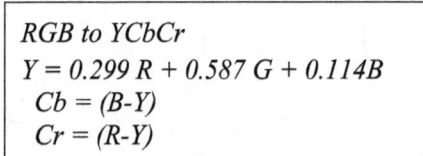

$$Y = 0.299\,R + 0.587\,G + 0.114B$$
$$Cb = (B-Y)$$
$$Cr = (R-Y)$$

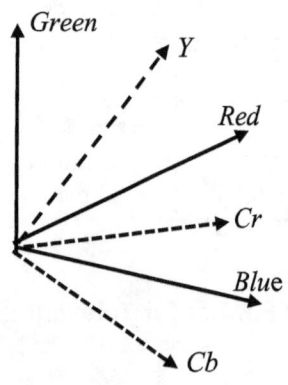

3D View of
Rd, Green and Blue

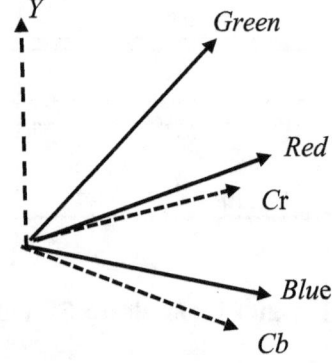

Color Coordinates Converted into
Y Cb Cr Coordiantes

Figure 1-21 *RGB* and *YCbCr* in Color Space

1.6 The Link DIG and the E&S CT-5

The Link DIG

What is not commonly known, is that the 1st RT CGI system with higher performances and AA was the Link DIG built by the APO Link Division of Singer in Sunnyvale, CA.

By 1975, Link had built an R&D DIG (Digital Image Generator) prototype that could output around 1500 edges/field (1/60 sec). Then, in 1977 the DIG production unit could produce 12,000 edges/field. This corresponds to 240,000 triangles per sec. I was one of the key architects and a main designer of the Link DIGs. The first DIG was delivered to NASA in Houston in late 1977. A total of 4 DIGs have been used to train all the Space Shuttle Astronauts in Houston before their missions into space [96]. A 5th DIG was also delivered to NASA Ames in Mountain View, CA, for their Vertical Motion Simulator [97]. Few people have heard about the Link DIGs, because they were designed under NASA or US military contracts and required security clearances to work on the projects.

Note: Although, the references from [82] and [83] rated the DIG performance at 12k images per frame (1/30 sec), it was actually 12k images per field (1/60 sec). This was probably due to a confusion in the marketing department at Singer Link. As the principal designer, I can attest for sure that the correct number is 12,000 edges/field (1/60 sec).

During the years I spent designing the first and fastest RT CGI systems at Link Flight Simulation, I was always faced with the requirements of high image quality and AA. When the DIG was designed, the 1kx1 Static Random-Access Memory chips (SRAM) was the densest semiconductor memory modules available. Even though, the DIG-1 had edge smoothing using analog circuits. The DIG-1 was also the first RT CGI system with Area-Based Anti-Aliasing.

There were 2 versions of the DIG: DIG-1 and DIG-2. For AA, the DIG-1 had analog edge smoothing. The DIG-2 had digital edge smoothing.

Because of its superior performances, the Link DIG was responsible to win important contracts against the competition: Space Shuttle Motion Simulator (4 DIG-1), F-111 Fighter Bomber (9 DIG-1), NASA the Vertical Motion Simulator at NASA Ames (1 DIG-1 with 4 windows, also used for Dog Fights), and 1 DIG-1 to All Nippon Airways (ANA) to train for take-off and landing in the Hong Kong airport. With gradual improvements, the DIG -2 continued to win contracts for several simulator/trainer programs for the Air Force (12 DIG-2 for B-52 Bomber, and 1 for F-117 Fighter-Bomber) and 40 DIG-2 for Army helicopters training program (AH-64 Apache, AH-1 Cobra, CH-47 Chinook and UH-60 Black Hawk). During a period of 12 years, a total of 70 DIGs were sold.

DIG Video Demo

In the DIG, the problem of face popping was solved with 'Coplanar Detail Faces' (CDF). The CDFs could be graciously introduced and removed from the scene by controlling their contrast when they were near Pixel size. This algorithm could accurately compute the projection size of polygons early in the geometric processor. There is a great YouTube Video demo of the DIGs at: [99] Link Flight Simulation Demo, Video, DIG-2 Demo, 1984:

Introduction

    https://www.youtube.com/watch?v=uy8sJ9AxvYI

There are also several references about the DIG delivered to NASA with 4 OTW scenes to simulate fighter-plane dogfights.

[97] NASA Ames Vertical Motion Simulator
   https://www.youtube.com/watch?v=0WaiAyU-3mU
   https://www.nasa.gov/simlabs/vms/technical-details
 DIG-1: Simulator Facility for Helicopter Air-to-Air Combat at NASA Ames
   https://apps.dtic.mil/sti/citations/ADA160693
   https://apps.dtic.mil/sti/pdfs/ADA160693.pdf
   NASA Ames Research Center (ARC):
     https://en.wikipedia.org/wiki/Ames_Research_Center

E&S CT-5 Demos with Texture

A few years later, the CT-5 from E&S was announced in 1981. The CT-5 and the DIG-1 had similar performances, although the DIG-1 was produced 5 years earlier. The DIGs used the SL-to-SL processing approach. The CT-5 and the GE Systems used a Face Buffer approach.

The CT-5 (Continuous Tone 5) was designed around 5 years after the DIG. At that time, face buffer and texture mapping became feasible [32].
By comparison, there are similar scenes in the CT-5 demos from E&S.
Refer to 'YouTube' videos about *Evans & Sutherland CT 5 Flight Simulator (1981) [86] [88]*

In this video there are examples of contrast decreasing with distance, simulated with translucency. In these cases, the decrease in contrast depends on distance only and is less natural than in the examples of details implemented with CDF in the DIG scenes.

[86] Evans & Sutherland (E&S) Wikipedia
  https://en.wikipedia.org/wiki/Evans_%26_Sutherland
 E&S History 2005:
  https://www.youtube.com/watch?v=FHhYAUgY3S0
  https://forum.beyond3d.com/threads/ct5-evans-sutherland-simulator-how-did-it-work.57664/
 Utah inventions: The birth of computer graphics
  https://www.ksl.com/article/36039333/utah-inventions-the-birth-of-computer-graphics

[88] E&S CT-5 Videos
 CT-5 Flight Simulator, 1981
  https://archive.org/details/CT5FlightSimulator
  https://www.youtube.com/watch?v=6W-qb_jHRhA
 Evans & Sutherland 'The Tactical Edge'
  Part 1: https://www.youtube.com/watch?v=06mbwNg1Vw4
  Part 2: https://www.youtube.com/watch?v=7e7_GiCc-HA

GE CompuScene
 [89] The Simulator Revolution
  https://www.airforcemag.com/article/1289simulator/

Chapter 2 **Aliasing**

The early computer-generated images were static rendering and usually had only one Sample Point per Pixel. Edges of the rendered triangles had stairsteps. This resulted into aliasing effects, referred to as 'Jaggies'. Many algorithms got developed to remove the Jaggies.

Some of the analytic techniques in this chapter might be new to the reader and difficult to understand in the first reading. But do not get discouraged. For the first reading, just scan through the titles and figures.

Also refer to the cited reference numbers shown in brackets like [xx]. After going back and reading a few times, you'll be surprised that you can understand most of it.

2.1 Aliasing and Anti-Aliasing

2.1.1 Aliasing

In CGI, television and movies, Aliasing is also referred to as: Jaggies, Face Popping, Edge Crawling, Narrow Faces Breakup, Moiré patterns and Distracting Artifacts [61].

Jaggies and Edge Crawling

Jaggies and Edge crawling occur when polygon edges transition vertically or horizontally and jump from Pixel to Pixel. Jaggies appear in static and dynamic images, when only one Sample Point per Pixel is used during rendering.

Face Popping

Face popping in-and-out of scenes occurs when some dimensions of displayed polygon faces are smaller than the Pixel size. Face popping also occurs when new polygons are introduced into a scene, or removed from a scene.

Moiré Patterns

Repetitive patterns in CGI can cause aliasing and Moiré patterns.
Moiré patterns aliasing occurs when using polygons to render repetitive patterns.
When modeling repetitive patterns in CGI, aliasing can be avoided by using texture maps [32]. Texture mapping can display repetitive patterns using several levels of resolution.

Distracting Artifacts

All these effects are considered as Distracting Artifacts.

2.1.2 Anti-Aliasing and Edge Smoothing

Anti-Aliasing (AA) consists of the methods that are used to prevent, or at least, minimize the unwanted effects of Aliasing. Such methods include Subpixel processing, Edge smoothing and also image filtering. Several methods for AA are presented in this book. These methods are related to Digital Signal Processing.

2.1.3 Digital Signal Processing

When processing electronic signals, there are 2 kinds of signals: **analog** and **digital** signals.

Analog signals

In nature, the signals are usually analog continuous signals. In the earlier days of electronics, these signals were processed with analog electronic circuits. A sound amplifier is a good example of analog circuit. The sound is converted to an analog electric signal by a microphone. It is amplified by an analog amplifier with a volume control to adjust loudness. Finally, it is converted back to sound by a speaker.

One of the problems with analog circuits, is that they have limited accuracy precision and may require frequent tuning. In the earlier TV, the circuits were all analog. They usually required periodical adjustments referred as 'tuning'.

With the advances in integrated circuit the encoding and decoding of TV signals have been replaced with digital circuits. At the input, the signals are converted from analog to digital (A2D). The A2D conversion consists of sampling the continuous analog signals and converting the measurements into sequences of binary numbers. After digital processing, the digital signals are converted back to analog signals with digital to analog converters (D2A).

Digital Signals

In CGI, the image data consist of digital signals consisting of sequences of binary numbers, that is numbers in base 2 consisting only of sequences of *1's* and *0's*.

Although these numbers could also be represented with decimal numbers in base10, inside of a computer, all the processing is done with binary numbers. Refer to later chapter '*Inside the Binary World*'.

Digital signals are represented with binary numbers and they accuracy is only limited by the number of bits that represent these signals. For processing TV signals, the number of bits to represent these signals is in the order of 10 to 12 bits. This corresponds to an accuracy of 1/1024 to 1/4096. As an example of digital signals, the sound and images are captured and recorded on CD and DVD compact discs. Another advantage of digital signal is that they can be compressed. The signals stored on CD and DVD are compressed digital signals. After being converted to digital, the signals are stable and don't need regular tuning.

2.2 Simple Example of Signal Sampling

As an example of signal sampling, let's consider a sprinter running *100m* in *10 seconds*.

This can be represented by a function $f(t) = d(t)$ where:
- $f(t)$ is a function of time
- $d(t)$ is the distance in *meter* (*m*).
- t is the time in *second* (*s*).

While running, the function $d(t)$ of the sprinter running *100 meters* in *10 seconds* is an analog continuous function. This function describes the increasing distance at any time during the *10 seconds*. But in order to represent that function in a graph, the distance has to be recorded at regular intervals to get sample points. In Figure 2-1, there are 2 examples with 2 different sample intervals.

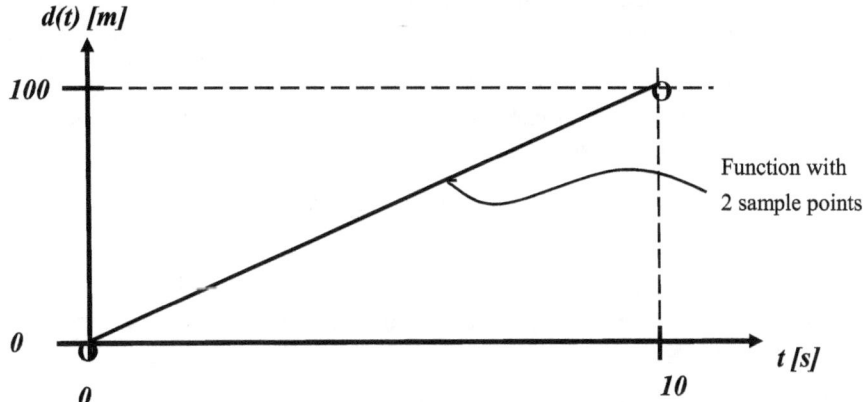

Function $d(t)$ with 1 sample per *10 seconds*

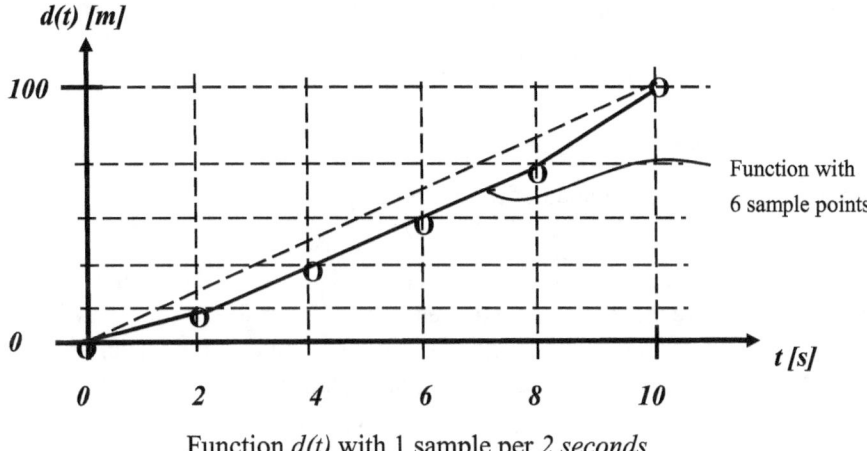

Function $d(t)$ with 1 sample per *2 seconds*

Figure 2-1 Sampling Example of Sprinter Running *100 meters* in *10 seconds*

Usually, the time starts at the beginning and is measured at the end. This corresponds to 2 samples points. In the first graph the function $d(t)$ is drawn using 2 sample points. Since there is no information about the function behavior between the 2 samples, the function can be represented with a straight line.

If we want more information, the distance can be sampled every *2 seconds*. In the 2nd graph, the function is drawn with the results of 6 measurements, the first measurement being *0 meter* at time *0 second*, the last one being *100 meters* at *10 seconds*. This graph represents a more detailed description of the sprinter progress.

During the first *2 seconds*, the progress is slower, because the sprinter starts at a speed of *0 m/s*. He accelerates until he reaches cruising speed. From *2 to 8 seconds*, he runs at almost constant cruising speed. During the last *2 seconds*, from *8 to 10 seconds*, the speed increases because of the sprint to the finish line. Again, there is no information about the behavior between samples, so the sample points are connected with straight lines.

Note that, if the sprinter was recorded in a movie at 24 samples per *second*, there would be 240 sample points from start to finish. In this case, the progress of the sprinter would be more complete and would be closer to the analog curve.

In this example, the samples are taken at equal time intervals. This can be referred as temporal sampling.

In another example, the sampling can be done by reading the times at equal distance intervals. This can be referred as spatial sampling. As example, a runner run 10 miles in a circular track, and the time samples are taken after every lap.

2.3 Anti-Aliasing in Real Time CGI Systems

The early RT CGI systems appeared in the 1970s. They were expensive and limited to NASA and US Military market. These customers wanted RT CGI Systems with good Anti-Aliasing features. For these systems there is a broader definition of 'Aliasing'.

2.3.1 Definitions of AA for RT CGI with the 5 A's

In 1980, the 'US Army Material Development and Readiness Command' produced a report about 'Computer Generated Imagery (CGI) Current Technology' [82]

From this report, there are several good definitions for the 5 A's.

Aliasing
In communications theory, the generation of spurious signals caused by sampling for a signal at a rate lower than twice its frequency. In a CGI scene, sampling refers to the spatial frequencies involved in both the computation of the scene and its display. The result is spatial and/or temporal image defects. Manifestations of aliasing include edge stair-step, scintillation of small scene surfaces, breakup of long narrow surfaces, positional or angular motion of edges in discrete jumps or steps, Moiré patterns in regions where there is periodic structure, double imaging, and loss of dynamic image integrity due to field tracking induced by edge motion perpendicular to the scanning direction.

Anti-Aliasing
Image processing techniques, usually involving low pass filtering, that reduce spatial and/or temporal aliasing phenomena. To avoid significant reduction in image resolution, it is generally necessary to perform the anti-aliasing on an image with higher resolution than the one to be displayed.

AOI

Area of Interest. Part of the visual display that contains a high-resolution terrain video presentation. The remainder of the display can be low-resolution supporting information such as featureless sky/earth or sky/checkerboard patterns.

Arc Minute

A measure of resolution as applied to human perception or acuity. One (1) minute of arc is equal to 1/3000th of the distance to an object or 12 inches at 3000 feet.

Artifacts

With respect to CGI systems, artifacts are those phenomena which are encountered in the engineering, operation and use of CGI visuals such as aliasing, flicker and the 'jumping' changes involved in dynamically changing the level of detail.

2.3.2 Spatial and Temporal Image Artifacts

In the following figures there are examples of Aliasing in CGI. These aliasing artifacts are very noticeable when the images are rendered with only one Sample Point per Pixel. Aliasing can be caused by Spatial and Temporal artifacts.

Spatial Artifacts

Spatial Artifacts are the unwanted effect caused by limited sampling resolution. These effects are noticeable in static or still pictures.

Temporal Artifact

Temporal artifacts are caused objects with spatial artifacts moving in the scene over time.

Edge Stairsteps and Crawling

In the following example, depending on their slopes, triangle edges are categorized as Horizontal (*HE*) and Vertical (*VE*) edges types,

In Figure 2-2, there are 2 examples with triangles. Each triangle has 2 *HEs* and 1*VE*. These 2 examples illustrate Spatial and Temporal Artifacts.

In both examples, the triangles edges are rendered with Stairsteps.

In the second half, the triangle has moved ½ Pixel left and ½ Pixel down.
When the triangle moves, the Stairstep pattern changes, resulting in Edge Crawling.

Aliasing

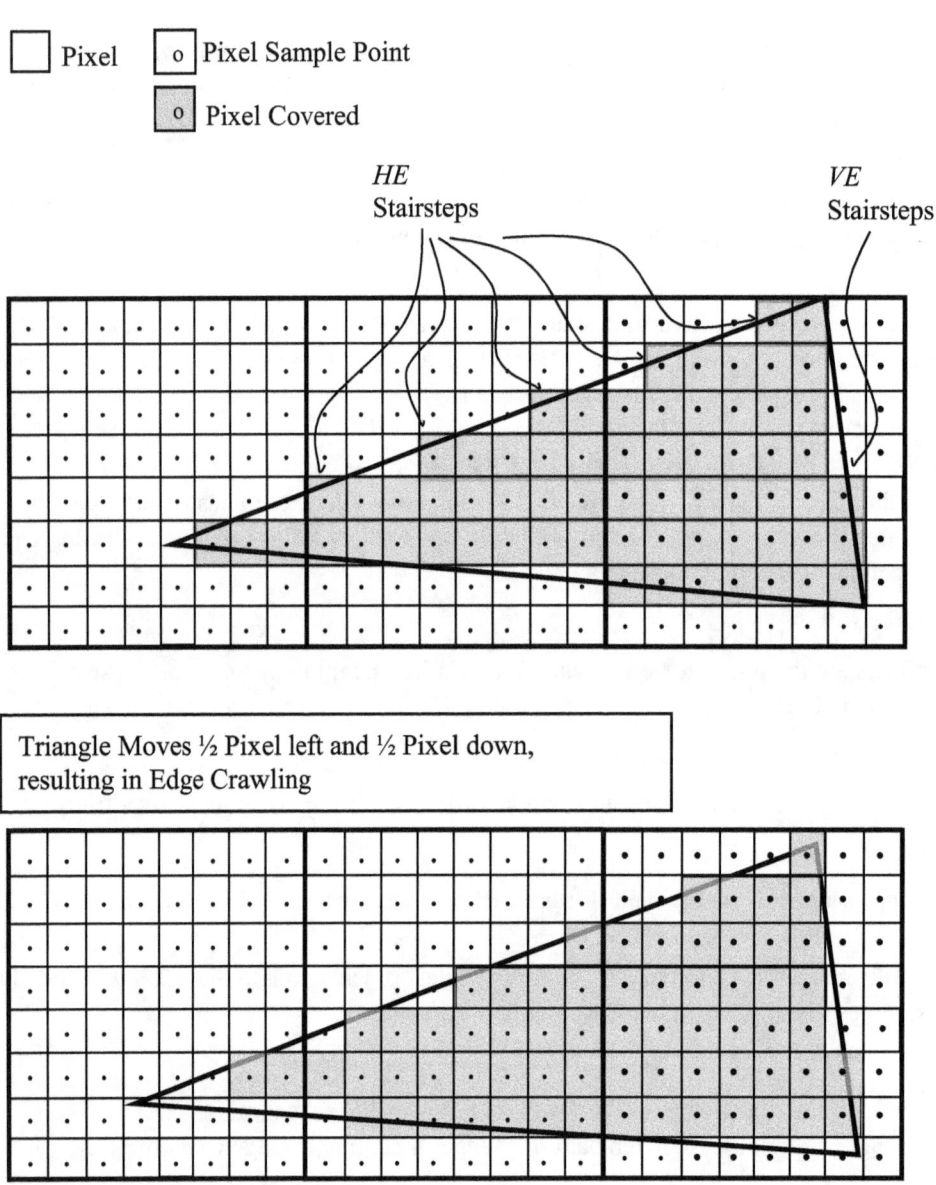

Figure 2-2 Edge Stairstep and Edge Crawling

Narrow Face Breakup

In Figure 2-3, there are 2 examples of Narrow Face Breakup.

When the width of narrow faces is near of smaller than the Pixel size, the rendering results in Face Breakup.

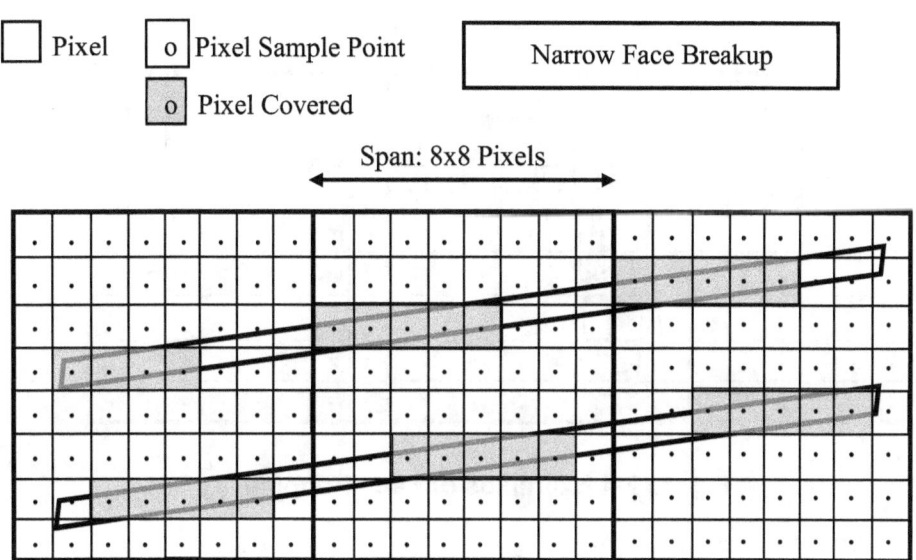

Figure 2-3 Examples of Narrow Face Breakup

Face popping

Face popping is a temporal artifact. It shows with objects going in-and-out of scenes when some dimensions of displayed polygon faces are smaller than the Pixel size.

In Figure 2-4 there are examples of face popping. These tiny faces are displayed only when the Pixel sample point is inside of the faces. In a moving scene, this results into faces popping in-and-out of the scene.

In the Link DIG, a special patented feature provided the capability to remove small face before their projected size reaches the Pixel size [105]. This capability was especially effective with runway stripes during landing or take-off, and with windows on buildings.

For coplanar faces, a new type of face was introduced: Detail Faces. Detail Faces are nested inside of coplanar Mother Faces. For coplanar Detail Faces, the contrast with their mother faces can be gradually reduced from full contrast to zero between size 4 Pixels to size 1 Pixel. At size 1 Pixel, the contrast reaches zero and the detail face can be gracefully introduced or removed in the scene without popping in-and-out of the scene.

Aliasing

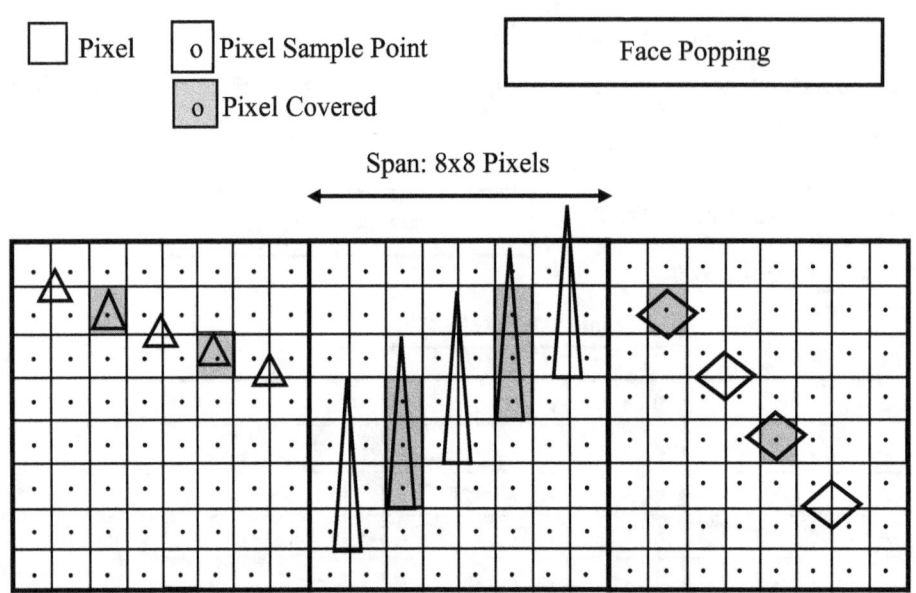

Figure 2-4 Examples of Face Popping

General Example of Moiré pattern [61]

In Figure 2-5, there is a general example of Moiré pattern.

In this example, a set of concentric circles is repeated. These overlapping concentric circles result in various Moiré patterns. In particular, in the lower part of the image, there is a pattern looking like a dragonfly or a spider. This was not intended. It is the result of Moiré pattern.

While this example does not relate to CGI, there are many examples of Moiré patterns in CGI. A typical example consists of displaying checkerboards or arrays of small repetitive pattern. This results in Moiré pattern when the size of the projected patterns become smaller than the Pixel size. Refer to the next examples.

Moiré Pattern when Displaying Checkerboard In CGI

All kinds of artifacts like squares or rectangles popping in-and-out of scene can occur when displaying a checkerboard pattern. The appearance of Moiré patterns depends on the projection size, viewing angle and movement of the checker board pattern.

Figure 2-5 Example of Moiré Pattern

Size of Checkerboard Squares when Compared with Pixel Size

When squares in checkerboard pattern are of the **same size or larger** than the Pixel size, they are displayed properly, but can show stair steps and crawling.

When they are **smaller** than the Pixel size, the under sampling produces squares or rectangles that can be much larger than the projected size. These squares or rectangles can pop in-and-out of scene.

Here are several examples displayed of checkerboards, some of them resulting in Moiré patterns. In these examples, a mask the size of an 8x8 Pixel Span is used to select the color at the center of each Pixel. Refer to the mask on the left side of the figures. In these masks, little holes at the center of Pixels select the color to display on the rendered Pixels. On the right side, the Pixels are displayed with the selected Pixel color.

When squares in checkerboard pattern are of same size or much larger than Pixels, they are displayed properly. Refer to Figure 2-6.

Aliasing

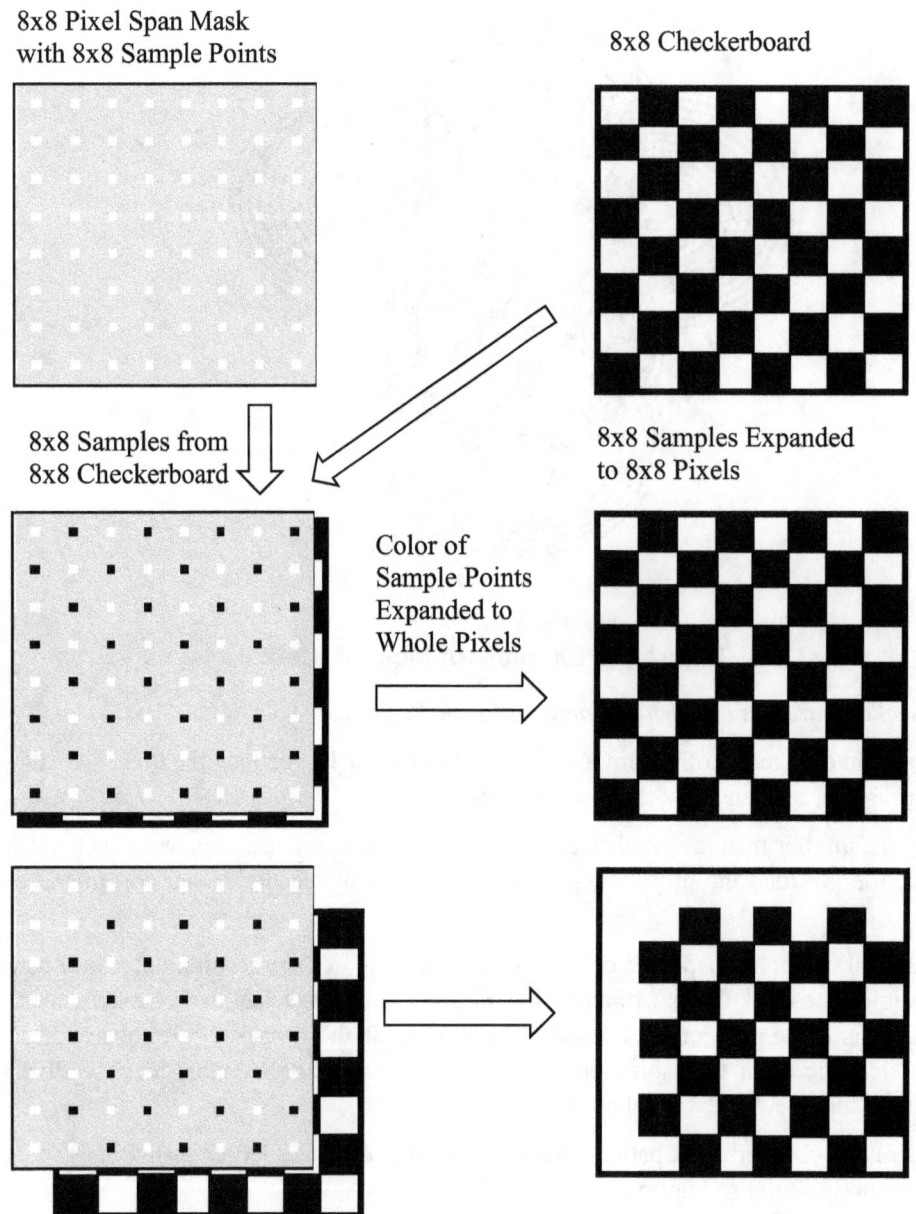

Figure 2-6 Checkerboard with Squares Equal to Pixel Size

Checkerboard Squares Greater than Pixel Size

When the checkerboard squares are greater than the Pixel size, the size of square or rectangle array of size NxN is unchanged. Refer to Figure 2-7.

Aliasing

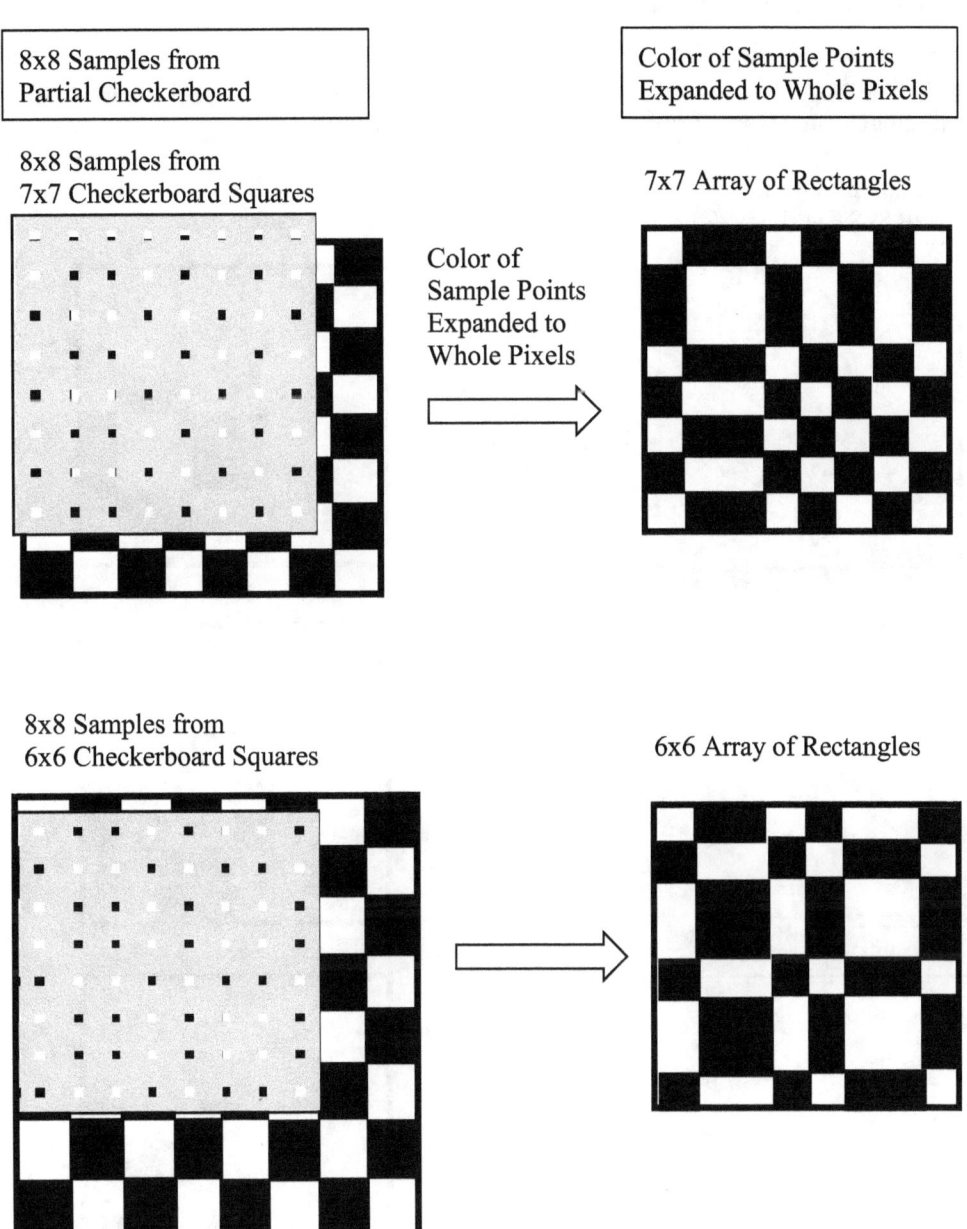

Figure 2-7 Checkerboard with Squares Greater than Pixel Size

Aliasing

Checkerboard Squares Smaller than Pixel Size

When they are smaller than the Pixel size, they start showing aliasing problems with Moiré patterns. In Figure 2-8, the small checker board moves in steps of ¼ Pixel to the right. The displayed squares jump from one pattern to another.

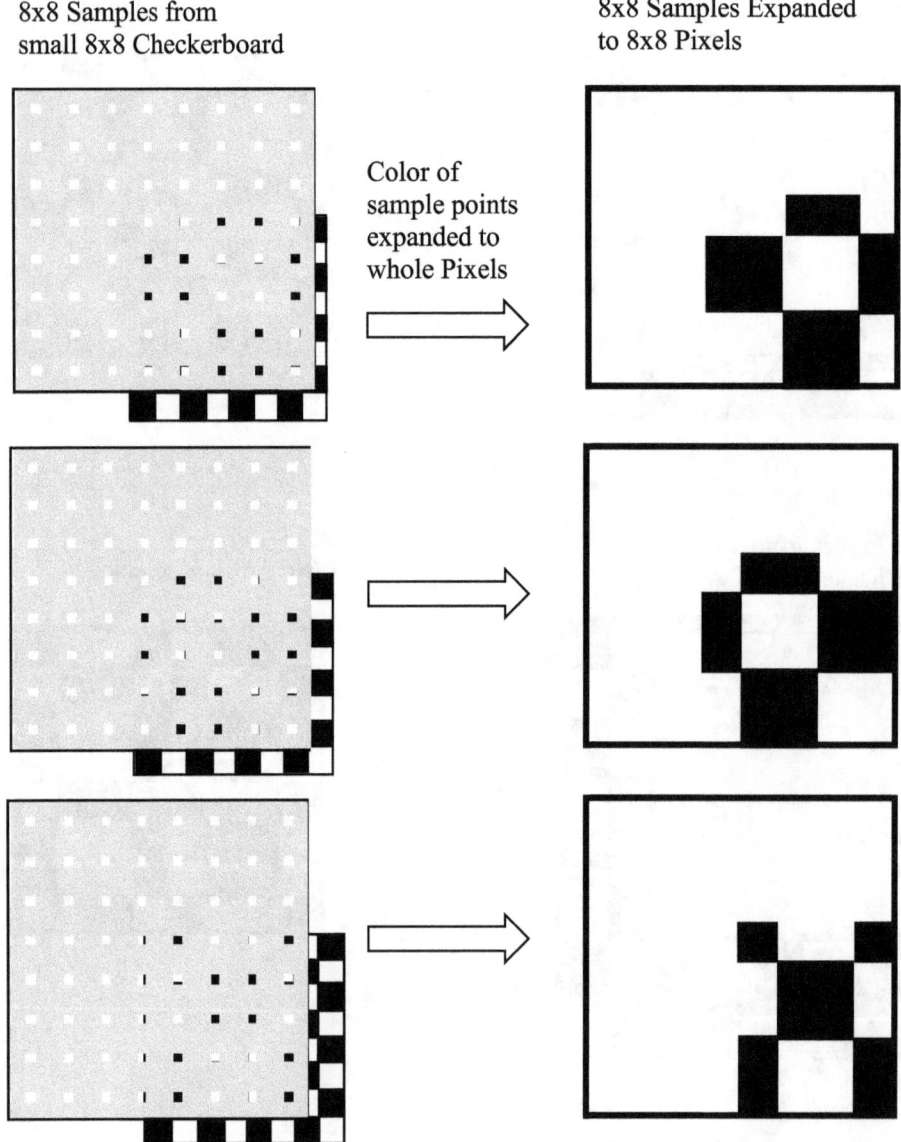

Figure 2-8 Small Checkerboard Moving 1/4 Pixel to the Right

When the checkerboard squares get much smaller the size of Pixels, the size of the displayed squares or rectangles can become much larger than their projected size. They also produce Moiré patterns. The aliasing also shows as the size of the displayed rectangle array decreases from NxN to smaller than NxN. Refer to Figure 2-9.

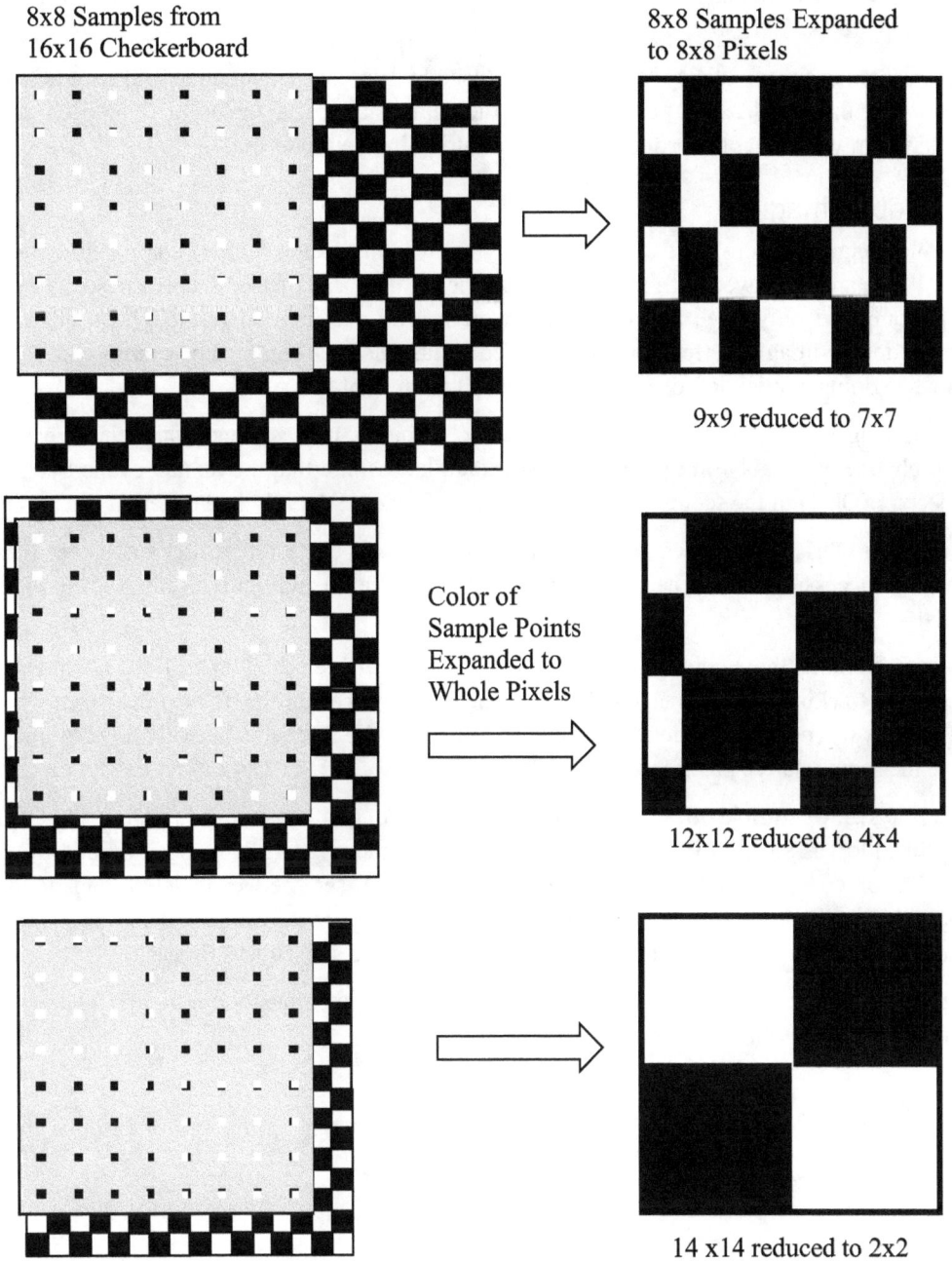

Figure 2-9 Displayed Squares from Shrinking Checkerboard.

Aliasing

Display Checkerboard using Texture Maps.

Instead of modeling checkerboard patterns with polygons and repetitive patterns, it could be implemented with texture maps. With texture maps the level of details would minimize and correct these Moiré patterns.

For example, texture maps of size MxN can be reduced by successive averaging into several level of details, starting at M/2xN/2, and reducing the dimension by a factor of 2 at each step. The CGI system will select the proper texture size during image rendering.

2.3.3 Double Imaging

The Double Imaging effect shows up when displaying dynamic scenes that are computed at frame rate of 1/30 sec and displayed with interlaced Scanlines at field rate of 1/60 sec. Because the same image is computed only once and displayed twice a 1/60 sec interval (although on alternate Scanlines), double imaging effect can be observed in fast moving scenes. For example, this can happen when doing a quick left or right turn, or a roll in an airplane.

Double Imaging can be observed when displaying 2 objects in the scene while their relative positions change noticeably on the display. For example, assume that the human eye is tracking one Object #1 (Obj1) in the scene while Object #2 (Obj2) moves rapidly in a different direction.

While tracking Obj1, both objects are projected in the viewer eye's retina. Let's consider what happens in 2 successive frames, each consisting of 2 fields: field0 and field1. Refer to example in Figure 2-10.

In field0 of 1st Frame, the 2 objects have a relative position between each other. Let's assume that the observer is tracking Obj1. When Obj2 moves, the eye moves according to the tracking of Obj1. After 1/60 sec, when field1 of the same frame is displayed, the 2 objects in the computed image still have the same relative position as in field0.

But after 1/60 sec, when field1 of the same frame is displayed, Obj2 has moved relatively to Obj1. In the retina, Obj1 is still in focus. But because the eye is tracking Obj1, the position of Obj2 in retina is recorded at a different position after the 1/60 sec between field0 and field1. But since Obj2 is moving relative to Obj1, the projection of Obj2 in the retina at field1 of 1st frame is expected to have moved at the middle of distances between 2 subsequent frames.

The expected position Obj2 at field 1 is different from the repeated position at field1. This result in having 2 images of Obj2 in the retina.

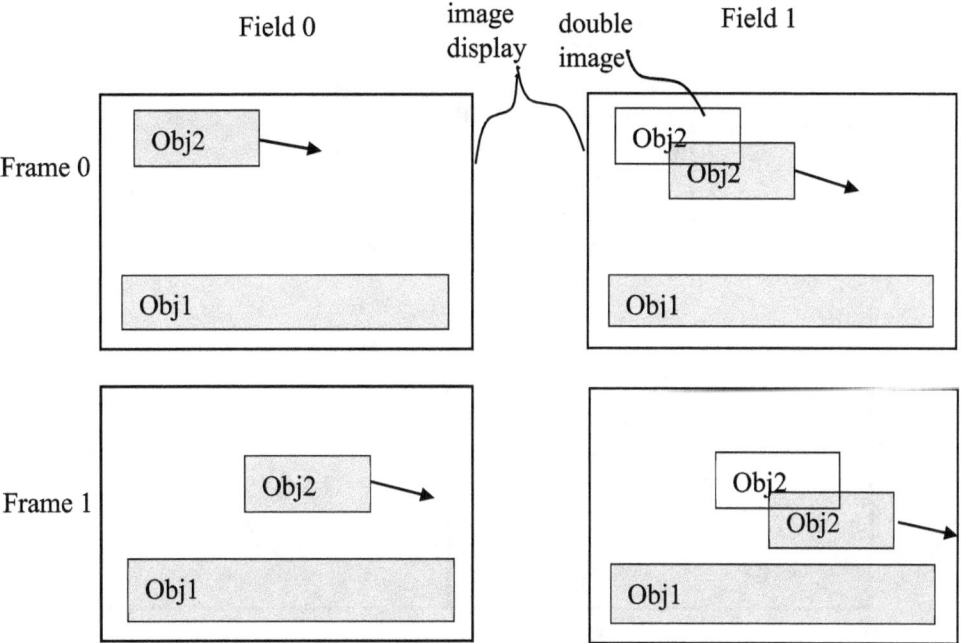

Figure 2-10 Example of Double Image

My experience with Double Imaging

I could not find a reference about Double Imaging in Wikipedia. Instead, I will describe my own experience to describe this effect.

When we started to evaluate our R&D DIG prototype at Link, it did not take long to observe Double Imaging in the CGI system for the first time in our CGI prototype system.

For the DIG testing and evaluation, we had a one window setup with a split screen display and parabolic mirror that presented the image at infinity. This setup was enclosed in a little black tent. We could control a flying airplane with switches and a simple joystick [81]. With this simple setup, it was like flying in the cockpit of a real plane.

We had designed the DIG prototype to compute the dynamic scenes at frame rate, that is the images were updated each 1/30 sec, while the same image was displayed in the two fields (1/60 sec each) on the interlaced display. It did not take long to observe Double Imaging and jerky images when doing quick left or right turns. For example, when an airplane does a turn, it first does a small roll, then turns. When doing turns in the simulated flight, the image also does a roll. In this case, I observed this effect while my eyes were concentrated on the image display. The horizontal horizon changed to around a 30-degree angle and I was able to observe Double Imaging in my eyes' peripheral vision. It was a jerky motion, similar to the 'ta-ta-ta' of a machine gun. Refer to the 'hill' in Figure 2-11.

Aliasing

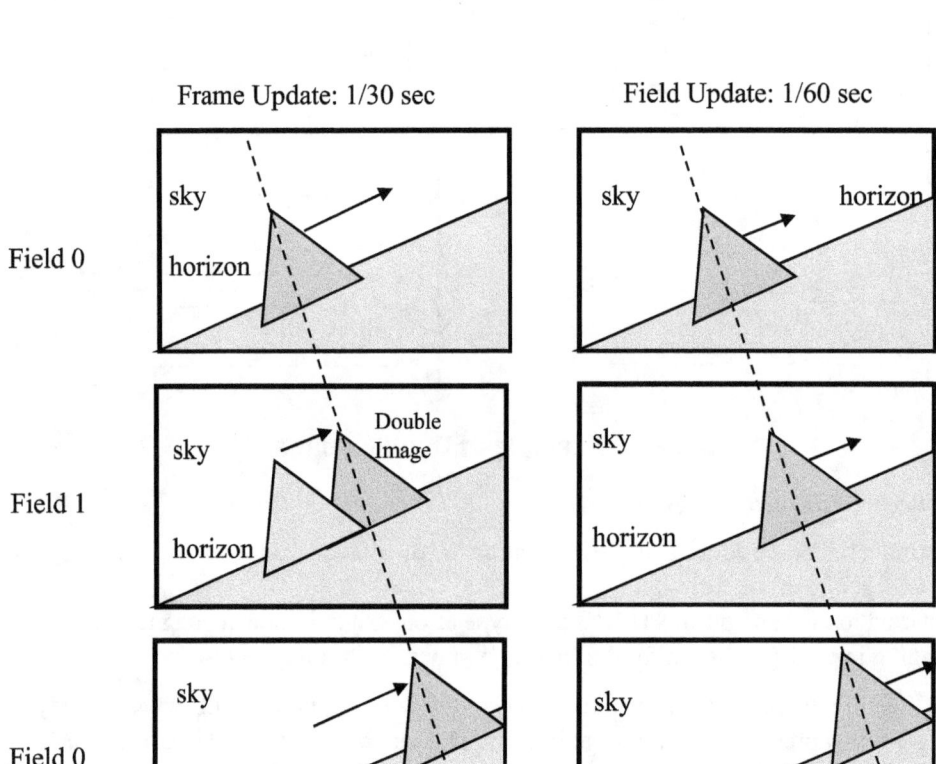

Figure 2-11 Double Imaging During Plane Roll

Double Imaging can be elusive

Since the Double Imaging effect depends on what object you are focusing on in the dynamic scene (or in the display surrounding), it is not always reproduceable. When repeating the experiment while looking at the scene elements that caused Double Imaging, this distracting effect disappears.

Double Imaging was a disappointment. We made small modifications to the DIG prototype in order to run at field rate of 1/60 sec. To our satisfaction, we observed no Double Imaging when using field update rate. We decided that all DIGs should be delivered with Field Update rate as the default. This also means that the number of edges per field would be roughly half the number of edges per frame. Because of this decision, the scene density was reduced by half. Aliasing Examples with Analog Signals

2.3.4 Definition of Aliasing in Broadcast TV

Before the advent of CGI, aliasing was observed on images produced by broadcast TV and even movies. On TV, a typical example can be seen when presenters wear ties or shirts with repetitive patterns of size of around a few *mm* or a fraction of an inch (around *1/8"*). In movies it can be observed when wheels of carriages seem to turn backward.

Here is a definition of 'Aliasing', according to Mariam Webster Dictionary [60]:

'Aliasing is an error or distortion created in digital images. It usually appears jagged outlines. We commonly observe aliasing on television. This occurs when there is an insufficient magnification produced by the lens of a TV camera focused on periodic structures such as the pattern of pinstripes in an announcer's shirt, bricks in the wall of a house, or seats in an empty stadium.'
— *Douglas B. Murphy,* Fundamentals of Light Microscopy and Electronic Imaging, 2001

2.3.5 Sine Function and Frequency

The most common repetitive analog signal is the sine function. For more details, refer to sine and cosine functions [46].

The sine and cosine functions are periodical functions. They repeat at equal intervals referred to as cycle or period. The frequency of periodic analog signal is measured in cycles per second [cyc/sec], or Hertz with symbol [Hz]. For example,

1 Hertz: *1 Hz = 1 cyc/sec*
1 kilo Hertz: *1 kHz = 1000 cyc/sec*
1 Mega Hertz: *1 MHz = 1000 kHz = 1000'000 cyc/sec*
1 Giga Hertz: *1 GHz = 1000 MHz = 1000'000'000 cyc/sec*

The cycle is measured in arc angles. The unit of arc angle is degrees *[deg]* or radians *[rad]*. For example, the angle for a full circle is:

1 full circle = 360 deg
1 full circle = 2Pi rad, where Pi = 3.14159265...

The constant Pi is an irrational number with an infinite non-repetitive and unending fraction. For example:

50 fraction digits of Pi: *Pi = 3.14159265358979323846264338327950288419716939937510...*

The cosine function precedes the sine function by 90 degrees, or Pi/4. Refer to Figure 2-12.

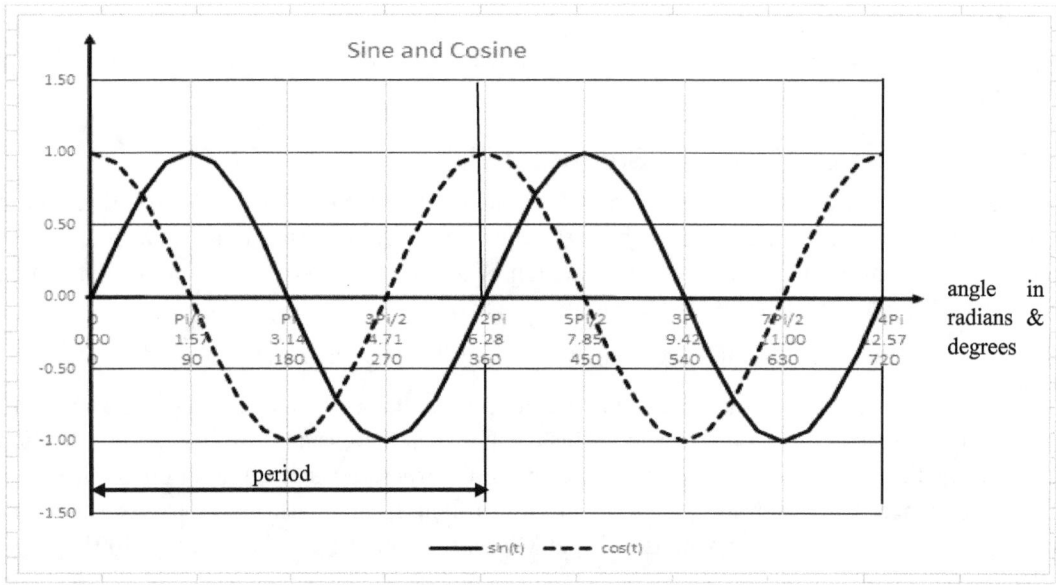

Figure 2-12 Sine and Cosine Functions

2.3.6 Aliasing when Sampling a Sine Function

In electronics, there are analog and digital signals. An example of analog signal is the processing of sound with a microphone, analog amplifier and speaker. The sound is converted from sound wave into electric signal in a microphone. It is then amplified with analog circuits and converted back into sound waves in a loud-speaker.

One of the weaknesses of analog signals is that their levels and amplitudes can drift over time or depending of the electric components. It needs to be calibrated. In older TV, the signal processing was done with analog circuits that needed calibration.

On the other hand, digital signals consist of numbers that are processed with digital circuits. The advantage of digital processing is that the numbers have stable values and can be safely reproduced. The CD and DVD are good examples of digital processing. Since sound and music are analog signals, they have to be sampled and converted to digital values before they can be stored in CDs or DVDs. Digital compression algorithms are then used to increase the density of data in CD and DVD (like JPEG, MPEG2, MPEG3, MP3 and HDTV).

2.3.7 Sampling Frequency and Nyquist Frequency

Aliasing is often caused when analog signals levels are digitized and the sampling frequency is not high enough to sample all the signal transitions. The critical sampling frequency for signal sampling is defined by the Nyquist frequency. For more info, refer to the Nyquist–Shannon sampling theorem [62].

When sampling periodic signals, there is no frequency aliasing when the sampling frequency fS is at least twice the signal frequency f. The Nyquist Frequency defines the minimum Sampling Frequency to prevent frequency aliasing [62].

> Definition of Nyquist Frequency:
>
> The Nyquist Frequency fN is defined as 2 times the frequency f of the sampled signal: $fN = 2f$
>
> When sampling a signal, the sampling frequency fS should be at least greater than the Nyquist Frequency fN to prevent aliasing: $fS > fN = 2f$

When the highest frequency of a signal is less than the Nyquist frequency of the sampler, the resulting sample sequence is said to be free of the distortion known as aliasing, and the corresponding sample-rate is said to be above the Nyquist rate for that particular signal.

> What is Frequency Aliasing:
>
> The Nyquist Sampling frequency is a requirement for preventing 'Frequency Aliasing'. There are other aliasing effects such as jaggies (edge stairsteps and crawling), faces popping and other distracting artifacts in CGI. For this reason, the definition of Nyquist frequency should be rephrased like:
>
> When sampling a signal, the sampling frequency fS should be at least greater than the Nyquist Frequency fN to prevent 'frequency aliasing'.

Frequency Aliasing when $f/fN > 0.5$

When the ratio of Signal frequency to Sample frequency f/fS is greater than 0.5, this results in aliased frequencies in the sampled signals. The frequency of the aliased sampled signal consists of a down and up mirror pattern limited by the Nyquist frequency.

The graph in Figure 2-13 shows how the frequency of a sampled signal results into aliased frequencies when $f/fN > 0.5$.

Aliasing

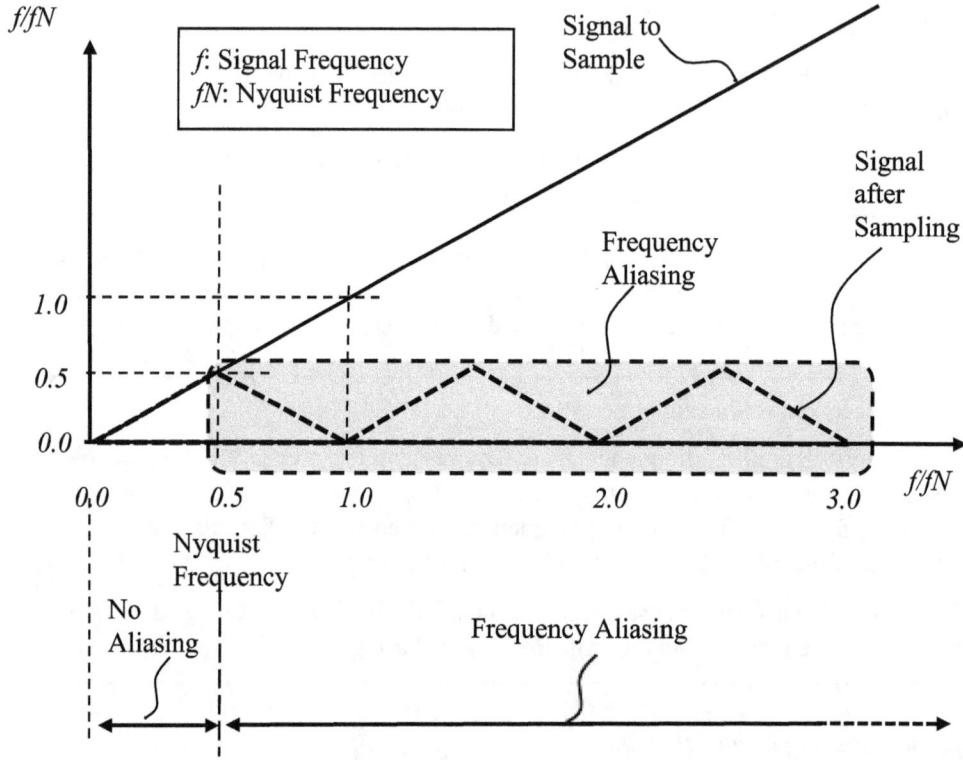

Figure 2-13 Signal to Sample and Signal after Sampling

2.3.8 Sampling of a Sine Function as Aliasing Example

Here is a typical example of aliasing that is caused by under-sampling.

A sine function is defined by its Amplitude (*A*), Phase (*t*) and offset Phase (*dt*):
$f(t) = A * sine\ (t + dt)$

The sine function is a periodic function, where a *Period P=2*Pi* is the time before the function repeats with the same values. A period, or cycle, corresponds to an angle of *2Pi* (or *360 degrees*).
$f(t) = A * sine\ (t) = A * sine\ (t + P)$

When a point rotates around a circle of radius 1 and centered a *x=0* and *y=0*, its projection on the *y* axis describes a *sine* function, and the projection on the *x* axis is a *cos*ine function.

The sine function repeats with the same values after each period. The 'frequency' is defined as the number of 'periods per second', measured in *cyc/sec,* or *Hz*.

The sine function represents an analog signal. Its values are continuous. For example, the early TVs were implemented with analog circuits, using vacuum tubes or transistors. The signals were continuous and their amplitude could be observed and measured with analog oscilloscopes. The new TVs use mainly digital circuits and a few analog circuits for interfaces.

On the other hand, digital computers deal only with binary numbers instead of continuous analog signals.

For more info about binary numbers and binary logic, refer to later chapter:
'Inside the Binary World'.

Binary logic consists of logic blocks separated by holding registers. Data in computers consist of bits (binary digits). Each bit can have only 2 states: *0* and *1*. For example, it takes 8 bits to represent and integer number from decimal *0* (binary '*0000'0000*') to *255* (binary '*1111'1111*'). Since the number of bits can be very large, groups of 8 bits are organized into bytes (B). Here, the quote symbol (') inside of number is used to facilitate reading. The value of each byte is between *0* and *255*. When bits are stored into memories, they are usually stored as 1, 2, 4 or 8 bytes. For example: *32 bits = 4 bytes = 4B*.

As another example it takes 10 bits to represent and integer number from decimal *0* (binary '*00'0000'0000*') to *1023* (binary '*11'1111'1111*'). Binary '*100'0000'0000*' = decimal '*1024*' is often referred as *1 kbit (kilo bit),* since the value is close to digital *'1000'*.

The computer operations are controlled by their main clock, which is a square wave of frequency around 1GHz. Registers data can change at the end of each clock cycle. The computer clock oscillates between *0* and *1*. The clock frequency corresponds to the number of clock transitions from *0* to *1* in a second. Generally, a computer can perform one operation per clock. The clock frequency of modern computer is around 1 GHz or more. That is, computers can perform 1000 million (1 billion) operations per second.

In the newer TVs, the processing of TV signals is also implemented with digital circuits. In order to accomplish this, the sine functions have to be sampled with analog to digital converters (AC to DC) to produce the sine function with a sequence of measured amplitudes. At the end of the processing, the signal can be converted back from digital to analog with DC to AC converters. Current display monitors can be driven by analog or digital RGB color signals.

Nyquist frequency

As mentioned above, there is an important requirement for sampling analog signals. In order to prevent 'aliasing', the 'sampling theory' defines the critical (or minimum) sampling frequency to be at least twice the largest frequency of the signals to sample. The minimum sampling frequency is the referred to as the **Nyquist frequency**.

2.3.9 Aliasing when Sampling a Sine Function

Here is an example of aliasing when sampling a *sin()* function.

In Figure 2-14, there are 6 examples of a *sin( )* function sampled with 6 different frequency ratios *fS/fN*. In Fig 2-15, same examples for *cos ()*.

There is no frequency aliasing for sampling ratios of *fS/fN < 0.5*. There is no interest in showing sampling frequencies below the Nyquist frequency. So, the lowest ratio starts at *fS/fN = 0.5*. In these figures, the Signals after sampling are compared with the Signals before sampling.

For the *sin( )* function, the sampling at frequency *ratios fS/fN= 0.0, 0.5, 1.0, 1.5, 2.0, ...* would be all 0.0. So, the sampling is delayed by 0.25.

Aliasing

For $fS/fN=0.25, 0.75.1.25.1.75, 2.25, ,...$, the non-zero samples are *1.0, -1.0, 1.0, -1.0, 1.0, ...*
Since the *cos( )* function starts at *cos(0)=1*, there is no need to delay the sampling.

For $fS/fN= 0.0, 0.5, 1.0, 1.5, 2.0, ...$, the non-zero samples are *1.0, -1.0, 1.0, -1.0, 1.0, ...*

The sample points are indicated with 'up-arrows'.

- *fS* is the Signal frequency
- *fN* is the Nyquist frequency
- $fS/fN = 0.5$ at the Nyquist frequency

In the sequence of examples, the ratio of sampling intervals is incremented in steps of *1/8=0.125*, starting at the Nyquist frequency of

$fS/fN = 4/8 = 0.5$.

Note that the indexes on the left of the graph is used only for identifying the cases.

Aliasing

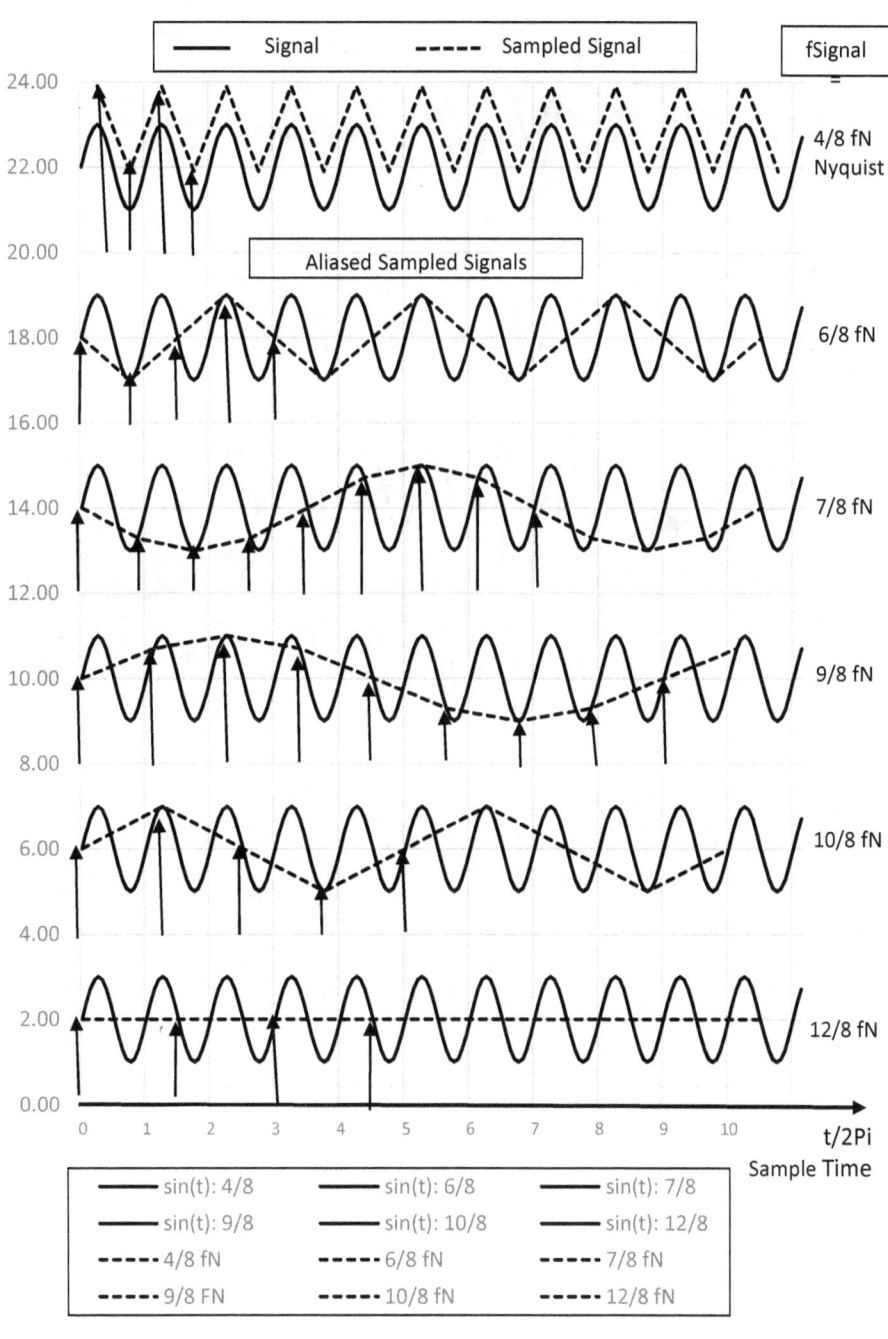

Figure 2-14 Aliasing when Sampling Sine Function

Introduction to Area-Based Anti-Aliasing for CGI

Aliasing

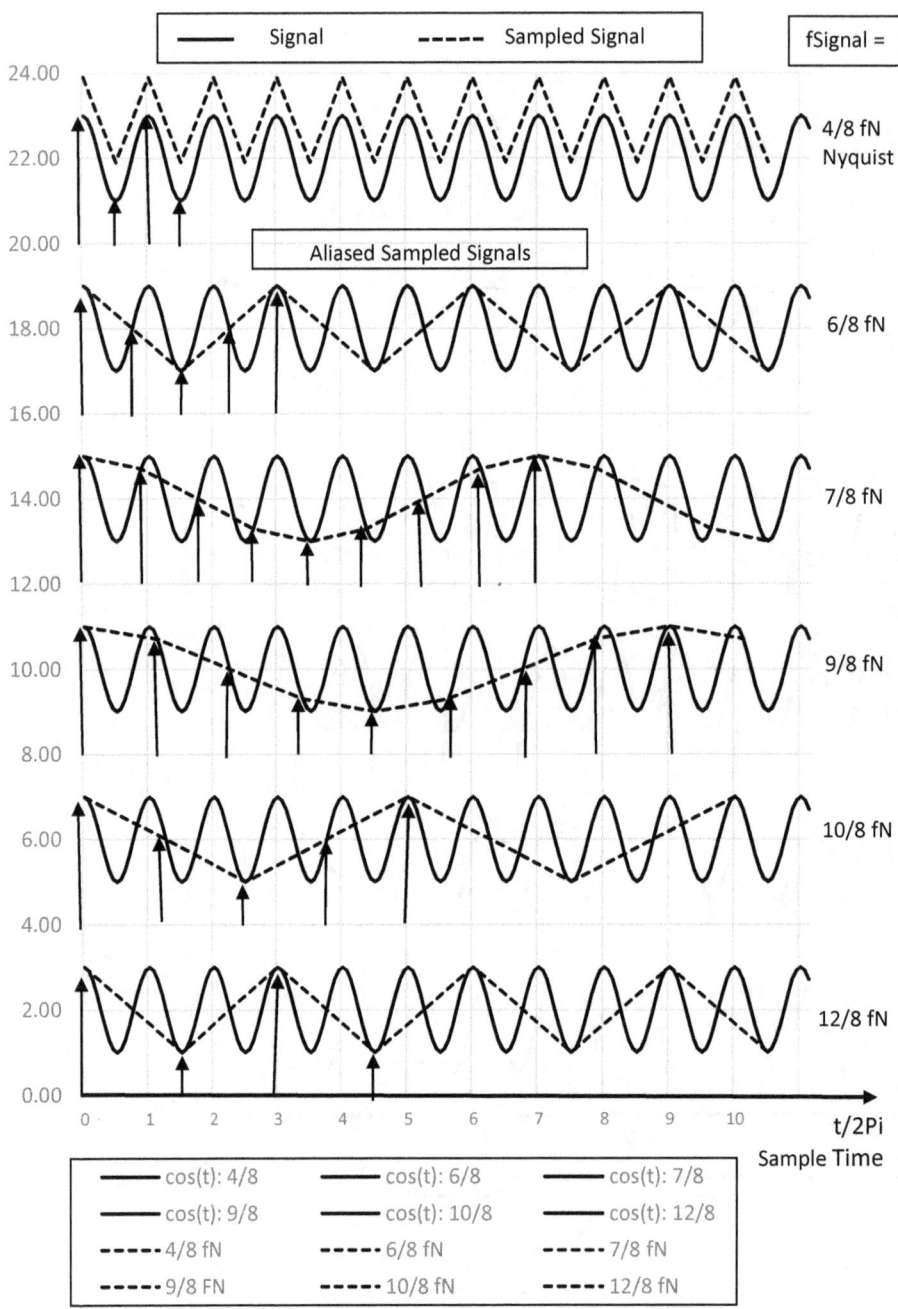

Figure 2-15 Aliasing when Sampling Cos Function

The results from these 2 examples are plotted in Figure 2-16. In this figure the frequencies for ratios of *f/fN* are shown *before* and *after* sampling.

Aliasing

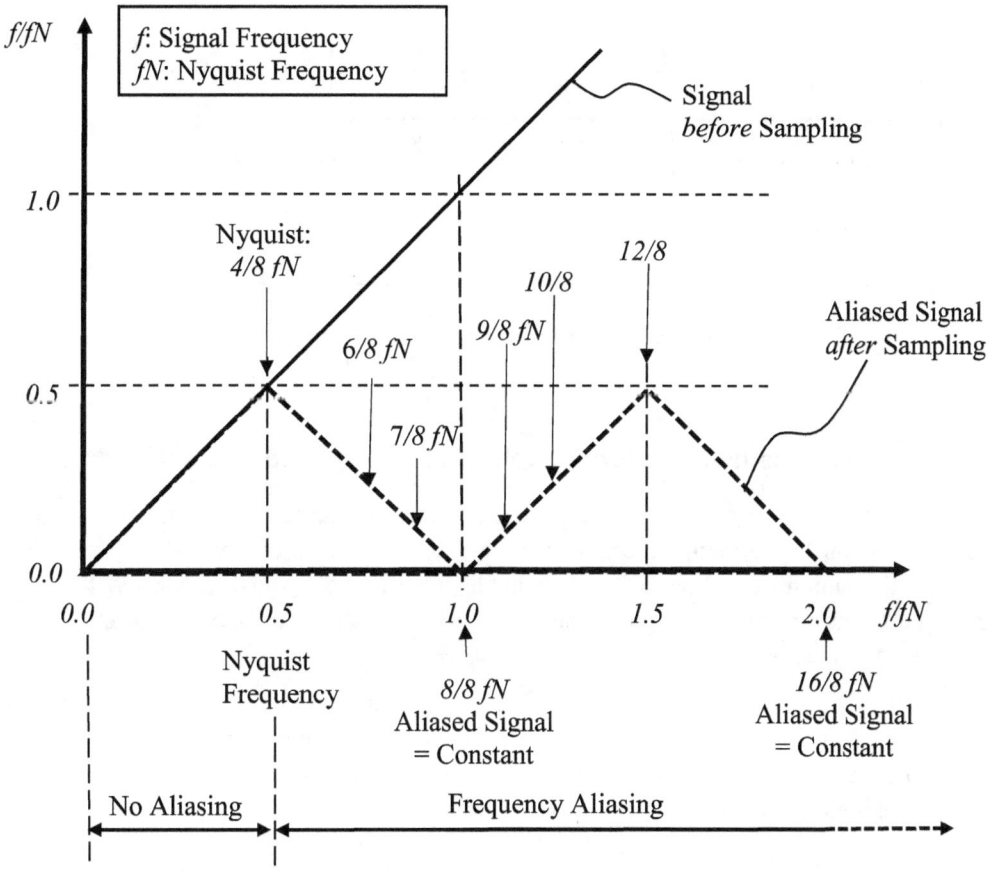

Figure 2-16 Signal to Sample and Signal after Sampling

In these examples, when the frequency ratios have integer values, like $f/fN = 0, 1, 2, 3, ...$, the aliased output samples have a constant value

For the $sin()$ function, when starting with $sin(0)=1$, the aliased samples would be all $sine(n*2Pi) = 0$ for $n= 0, 1, 2, 3, ...$. For the $cos()$ function, when starting with $cos(0)=1$, the aliased samples would be all $cos(n*2Pi) = 1$, for $n= 0, 1, 2, 3, ...$. For other starting values, the samples would have a constant value.

$sin(n*2Pi + offset) = constant$, for $n= 0, 1, 2, 3, ...$.

2.3.10 Sine and Cosine Functions after Sampling

In the above examples, the sampled values are shown connected with line segments. In reality, the sampled functions consist of sequences of unconnected points. In case of signals consisting of sine and cosine functions after sampling, the analog signals can be recovered by applying filters or scaler functions. But there is a problem when sampling at the Nyquist frequency $fN = 2fS$.

Depending on the sample point, the output could be a constant value. Refer to Figure 2-17. In this example, the function '$cos(t)$ for $fN=2*fS$, or $fS/fN=0.5$' is sampled twice per cycle.

Introduction to Area-Based Anti-Aliasing for CGI

Aliasing

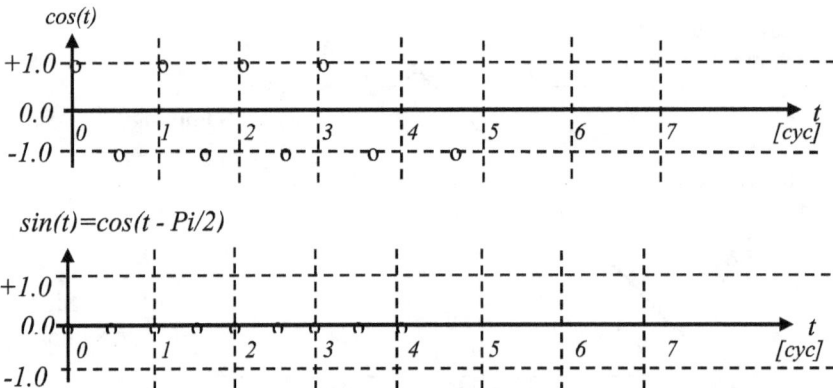

Figure 2-17 Cosine Function Sampled at Nyquist Frequency (*fN=2*fS*)

When the amplitude at points is maximum, there is enough information for reconstructing the sine and cosine function by applying filters. But, note that in the case of *cos(t - Pi/2)*, the output amplitude of the samples are all zero. This is what happens at the Nyquist frequency. There is no aliasing. The frequency of the output signal is the same as the frequency of the input signal, although the amplitude is zero.

So, the Nyquist frequency is no warranty for the output amplitude being the same as the input amplitude. It is only the limit for output without frequency aliasing. In order to have the same amplitude, the frequency limit should be *fN = 4*fS*. In this case, the output amplitude would be the same as the input amplitude. Refer to Figure 2-18.

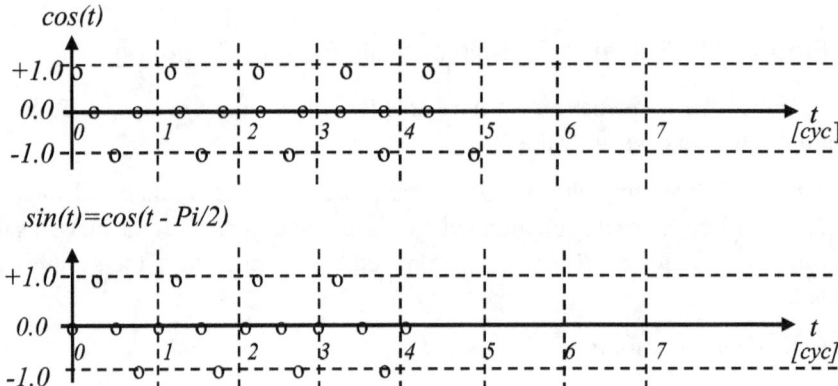

Figure 2-18 Sin and Cos Func Sampled at Twice the Nyquist Freq (*2fN=4*fS*)

2.4 Sampling of TV Signals

As mentioned earlier, there are different TV standards in the world. In particular the image refresh rate (or field rate) is 60 Hz in the US and 50 Hz in the European countries. On top of that, the detail standards can vary from country to country. In order to exchange TV programs across different countries, the ITU (International Telecommunication Union) developed standards to store TV images into a common digital format.

2.4.1 Standard TV

There are two recommendations documents from the ITU to define the standard of exchanging TV signals between different analog TV formats [43].

ITU-R BT.601 (or its former name CCIR 601) is a standard originally issued in 1982 by the CCIR for encoding interlaced analog video signals in digital video form. It includes methods of encoding 525-line 60 Hz and 625-line 50 Hz signals, both with an active region covering 720 luminance (intensity info) samples and 360 chrominance (blue and red color info) samples per line.

BT.601 provides interlaced video data, streaming each field separately, and uses the $YCbCr$ 4:2:2 color encoding system. The sampling frequency for Pixels is 13.5 Mz. The Luminance is transmitted at 13.5MHz. The Color info is also transmitted at 13.5 MX, but with alternating component. The resulting transmission rate for Cr and Cb is 6.75 MHz.

ITU-R BT.656 describes a digital video protocol for streaming uncompressed PAL (Germany, 50 Hz and 625 lines) or NTSC (US, 60 Hz and 525 lines) Standard Definition TV signals. The protocol builds upon the 4:2:2 digital video encoding parameters defined in ITU-R BT.601,

BT.656 data stream is a sequence of 8-bit or 10-bit words, transmitted at a rate of 27 Mword/sec. The transmitted word sequence of Pixel pairs consisting of 4 words 'Y, Cr, Y, Cb' is transmitted at 6.75 MHz. (4*6.75 Mword/sec)

The ITU (International Telecommunication Union) is based in Geneva, Switzerland. Its global membership includes 193 countries and around 900 business, academic institutions, and international and regional organizations.

The CCIR is the 'Comité Consultatif International pour la Radio', a forerunner of the ITU-R.

Although the number of Line for PAL and NTSC are different, it is compensated by having 25 frames/sec and 30 frame pre sec, respectively.

In Table 2-2, there is the list of parameters for the NTSC (US), PAL (Germany) and SECAM (France) standards.

Aliasing

Parameters	525-line, 60 field/s	625-line, 50 field/s
Standard	NTSC	PAL, SECAM
Coded signals	Y, C_B, C_R	Y, C_B, C_R
Number of samples per total line for each signal	858	864
# Lines /Frame	525	625
# frames/sec	30	30
Total #cycles/sec	2*858*525*30 = 27'027'000	2*864*625*25 = 27'000'000
Transfer frequency	27.0 MHz	27.0 MHz
Sampling frequency for each Pixel	13.5 MHz	13.5 MHz
Sampling frequency Y	13.5 MHz	13.5 MHz
Sampling frequency Cb or Cr	6.75 MHz	6.75 MHz
Form of coding	8 or 10 bit samples	8 or 10 bit samples
Duration of the digital active line expressed in number of samples	720	720
Form of coding	Y, Cb, Y, Cr	Y, Cb, Y, Cr

Table 2-1 TV Digital Encoding

In Figure 2-19, there are examples of the data sampling and transfer for *Y, Cb*, and *Cr*.

For the color information, TV images use the *YCbCr* color format instead of *RGB*, for the following reason. In the *YCbCR* format, the *Y* component represents the intensity or gray shades. For Black and White TV, the image can be displayed with the *Y* component only. The *YCbCr* format could be used for Black and White TV, as well as Color TV.

For a practical point of view, when you need to adjust the contrast and brightness in a TV set, you are modifying the *Y* component. When you adjust the color, you are modifying the *Cb* and *Cr* components. It would be hard to adjust the image brightness if you had to manipulate the three *RGB* components.

It was determined through experiments that the human eye is more sensitive to gray shade changes than color changes. This allowed sampling of the *Y* component at the Pixel frequency and the *Cb* & *Cr* components at half the Pixel frequency. The French went one step further by alternating the sampling of the *Cb* and *Cr* component from *SL* to *SL*. Each component was sampled on one *SL* then sent a 'one *SL* delay line' so that it could be reused on the next *SL*. At that time, it allowed the colors in the SECAM standard to be more stable than in the NTSC US standard.

Aliasing

By using the *YCbCr* format, the color can be represented in a 16-bit format when the *Cb* and *Cr* components are sampled at half the frequency of *Y* component. During the transfer of color data, the *Cb* and *Cr* components alternate from Pixel to Pixel.

While the Standard TV standards have been replaced by HDTV standards since the early 2000s, they are still used for transmitting TV image in local TV surveillance and monitoring systems. While working at MetaVideo in Los Gatos CA, I have designed several chips for TV surveillance camara systems.

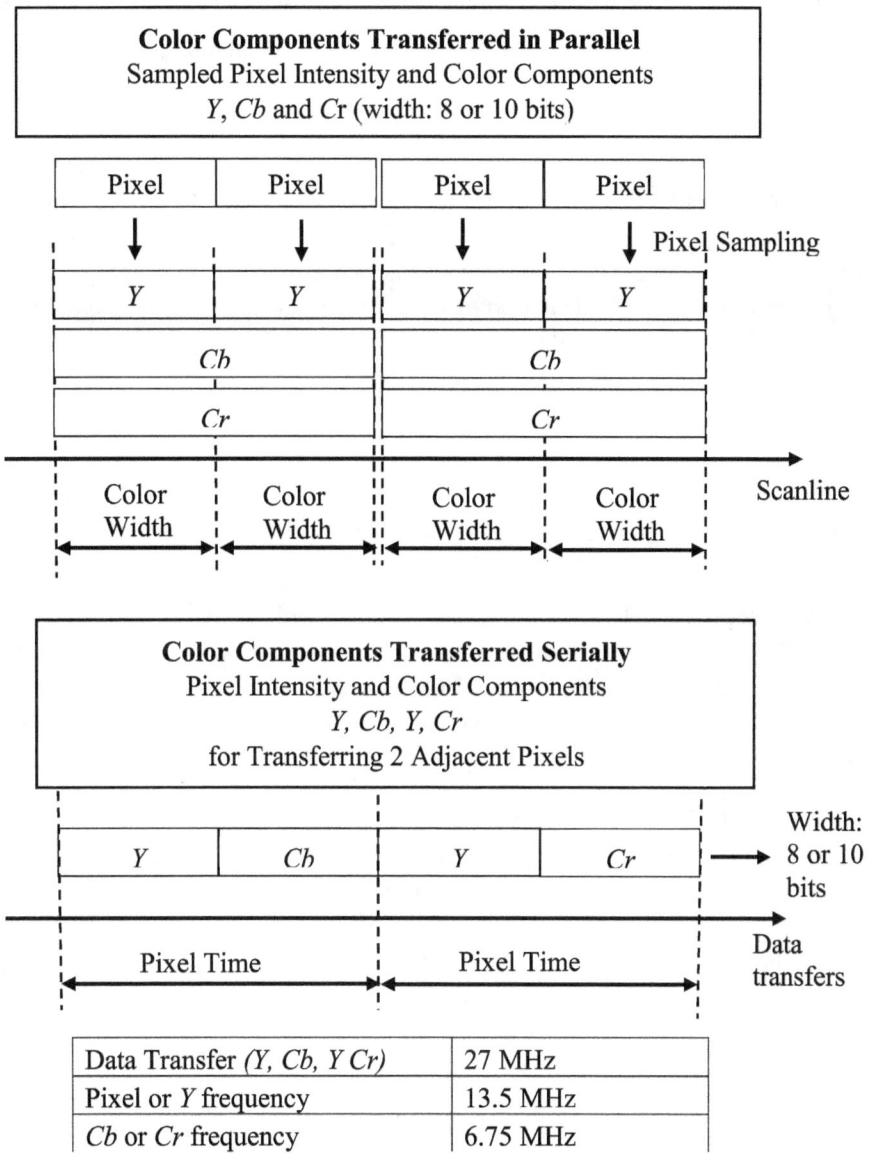

Figure 2-19 Pixel Data Sampling and Transfer

Aliasing

2.4.2 High-Definition TV (HDTV)

HDTV as it is known today first started official broadcasting in 1989 in Japan. It was widely adopted worldwide at the beginning of the 2000s.

HDTV has a better image quality and resolution than Standard TV. Another advantage of HDTV is that it can be broadcast within a smaller bandwidth. The TV channels for Standard TV occupy a bandwidth of 8 MHz per channel. HDTV signals are **compressed** and can send more detailed images with 8 time less bandwidth. HDTV can be transmitted within the same channels, but instead of 1 channel of STV, up to around 8 HDTV channels can be transmitted within this bandwidth.

With HDTV, the ITU standards (ITU-R BT.601 and 656) have been replaced by HDTV standards like H.264 and H.265. Refer to [44].

H.264

Advanced Video Coding (AVC), also referred to as H.264 or MPEG-4 Part 10, Advanced Video Coding (MPEG-4 AVC), is a video compression standard based on block-oriented, motion-compensated integer-DCT coding on block size. It is by far the most commonly used format for the recording, compression, and distribution of video. It supports resolutions up to and including 8K.
H-264 Block Sizes: 4x4 or 8x8 Pixels

H.265

High Efficiency Video Coding (HEVC), also known as H.265 and MPEG-H Part 2, is a video compression standard designed as part of the MPEG-H project as a successor of Advanced Video Coding (AVC, H.264)

While AVC uses integer discrete cosine transforms (DCT) with 4×4 and 8×8 block sizes, HEVC uses integer DCT and DST transforms with varied block sizes between 4×4 and 32×32. When compare to AVC, HEVC offers from 25% to 50% better data compression at the same level of quality or substantially improved video quality at the same transmission rate.
H-265 Block Sizes: 4x4, 8x8, 16x16 and 32x32 Pixels.

2.5 Aliasing with Digital Signals

In CGI, instead of sampling analog signals, the samples are taken from scene elements consisting of 3D triangles projected onto a 2 D image. During rendering, the image is constructed by sampling triangles in 2D geometric space to assign colors to the image Pixels. Only one color can be assigned to each Pixels. When taking only one Sample Point per Pixel, aliasing occurs where triangles cover only portions of Pixels.

2.5.1 Point Sampling and Z-Buffer
Single Sample Point and Z-Buffer

In the 1960s, with the advent of minicomputers, several universities started to produce 3D images from computers. Because of the amounts of computations, the images were simple. But soon many algorithms were developed and the images became quite complex and realistic.

For images generated by computer, the color and depth of the computed Pixels are saved in a frame buffer in computer memory. The frame Buffer consists of a Color-Buffer and a Z-Buffer. When 2 objects that are projected onto the image overlap in depth, the hidden portions of these object have to be ignored. When rendering the triangles on the image, for each Pixel, the Z-depth is used to select the triangle closest to the viewpoint. Because of the memory requirement, only one Sample Point can be saved in memory. When selecting only one sample, the quantization effect produces stairsteps on the edges of projected triangles or breakup of narrow faces. These stair steps are also referred to as Aliasing or Jaggies. This can be fine for static images, but not for dynamic images and movies.

When only one Sample Point inside of a Pixel (*Pix*) is used to produce dynamic scenes in CGI, the lack of resolution amplified these adverse distracting effects. The edge stairsteps results in edge crawling and small faces popping in out of the scene.

Multiple Sample Points

One of the AA methods for reducing the jaggies consists of taking several samples to render each Pixel. There are several ways for selecting these samples. For example:

- Render an image at higher resolution, then reduce the image to a lower resolution with filtering. This is the approach used by Super Sampling AA (SSAA). This approach is equivalent to taking NxN Samples to render each image Pixel.
- Another approach is to sample several points inside of image Pixels, referred to as Subpixels and construct several images using these Subpixels. The final image is obtained by taking the average of these images. The array of Subpixels within a Pixel is often referred to a Bed of Nails (BON). This is the approach used by Multi Sample AA (MSAA). This approach is equivalent to taking Nx1 Samples to render each image Pixel.
- The ideal solution would be to process the Subpixels in one pass, without rendering an image for each Subpixel. This is the approach proposed with Area-Based AA (ABAA). This approach is equivalent to sampling N Subpixel-Areas to render each image Pixel.

2.5.2 Sampling Frequency and Nyquist Frequency

In a previous section, the Nyquist frequency was introduced for periodic analog signal. Here, the Nyquist frequency is introduced for Pixel sampling with Pixel frequency (fP).

During rendering, the decision to display polygons depends on their displayed size and the sample points. The sample points can be the Pixel center, or, several Subpixel sample points. In general, there is no frequency aliasing when the polygon width is greater than the distance between 2 Sample Points. The Nyquist Sampling Frequency (fN) defines the minimum frequency (f) of the sampled signals to prevent frequency aliasing [62].

Aliasing

> Definition of Nyquist Frequency:
>
> The Nyquist Frequency fN is defined as 2 times the frequency f of the sampled signal: $fN = 2f$
>
> When sampling a signal, the sampling frequency fS should be at least greater than the Nyquist Frequency fN to prevent aliasing: $fS > fN = 2f$

When the highest frequency of a signal is less than the Nyquist frequency of the sampler, the resulting sample sequence is said to be free of the distortion known as aliasing, and the corresponding sample-rate is said to be above the Nyquist rate for that particular signal.

> What is Aliasing:
>
> The Nyquist Sampling frequency is a requirement for preventing 'Frequency Aliasing'. There are other aliasing effects such as jaggies (edge stairsteps and crawling), faces popping and other distracting artifacts. For this reason, the definition of Nyquist frequency should be rephrased like:
>
> When sampling a signal, the sampling frequency fS should be at least greater than the Nyquist Frequency fN to prevent 'frequency aliasing'.

Nyquist Frequency and Pixel Frequency

When sampling signal and displaying these signals, several frequencies need to be defined:

- f: Signal frequency or Pattern frequency
- fP: Pixel frequency
- fS: Sample frequency
- fN: Nyquist frequency

2.5.3 Checkerboard Pattern with 1 Sample per Pixel

In the following examples, the Pixel color is obtained with only 1 sample per Pixel (sample point at center of Pixel). A checkerboard pattern is used to illustrate how the Nyquist Frequency applies to Pixel sampling.

Rendering a Checkerboard Pattern

When rendering a checkerboard pattern, the pattern frequency is the frequency of the repeating pattern. The pattern period consists of '1 white square and 1 black square'.

So, the Sample frequency of the checkerboard pattern should be at least 1 sample per square.

- $f\,(pattern) = 2\,squares/period$.

In order to sample a pattern without aliasing, the sampling frequency should be at least greater than twice the Signal frequency, or Pattern frequency.

That is *fS = 1 sample/square = 2f*   (twice the pattern frequency)

Checkerboard with Squares Equal to Pixel Size

When sampling with 1 Sample Point per Pixel, the Nyquist frequency should be at least equal to the Pixel frequency is. It takes 2 cycles to represent a cycle of white and black squares. When sampling the checkerboard pattern at 1 sample/Pixel and 1 square per Pixel, the Pattern frequency is *f (pattern) = fP/2*

where *fP = Pixel frequency*.

Refer to Figure 2-20.

In Figure 2-21, there is an example of a checkerboard where each square is equal to 1 Pixel. There are 2 samples, 1 taken on the bottom-right moving and 1 taken on the top-left. As can be seen, the rendered 8x8 pixel-span is unchanged. This is different from the sine being sampled across a half cycle (180 degrees or Pi radians). Compare with analog 'Sampling a Sine Function' in a previous section.

Aliasing

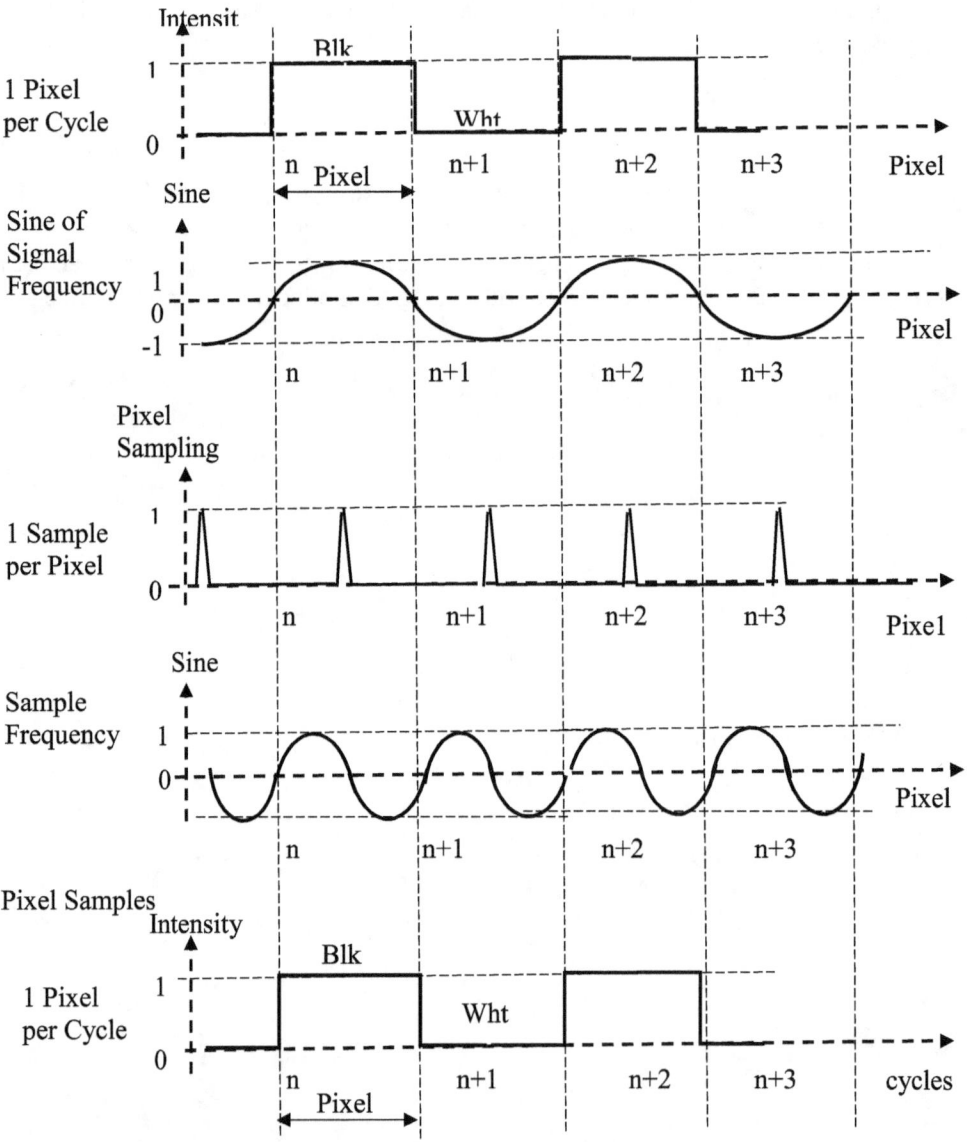

Figure 2-20 Sampled Signal with 1 Sample per Pixel

Aliasing

Using 1 Sample per Pixel: Nyquist Frequency = Pixel Frequency

Checkerboard Pattern Frequency = 1 square per pixel = NyquistFrequency /2
Nyquist Frequency = 2* Pattern Frequency

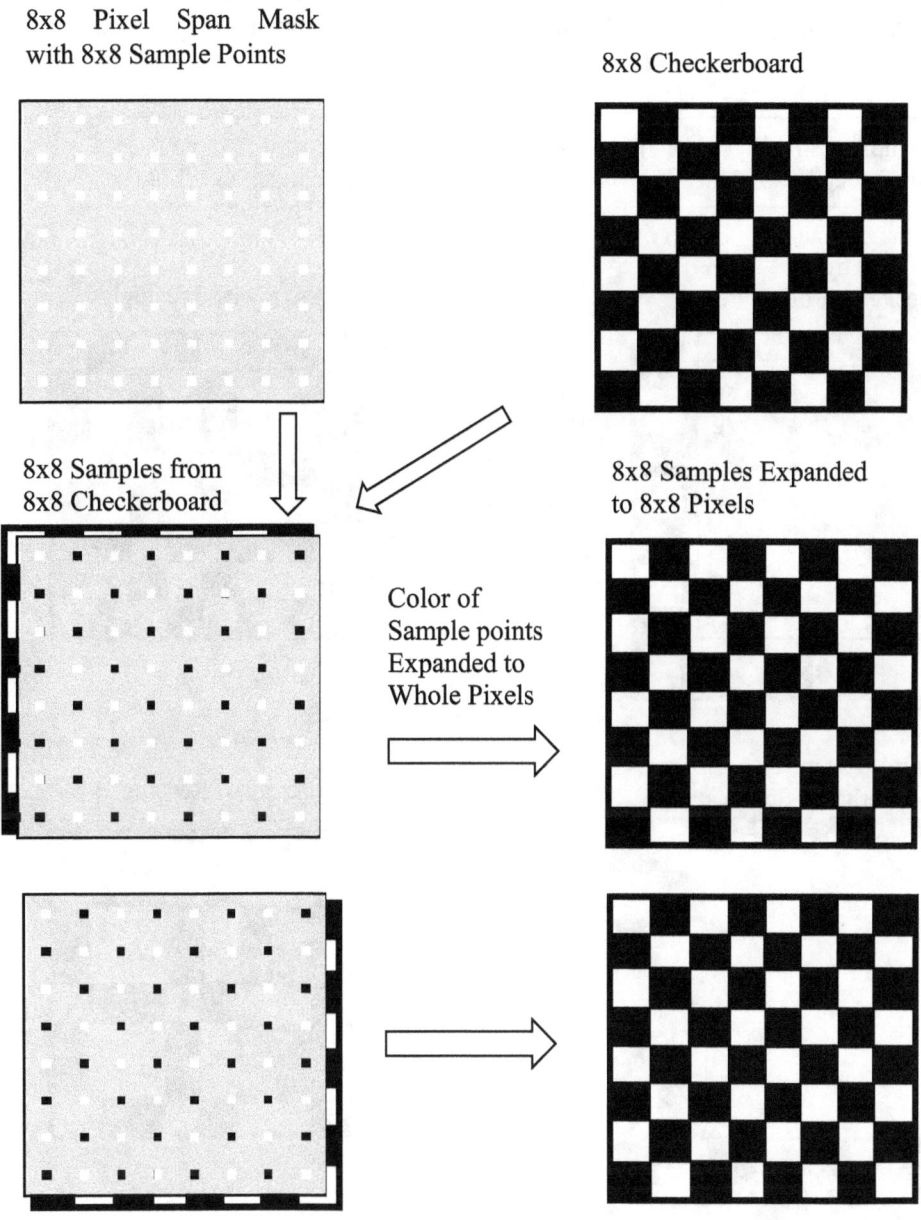

Figure 2-21 Checkerboard with Squares Equal to the Pixel Size

Aliasing

Checkerboard Squares Greater than Pixel Size

Ther is no frequency aliasing when there is at least 1 sample per Pixel.

When squares in checkerboard are larger than Pixels, the squares are displayed properly (as squares or rectangles). In this case when the pattern frequency is less than half the Pixel frequency, there is no 'frequency aliasing; In the sampled image, there is either a square or a rectangle for each sampled square. Refer to Figure 2-22.

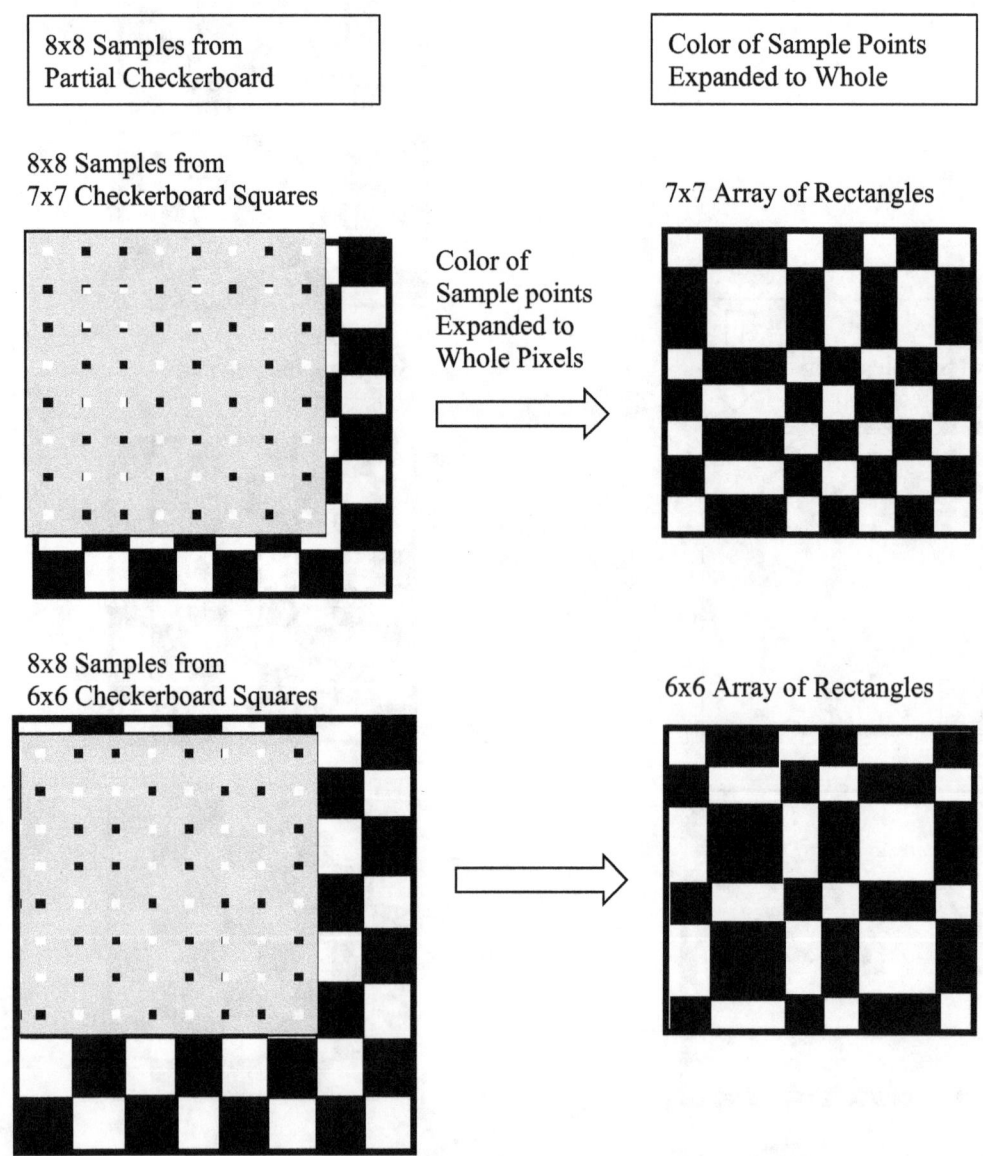

Figure 2-22 Sampling when Sample Freq > Nyquist Freq

Aliasing

Checkerboard Squares Near Pixel Size

- When the rendered squares in checkerboard pattern are **larger** than the Pixel size, they will show no frequency aliasing.
- When the rendered squares in checkerboard pattern are **equal** to Pixel size, they is no frequency aliasing.
- When the rendered squares in checkerboard patterns are **smaller** than Pixel size, they show frequency aliasing. The under sampling produces squares that are larger than the projected size. They also produce Moiré patterns.

Refer to Table 2-2 and Figure 2-23 for examples when the Sample Frequency is near the Nyquist Frequency.

Checkerboard Squares	fS vs fN	Freq. Aliasing	Comment
Greater than Pixel size	>	No	Squares or Rectangles
Equal to Pixel size	=	No	Squares
Smaller than Pixel size	<	Yes	Larger Rectangles Moiré patterns

Table 2-2 Checkerboard Squares Near Pixel Size

Checkerboard Squares Smaller than Pixel Size

When checkerboard squares are smaller than a Pixel, many distracting aliasing effects occur.

- In-and-out face popping
- Edge Crawling
- Moiré patterns

Refer to 3rd example in the figure, when the Sampling Frequency < Nyquist Frequency

Aliasing

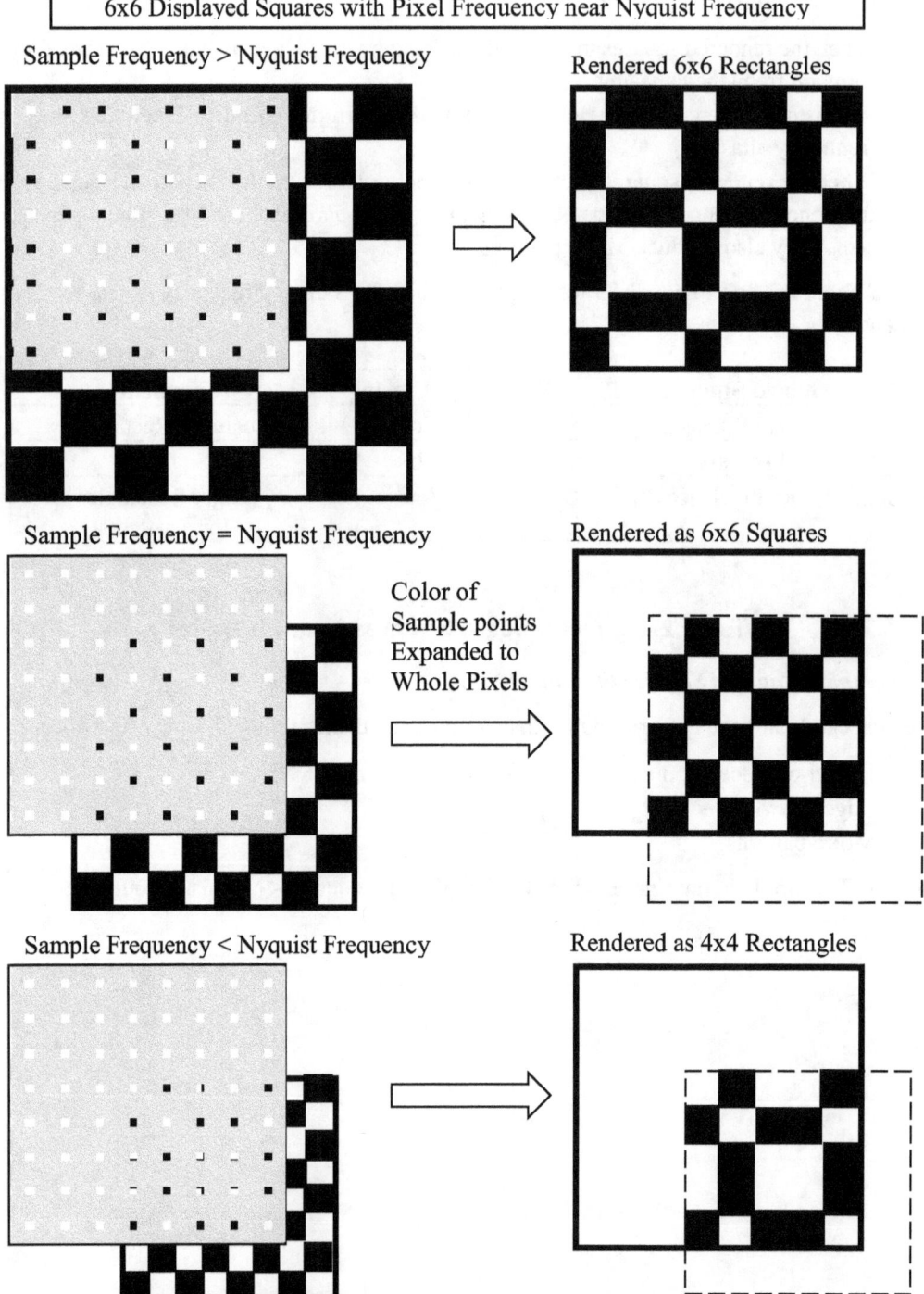

Figure 2-23 Checkerboard with Squares Close to the Pixel Size

Aliasing

Checkerboard Squares Equal to Half Pixel Size

There is an interesting case when the checkerboard squares are equal to half the Pixel size. In this case the sample frequency is equal to ½ Nyquist frequency: $fS = fN/2$.

Refer to Figure 2-24.

In this example the sampled array of 6x6 checkerboard squares results in a display of a Black or White square of size 3x3 Pixels.

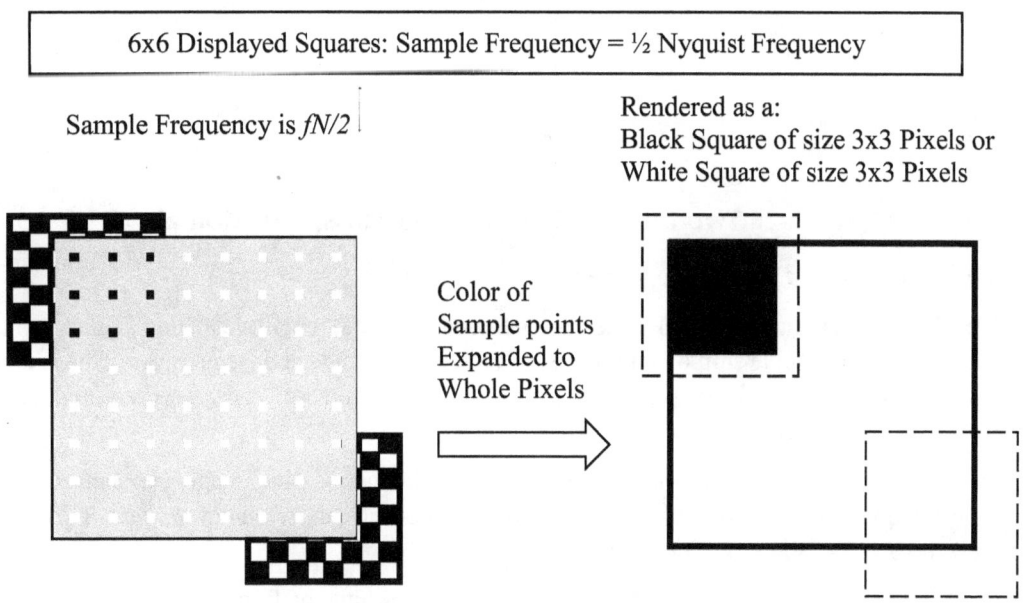

Figure 2-24 Pixel Frequency Equal to 1/2 Nyquist Frequency

2.5.4 Box Filter and Frequency Response

In Sample Theory, the sampling region in the image is referred to a Fourier window [62]. Within the window the weights to the Sample Points are represented by a function. Outside of the window, the sample weights are '0'. When the image is rendered with N Sample Points per Pixel and all the samples have the same weight, the sample window is a square window. This square window represents a 'Box Filter'.

Refer to Figure 2-25.

Aliasing

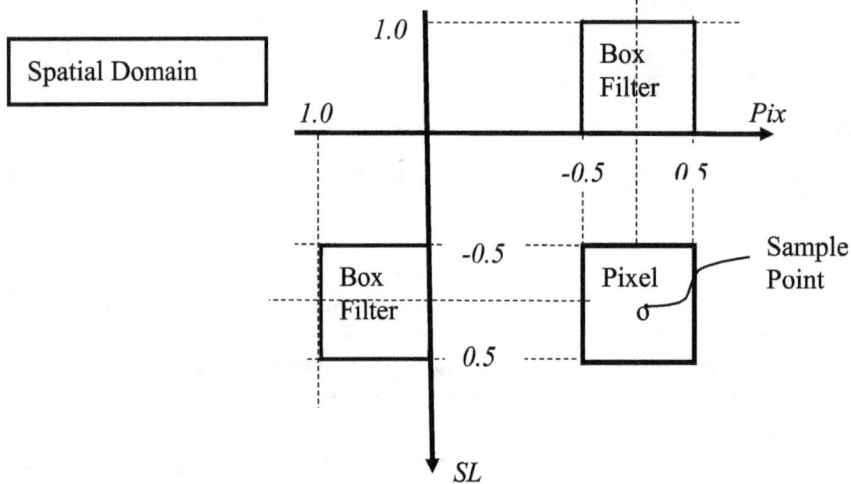

Figure 2-25 Two-Dimensional Box Filter in Spatial Domain

Fourier Transform and Frequency Response

The French mathematician, Joseph Fourier, has demonstrated that repetitive analog signals can be decomposed into an infinite sum of sine waves of various amplitude and frequencies. This is done by using the Fourier Transforms [62]. So, a signal in 'time domain' can be represented by its frequencies in 'frequency domain'.

As an example, when an image is rendered in *spatial domain*, the image elements can be decomposed in a sum of signals *sine(n*t)* at different frequencies, in *frequency domain*. This is the frequency response of the sampling window.

The sampling window has a frequency response that indicates how the frequency of the signal will be rendered. The single point sampling (N=1) can be represented by a Box Filter in the 'spatial or time domain'. The frequency response is represented by a *sinc()* function in the 'frequency domain'. Refer to 'Nyquist and *sinc()* function' in Wikipedia [62].

$sinc(Pi * x) = sine(Pi * x) / (Pi * x)$, where x is the signal angle in radian.

Refer to Figure 2-26, 'Box Frequency Response with *sinc()* Function'.

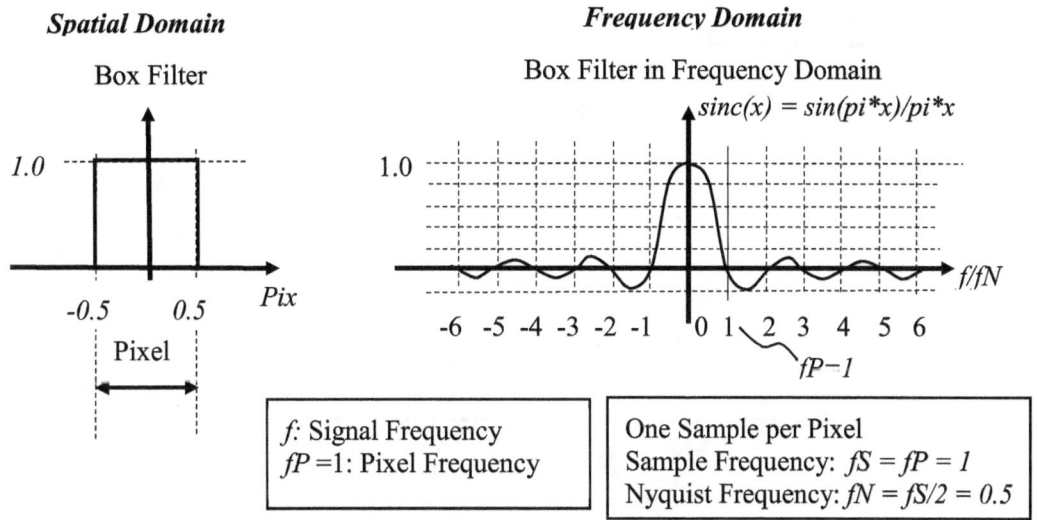

Figure 2-26 Box Filter in Spatial Domain and Frequency Domain

Frequency Aliasing and Aliasing Effects

According to the sampling theory, aliasing occurs when the frequency of the signal is more than half the Nyquist frequency (f > fN/2). This is what I will refer to as 'Frequency Aliasing'. In CGI, other distracting artifacts are also referred to as 'Aliasing'. I will refer these as 'Aliasing' or 'Aliasing Artifacts'.

When sampling within a Pixel, the Pixel frequency(fP) is equal to 1:

$fP = 1$;

With 1 Sample Point per Pixel, the sample frequency (fS) is equal to the Pixel frequency (fP).
$fS = fP$

To prevent aliasing, the sample frequency (fS) should be at least twice the Nyquist frequency (fN).
$fS >= 2fN$

To prevent aliasing, the signal frequency (f) should be no more than the Nyquist frequency.
$f < fN = fP/2$

The signal frequency (f) is limited to half the Pixel sample frequency (fS).

Refer to Figure 2-27 and 2-28.

When considering the frequency response, there is significant 'Frequency Aliasing' when the signal frequency (f) becomes greater than the Nyquist frequency of fN=0.5. This explains the Moiré patterns with the checkerboard when the size of the squares becomes smaller that the Pixel size.

Aliasing

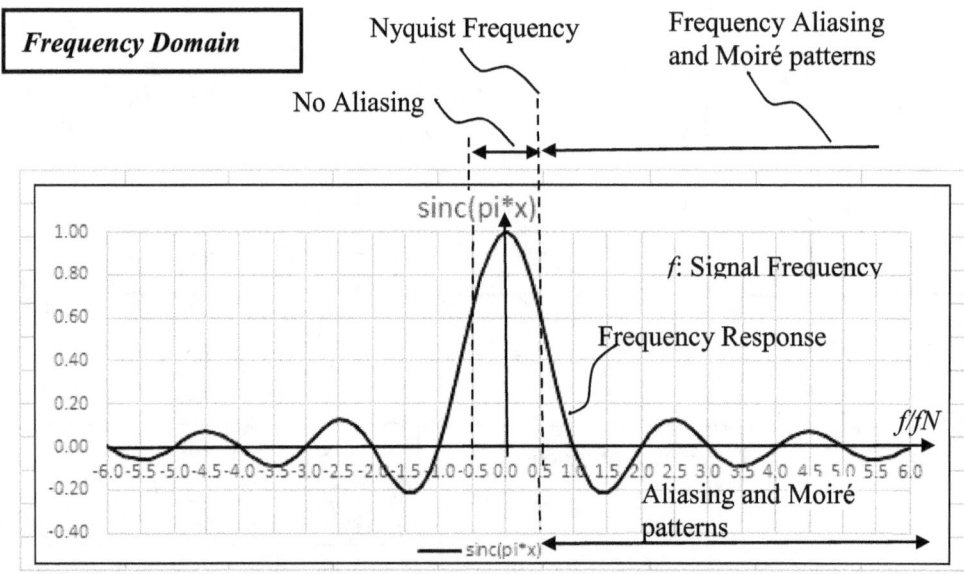

One Sample per Pixel: $fP = 1.0$; $fN = fP/2$;

Figure 2-27 Box Frequency Response with sinc() Function

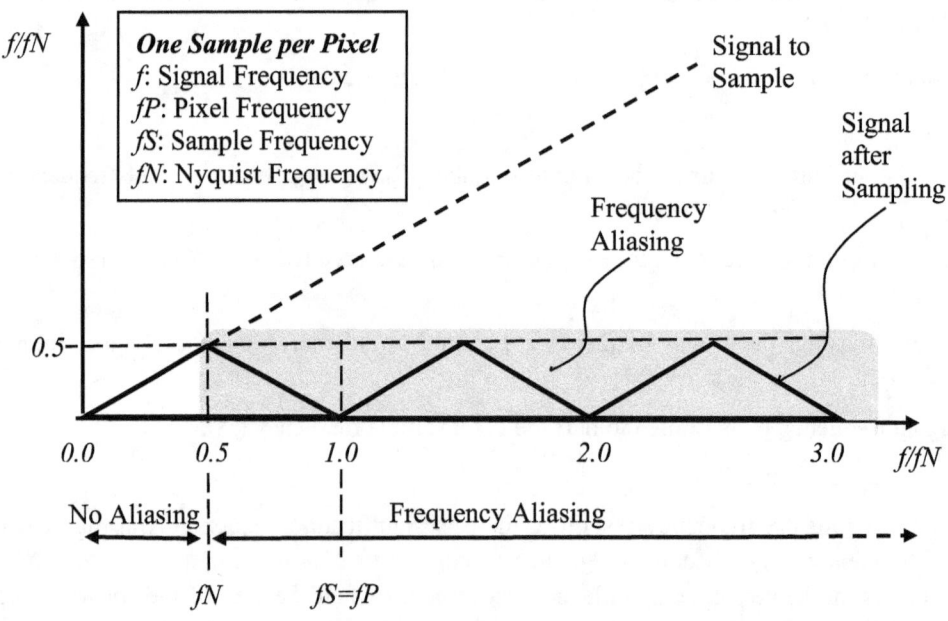

Figure 2-28 Signal to Sample and Signal after Sampling

Chapter 3 **Anti-Aliasing**

The purpose of Anti-Aliasing (AA) is to reduce, if not eliminate, distracting artifacts in Computer Generated Imagery. Most aliasing artifacts result from using only one sample point per pixel when computing the 2D image. These artifacts are more noticeable in real-time CGI applications, such as when simulating visual scenes for flight training or running computer games. Aliasing artifacts can be reduced by doing subpixel processing. Among the prior art for AA are two methods relying on point sampling: Super-Sampling Anti-Aliasing (SSAA) and Multiple-Sample Anti-Aliasing (MSAA).

The SSAA approach has been used in non-real-time applications. In this approach, a 512x512 image is first computed at higher resolution, such as 2048x2048, for example. It is then reduced through averaging or filtering to produce a 512x512 image. It is computation intensive and cannot be used for RT CGI applications. Since there are no time constraints, large images can be computed offline using high-speed general-purpose computers.

For RT CGI applications, algorithms are limited to methods that can produce new images at rate of at least 50 images per second. A more efficient approach is to use a smaller number of random (or sparse) Subpixel samples. The Multi-Sample Anti-Aliasing (MSAA) approach for RT CGI AA relies on taking Multiple Sample Points (or Subpixels) within image Pixels. For example, this reduces the number of Samples from NxN to 1xN. Also, see references [64] and [65].

This book presents a new approach referred to Area-Based Anti-Aliasing (ABAA). While the most common approaches to AA rely on point sampling, ABAA relies on Pixel sub-area sampling. ABAA relies on the computed covered area of Pixels to determine the mixed color of Pixels. This method is quite simple and efficient, with no cost or processing speed penalties. It produces more consistent results than SSAA or MSAA, at a lower cost. Using the same number of subpixels, it produces better image quality then MSAA.

3.1 SSAA and MSAA

For CGI, the most common algorithms assign Subpixels inside of a Pixel and use Subpixel point sampling. The resulting Pixel color is the color mix that is the average of the selected Subpixel contributions. When all the subpixels have the same weight, this corresponds to a Box Filter.

The Pixels are divided into Subpixels (2, 4, 8, 16, 32 or 64) and use a variety of filters. The colors are expressed with binary numbers. There is an advantage of using a power of 2 for the number of Subpixels. This makes it easier for dividing the sum of colors during averaging. With binary numbers, dividing by $2**N$ is done by shifting binary numbers N places to the right.

3.1.1 Super Sampling AA (SSAA)

For non-RT CGI, the early approach was SSAA. This is accomplished by computing an image at a higher resolution than that of the target image using one Sample Point per Pixel. Then the high-resolution image is reduced to the desired resolution with filtering. Since there are no time constraints, large images can be computed offline using high-speed general-purpose computers. For example, when doing a Super-Sampling at 4x4 resolution, an image of 2048x2048 Pixels is computed. The image is then reduced to a 512x512 Pixels image thru filtering. In this case the computing time will be roughly 4x4=16 time larger.

A similar result to SSAA can be obtained by sub-dividing Pixels into an array of Subpixels that have same relative positions within the Pixel. This way, there is no need to use a 2 step-process that require producing a high-resolution image before being downscaled and filtered into a lower resolution image. By using Subpixels, the sampled image and displayed image have the same number of Pixels. With SSAA, the samples are organized in a uniform NxN array of Subpixels. The set of Subpixels is often referred to a Bed of Nail (BON). In most implementations, the Pixel color is obtained by the average of the Subpixel contributions. This corresponds to a Box Filter. Refer to figure 3-1.

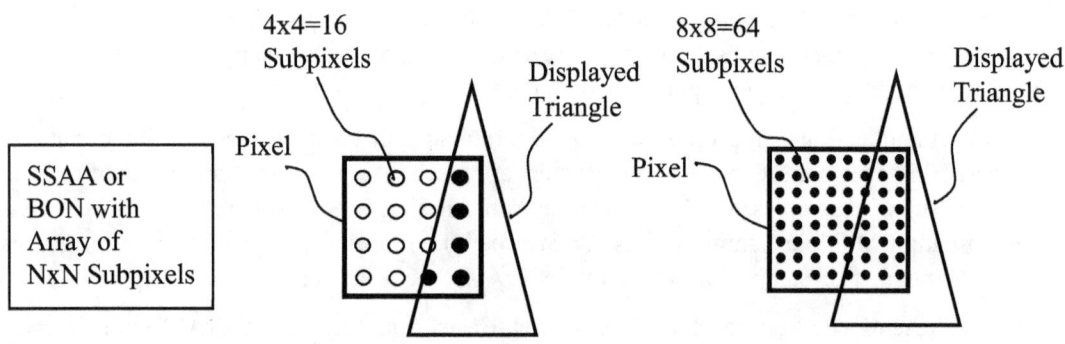

Figure 3-1 Examples of Pixel Divided into Subpixels or Bed of Nails

3.1.2 Multi-Sample AA (MSAA)

For RT CGI, SSAA is too time consuming. The MSAA approach is derived from SSAA. With MSAA a decimated set of 1xN samples is selected and spread inside of the Pixel in a non-uniform, or sparse, distribution. The square Box Filter is the fastest approach and it produces good results. The most common algorithm is to divide the Pixels into $N=4$ or 8 random (non-arrayed) Subpixels and use a. As will be shown later on, there is a disadvantage when Subpixels are arranged in rows and columns.

For MSAA, when all Subpixels have the same weight, the sparse distribution of N Subpixels is more efficient for a Box Filter than an array of NxN Subpixels. But, as will be shown, the results with MSAA depend on the polygon edge directions.

The set of Subpixels is often referred to a Bed of Nail (BON). The BON approach is similar to MSAA, but instead of computing multiple images followed by averaging these images, the covered Subpixel or BON can be detected in one or a few cycles.

This is the solution used for real-time AA. In most approaches the Pixel is divided into a number of Subpixels sample points. Here, N indicates the number of Subpixels.

In Figure 3-2, there are examples of Pixels divided into Subpixels for MSAA.

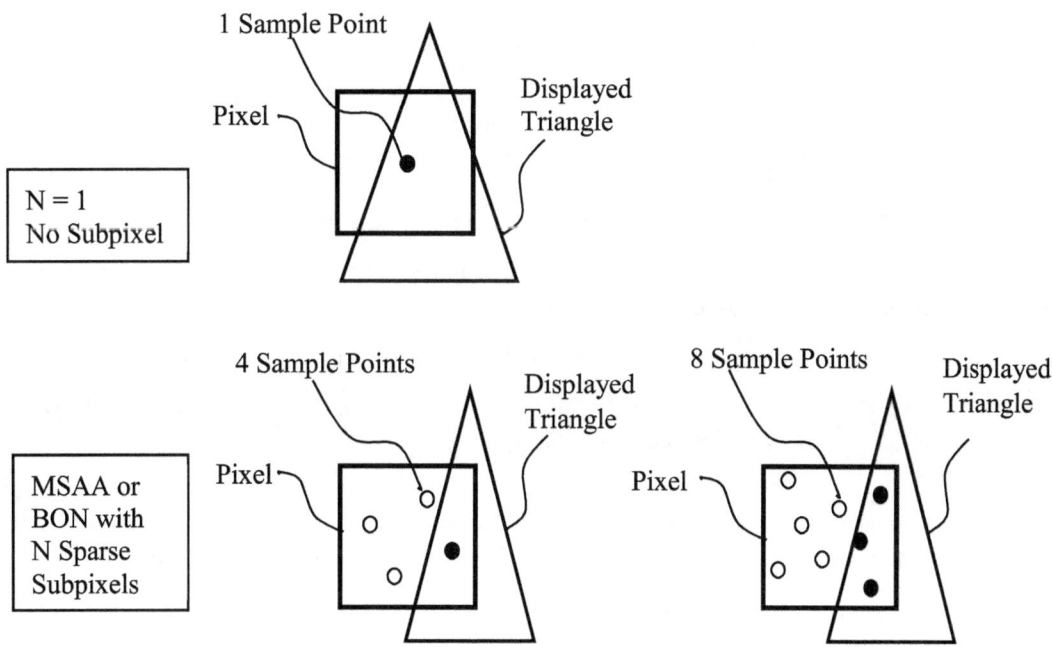

Figure 3-2 Examples of Subpixels for MSAA

Single Sample Point: N=1

In the simple implementation, there are no Subpixels, that is N=1. There is only one Sample Point at the center of the Pixel. As demonstrated, this approach results in aliasing artifact and is unsuited for most applications.

Multi-Sample: N>1

When N>1, there are many possibilities for dividing a Pixel into Subpixels. The Subpixels are organized as sparse N Subpixels. After the image is computed for all Subpixels, the final image is obtained by averaging all these images.

Box Window

When the filter is a Box Filter, all Subpixels have the same weight. In this case, the final image is obtained by straight averaging. In this case the use of Sparse Subpixel is more efficient.

Anti-Aliasing

Bartlett Window

With SSAA, the Subpixels within the Pixel can be weighted according to their distance to the center of the Pixel. This is the case with the Bartlett or Triangle Window. In this case, the final image is obtained by doing a weighted average of the computed images. In this case the use of arrays of Subpixel produces more accurate results.

3.2 Processing Subpixels as Bed of Nails

The BON approach is similar to MSAA, but instead of computing multiple images followed by averaging these images, the covered Subpixel or BON can be detected in one or a few cycles.

The covered Subpixel can be detected as follows.

Refer to Figure 3-3, Edge to Subpixel Distance in *(x_i, y_i)* Coordinate System

In this figure, there is a Pixel and an Edge defined in an *(x_i, y_i)* coordinate system. The Subpixel Distance is defined from the Edge to the Sample Point at the center of the Pixel.

In the *(x_i, y_i)* coordinate axis system, the edge can be represented by its equation:
$ax_i + by_i + c = 0$

The normal to the edge can be derived from this equation:
$N = (a, b)$.

The normal distance of any point *(x_i, y_i)* on the line edge can be obtained by replacing the point coordinates in the equation. The normal distance of the line edge to the origin *(0, 0)* is: c.

The normal distance of the Pixel center *(x_1, y_1)* the line *(x_i, y_i)* can be obtained by replacing the point *(x_1, y_1)* in the line equation. The normal distance d of the Pixel center *(x_1, y_1)* to the line edge is

$d = a*x_1\ b*y_1 + c$.

Since the edge belongs to a triangle, there is an *in-side* (visible) and *out-side* of the edge. In this example, the points on the left of the edge are *outside* of the triangle. The points on the right side of the edge are *inside* of the triangle. So, if $d>0$, the point is *inside*, else it is *outside*.

When there are several Subpixels, each Subpixel is tested against the edge.

Anti-Aliasing

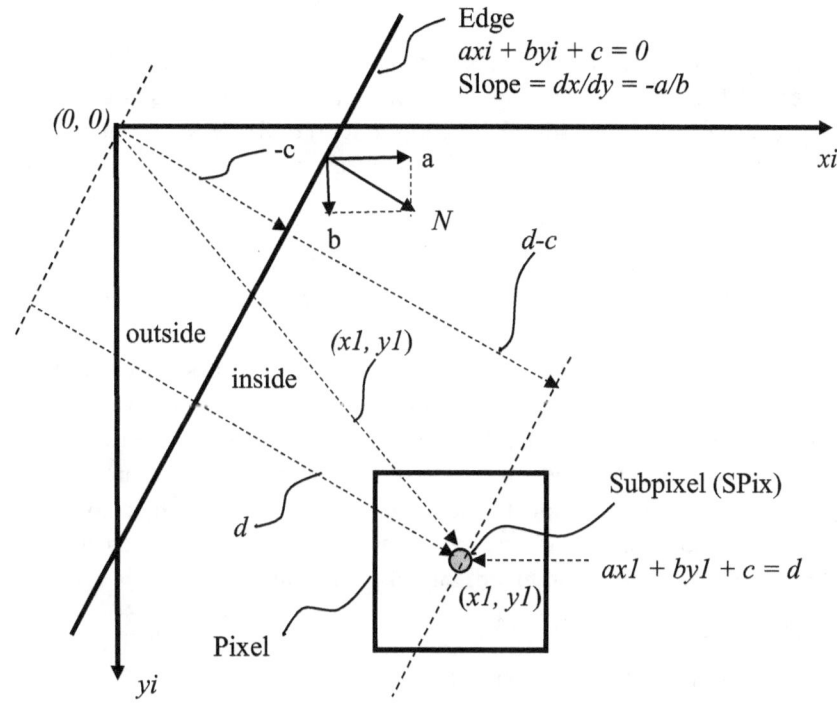

Figure 3-3 Edge to Subpixel Distance in (xi, yi) Coordinate System

3.3 MSAA and the 8 Queens Puzzle

When implementing MSAA, there are several factors that affect the image quality and performances. The quality of the MSAA implementation depends on the number of Subpixel and how they are distributed within the Pixel.

- How many Subpixels to select.
- How to select Subpixels the Subpixel distribution for optimum performances.
- All Subpixels have the same weight.

The performance depends on how and when the distances to Subpixels are computed. The distance can be computed in real-time, or precomputed and stored into a look-up table. That table is then accessed using the entry and exit points of the edge intersecting the Pixel.

In this section, the selection of $N=8$ Subpixels will be analyzed. All Subpixels have the same weight. Assuming that the triangle has an intensity i, where i can be an RGB color component on the triangle area. When a Pixel is fully covered by a triangle, the triangle contribution is $100\% * i$. Each Subpixel will have a contribution of $i/8$.

One approach is to use solutions to the '8 Queens Puzzle' [61].

Anti-Aliasing

The 8 Queens Puzzle

In the literature, the selection of Subpixel within a Pixel is often referred to as "Solutions to the 8 Queens Puzzle". The idea is to position 8 Queens on a chess board, so that no Queen can attack another Queen. This algorithm provides good solutions for MSAA, but there are acceptable solutions that do not satisfy as solution to the '8 Queens Puzzle'.

Selecting 8 Subpixels as a Solution to the 8 Queens Puzzle

The distribution of 8 Subpixels inside of a Pixel can be simulated with a chess board with *8x8=64* square locations. In this approach, each of the 8 Subpixels will be assigned one of the 64 squares and reside at the center of the assigned square. For simulation purpose, all 8 Subpixels will be assigned the same set of moves or properties from one selected chess piece, such as: Queen, Rook, Bishop or Knight. Since the Queen has access to moves from the Rook (0 degrees and 90 degrees, and Bishop (+/- 45-degree diagonals), the Rook and Bishop are not considered. For this reason, the Queen is a good choice for selecting Subpixels. When all Subpixels are considered as Queens, none of them is under a Queen threat. The Knight is another chess piece of interest since it can attack a Queen without being under Queen attack. Although the Queen has more power than Knights, the Knights can be useful in looking for good solutions.

Knights and Queens

Refer to Figure 3-4, Knights and Queens

In this figure, there are 2 solutions that satisfy the 8 Queens Puzzle. For each solution, a Pixel is organized as an array of 8x8 Subpixels locations. For a solution with 8 Subpixels, only 8 locations are selected among the possible 64 locations.

On the left Pixel, the 8 Subpixels are identified with the K letter. Although this arrangement is a solution to the 8 Queens Puzzle, the K is selected to show the Knight threats capability. The Knight moves 2 horizontal or 2 vertical spaces, followed by 1 diagonal space.

On the right Pixel, the Subpixels are identified with the Q letter, to show that it is a solution to the 8 Queens Puzzle.

What is interesting with these 8 Queens assignments is that the Queens on the right figure are obtained from the left figure **by swapping 4 Knights in lower half with 4 Knights in upper half.**

Both are solutions to the 8 Queens Puzzle. But after a quick analysis, it turns out that the assignment with the Queens on the right side is better. In order to identify the Subpixels that are aligned, the lines that connect pairs of Subpixels are assigned a number. The sets of parallel lines that connect Subpixels are identified with the same number.

Refer to Table 3-1

In this table, the cases with aligned Subpixels are identified. For each line direction, the number of parallel cases is counted. The best selection for AA should have the minimum of aligned Subpixels and the minimum number of parallel cases.

In the 8 Knights assignment, 4 Knights are aligned, which would make it a bad selection for an AA solution.

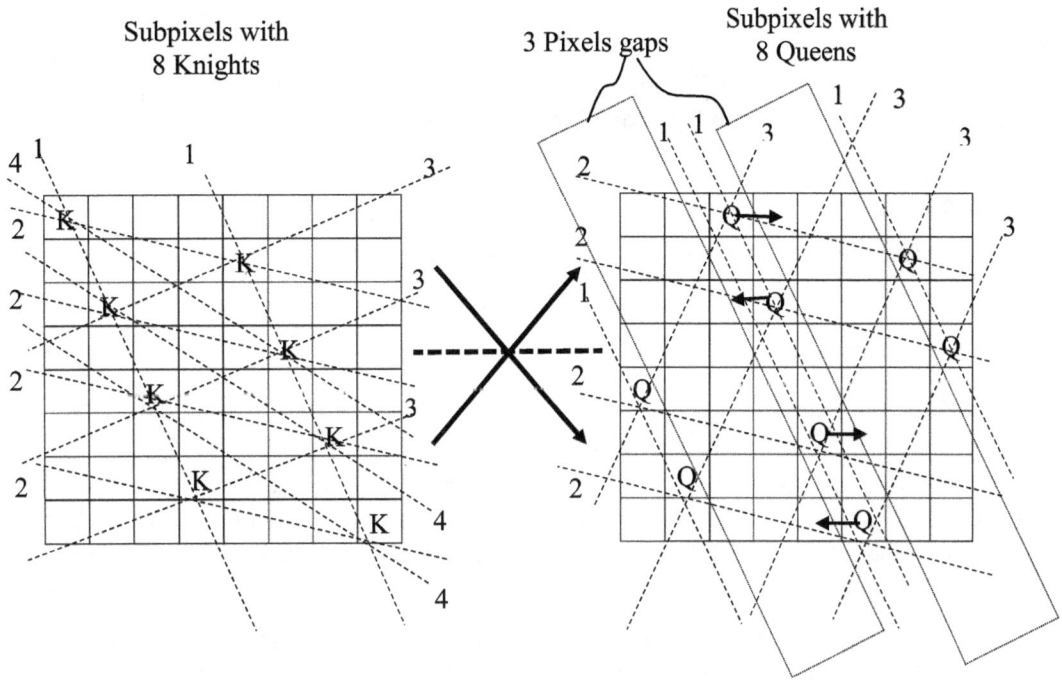

Figure 3-4 Knights and Queens

Subpixels with 8 Knights			
Case	#Cases	#SPix	di
1	2*4=8	4	1/2
2	4 pairs	2	1/4
3	3 pairs	2	1/4
4	3 pairs	2	1/4
5,6	2*2pairs=4	2	1/4
7..10	4*1 pair	2	1/4
total	28		
di is fractional intensity jump			

Subpixels with 8 Queens			
Case	#Cases	#SPix	di
1	4 pairs	2	1/4
2	4 pairs	2	1/4
3	4 pairs	2	1/4
4..7	4 * 2 pairs	2	1/4
8..19	12 *1 pair	2	1/4
total	28		
di is fractional intensity jump			

Table 3-1 Intensity Jumps for Knights and Queens

Introduction to Area-Based Anti-Aliasing for CGI

8 Knights Solution

In the case of Knights, there are 2 parallel cases (1) where 4 Knights are aligned.

When 2 sets of 4 Knights are aligned, there are only 2 steps per Pixel. Each group of 4 Knights correspond of 5 pairs. So, these 2 sets of 4 Knights amount to 10 pairs.

There is 1 case (2) with 4 parallel pairs of Knights. This results into 4 steps per Pixel (4 pairs) amount to 4 pairs.

There are 2 cases of 3 parallel pairs of Knights (3, 4). This result into 5 steps per Pixel (6 pairs)

Then, 6 cases remain with 1 or 2 aligned pairs (5…10), corresponding to 6 or 7 steps per Pixel.

8 Queens Puzzle's Solution Derived from 8 Knight Solution

In the case of the Queens, there are 3 cases where 4 pairs (1,2,3) are aligned. This amount of 12 pairs. There remain 16 pairs where 1 or 2 pairs are aligned.

The solution with the Queens on the right Pixel is better than the solution with the Knights on the left Pixel. The 8 Queens Puzzle solution has 16 cases where 1 or 2 pairs are aligned (4…19). This is better than the 8 Knights solution where there are only 6 cases where 1 or 2 pairs are aligned (cases 5…10).

One of the weaknesses of this solution, is that there are 2 parallel gaps of around 3 Pixel wide. For edges parallel to these gaps, there will be a degradation of antialiasing. When an edge that is parallel to these gaps moves from left to right the following behavior is expected. There is no transition for a distance of 3 Pixels, followed by 4 transitions across 4 sample points in the space of ½ Pixel, followed by no transition for a distance of 3 Pixels. These gaps can be reduced as shown by moving 4 queens, as shown with the little arrows. This solution should be better, although it is not an 8 Queens solution.

By comparison, the gaps for horizontal or vertical edges are only 1 Pixel wide.

Best Case

No matter how the Subpixel are selected, it cannot be avoided that at least 2 Subpixels can be aligned along some random triangle edge. When 2 Subpixels aligned with a triangle edge, this will reduce the number of intensity steps by 1.

In the best case, each line connects only 2 Subpixels. The minimum set of lines can be counted as follows:
Counting Subpixel pairs:
Subpixel 0, 7 pairs: 0-1, 0-2, 0-3, 0-4, 0-5, 0-6, 0-7
Subpixel 1, 6 pairs: 1-2, 1-3, 1-4, 1-5, 1-6, 1-7
Subpixel 2, 5 pairs: 2-3, 2-4, 2-5, 2-6, 2-7
Subpixel 3, 4 pairs: 3-4, 3-5, 3-6, 3-7
Subpixel 4, 3 pairs: 4-5, 4-6, 4-7
Subpixel 5, 2 pairs: 5-6, 5-7
Subpixel 6, 1 pairs: 6-7
Given 8 Subpixels, there are: 7+6+5+4+3+2+1= 28 possible pairs

Selecting a Solution

In order to analyze the solutions, the following criteria will help in finding a good solution.

- Avoid solution where no more than 2 Queens are aligned.
- Avoid solutions with large gaps.

In reference [61] from Wikipedia, there are many proposed 'Solutions to 8 Queens Puzzle'. Solution 10 has the additional property that no three queens are in a straight line. Refer to Figure 3-5.

But in this example, there are 3 cases where 3 Queens are almost aligned. Also, there is a 3 pixels gap.

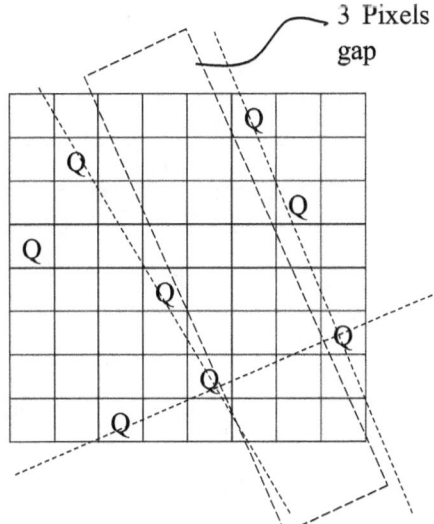

Solution 10 from Wikipedia: No three queens are in a straight line.

Figure 3-5 Solution where no more than 2 Queens are aligned

In order to analyze the solutions, the following criteria will help in finding a good solution.

- Select the solutions where no three queens are in a straight line.
- Select solutions where there are no more than 2 parallel pairs.
- Avoid solutions with large gaps.

Other Examples of 8 Queens Solutions

In Figure 3-6, there are four examples of 8 Queen Solutions

In each of these four 8 Queen examples, there are at least 2 cases with 2 pairs of parallel Subpixels. In examples 1 to 3, there is at least one case with 3 aligned Subpixels (2 cases in example 1).

In example 4, there are no case with more than 2 aligned Subpixels. So, the Subpixel distribution in example 4 should be the best approach.

Anti-Aliasing

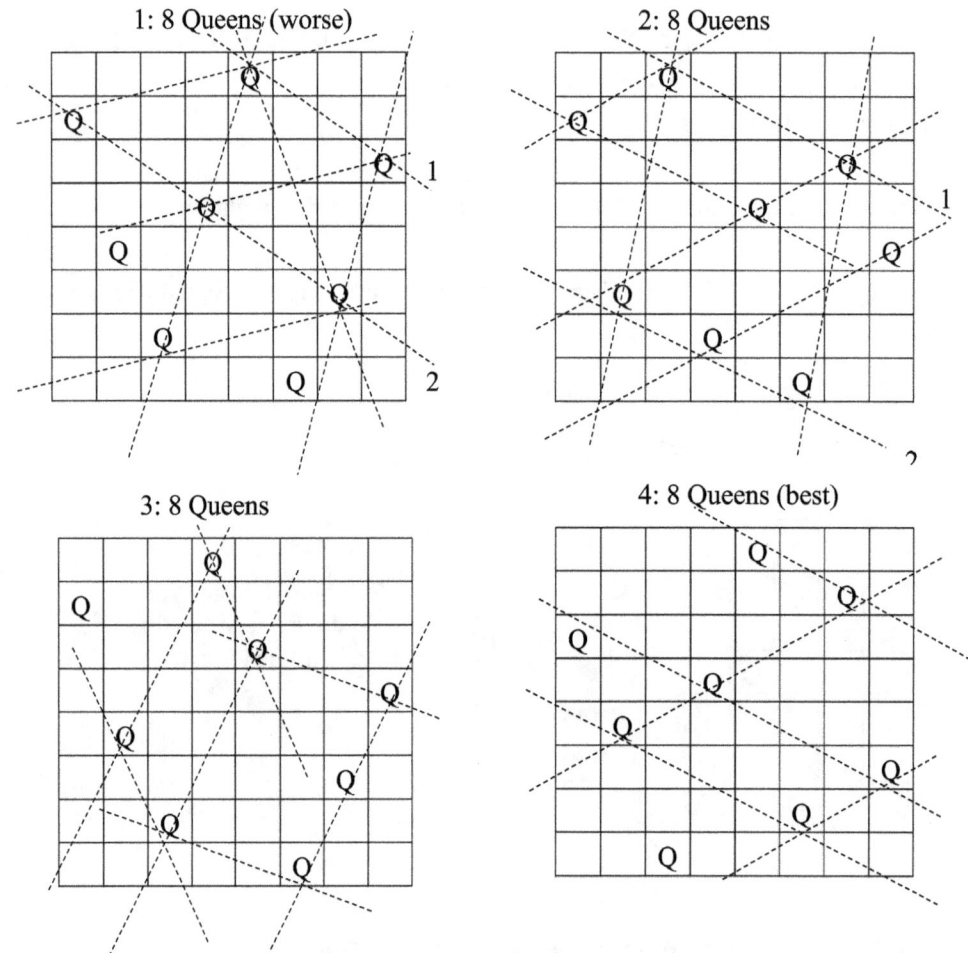

Figure 3-6 Four Examples of 8 Queens Solutions

Anti-Aliasing

Gaps > ¼ Pixel in 8 Queens Solutions

Besides aligned Subpixels, the gaps between aligned Subpixel should be considered. When there are gaps greater than a Subpixel wide between groups of Subpixels, narrow faces < ¼ Pixel wide would pop in-and-out of scenes.

In Figure 3-7, several gaps greater than a Subpixel wide are identified in these four 8 Queens Solutions. Here, examples 3 & 4 are the best solutions. Also, by moving 4 queens in example 4, the gaps can be reduced to 2 pixels wide. In this case, example 4 would be the best solution, although some Queens would be under attack at 45 degrees.

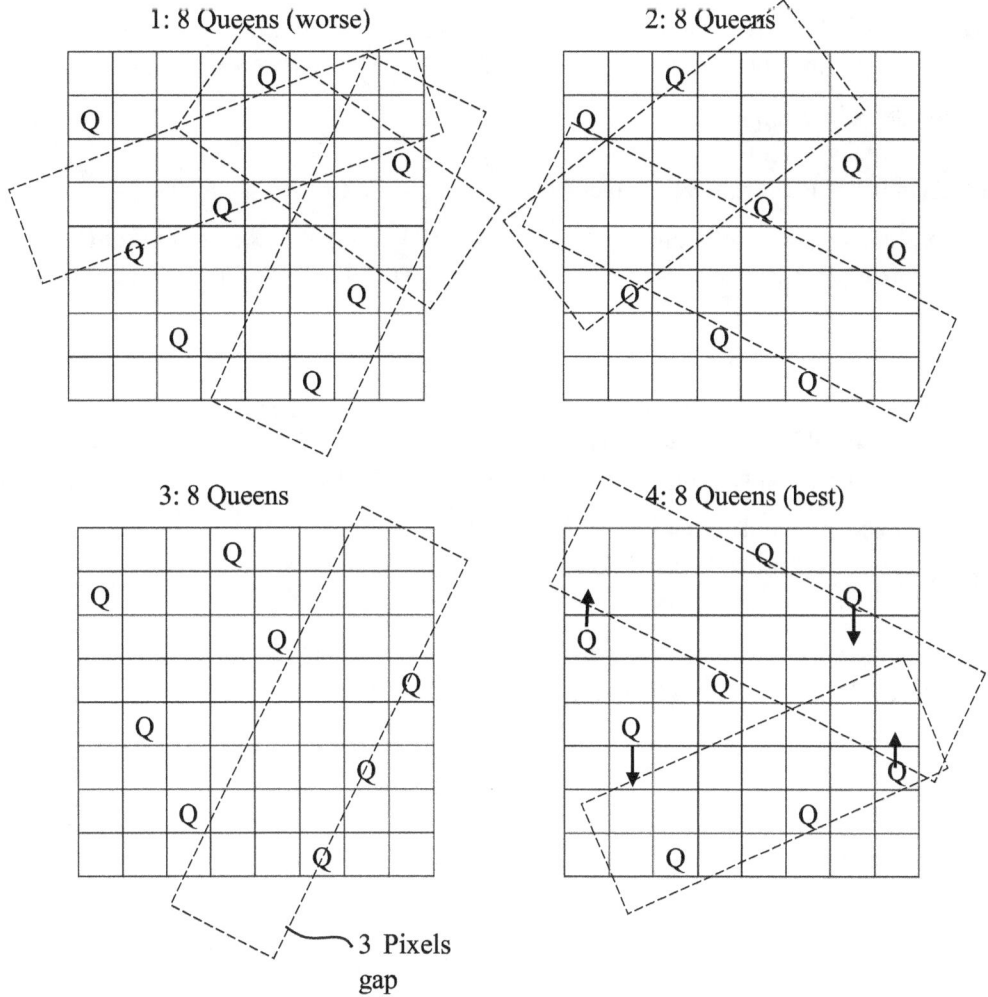

Figure 3-7 Identified ¼ Pixel Gaps in 8 Queens Solutions

3.4 Introducing Area-Based Anti-Aliasing

In this book, a new approach to anti-aliasing is presented, Area-Based Anti-Aliasing (ABAA). ABAA uses Subpixel areas samples instead of Subpixel point samples. There are many advantages of ABAA over MSAA.

Refer to Figure 3-8.

In this figure, there are examples of Pixel subdivided into 4 and 8 Subpixels using two 2 different approaches: ABAA vs MSAA.

3.4.1 ABAA vs MSAA

Subpixel Areas with ABAA

On the left side, using ABAA, each Pixel is decomposed into 4 or 8 Subpixel Areas. There many ways to represents the Subpixel Areas. A few examples are shown here.

- Single Point Sample
- Example of Pixel with 4 Subpixel Areas
- Example of Pixel with 8 Subpixel Areas

The 4 & 8 Subpixel Areas solutions are derived from the 4x4 Subpixel Areas of the DIG. This was made possible by changing the shape of the Subpixels, so that the same Subpixel area can be used for both HE and VE.

Subpixel Sample Points with MSAA

On the right side, MSAA uses Subpixel Sample Points for Super-Sampling. In the MSAA approach, each Pixel is subdivided into 1, 4 or 8 Subpixel Sample Points. There are many ways to arrange Subpixels as Sample Points. Two examples are shown here.

- Pixel with 1 Sample Point
- Pixel with 4 Sample Points
- Pixel with 8 Sample Points

In the MSAA approach, several images are computed using different sample points within a Pixel. The AA image is obtained by computing the average of these images.

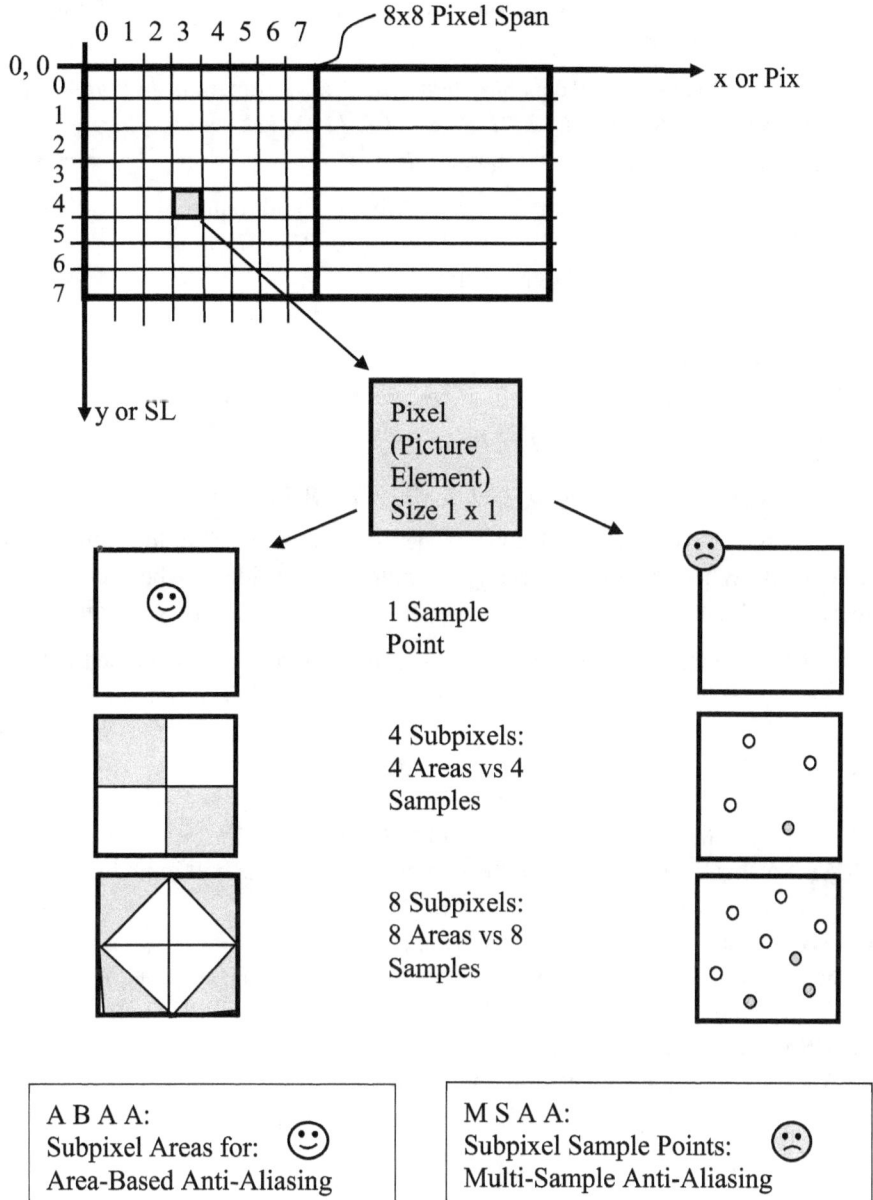

Figure 3-8 Comparison of Subpixels with ABAA and MSAA

Understanding Binary Numbers

The ABAA algorithm will be explained in the following Sections. But, in order to have a full understanding of the algorithm the reader should have some understanding of binary numbers. In order to describe the algorithm, the image is decomposed into small square areas of size 8x8 Pixels. These square areas of 8x8 Pixels are referred to as 'two-dimensional Spans', or simply 'Spans'. In

Anti-Aliasing

the final steps of the AA HW implementation (and also SW implementation), the operations are performed with binary numbers.

In the HW, the number 8 is represented as *bin 1000*. The Pixel numbers from *0 to 7* can be represented with 3 bits: *bin 000, 001, 010, 011, 100, 101, 110, 111*
This can also be represented by 8 octal numbers: *0, 1, 2, 3, 4, 5, 6, 7*

This is the reason the size of spans is not *dec 10x10*, which would require 4 bits to identify Pixels from *0 to 9*: *bin 0000, 0001, 0010, 0011, 0100, 0101, 0110, 0111, 1000, 1001.*
This can also be represented by 10 octal numbers: *0, 1, 2, 3, 4, 5, 6, 7, 10, 11*
This would be ackward for many reasons.

This is also true for Subpixels:
4 Subpixels from *0 to 3* are numbered with 2 bits as: *bin 00, 01, 10, 11*
8 Subpixels from *0 to 7* are numbered with 3 bits as: *bin 000, 001, 010, 011, 100, 101, 110, 111*

3.4.2 Comparison of MSAA vs ABAA with 4 or 8 Subpixels

Given a Pixel with N Subpixels, as an edge moves across a Pixel, that should result into N distinct intensity increments. When the Pixel intensity (or color) is considered, these corresponds to N intensity steps. With ABAA, there are always N distinct and equal intensity increments.

1. With MSAA, there are always several cases where 2 Subpixels are aligned with a polygon edge. When a moving edge that is aligned with a pair of Subpixels crosses these Subpixels, the Subpixel count jumps by 2. Consequently, the Subpixels sequence will increment by 1 and sometimes 2 or more Subpixels at a time.
   For 4 Subpixels, there are 3+2+1=6 Subpixel pairs.
   For 8 Subpixels, there are 7+6+5+4+3+2+1=28 Subpixel pairs.
   With ABAA there is no case where the number of Subpixels will jump by 2.
2. With MSAA the N increments are not evenly spaced.
   With ABAA, the N increments are evenly spaced.
3. With MSAA, the detection of covered Subpixels is not always accurate.
   With ABAA, the detection of covered Subpixels is accurate (1/16 Pixel)
4. With MSAA the covered Subpixels are detected with multiple operations.
   With ABAA, for each edge position, the number of covered Subpixels is derived in one operation, according to the sampled area. There is no need for Multi Sampling.

3.5 Selecting Subpixels for AA

In this section, there are several examples comparing ABAA with SSAA and MSAA.

For RT CGI, most algorithms assign Subpixels inside of a Pixel and use Subpixel point sampling. The resulting Pixel color is the color mix that is the average of the selected Subpixel contributions. Both MSAA, BON and ABAA use a similar approach, where all the Subpixels have an equal weight. The filter corresponds to a square box. This is a fast approach that produces good results. For MSAA, when all Subpixels have the same weight, the sparse distribution of Subpixels is more efficient for a Box Filter than SSAA with arrays of NxN Subpixels.

In the following figures, there are several examples of Subpixel distributions within Pixels and the expected result when a triangle intersects that Pixel. The Subpixels can be organized into an N*N array of Subpixels, or as sparse 1xN Subpixels. In each of the following examples, there are 4 displayed triangles intersecting a Pixel. The same triangles are used for the 4 examples. On the left side, the first triangle intersects the Pixel, but all Subpixels are covered. So, the Pixel is completely covered. In the other 3 cases, the Pixels are partially covered. The triangles cover various fraction according to the covered Subpixels. As can be observed, the fraction of covered Subpixels can be different, depending of the Subpixel distributions and the triangle position. Depending of the organizations of the Subpixels, the Pixel coverage can vary for the same triangle vs Pixel geometry.

SSAA with array of 4x4 or 8x8 Subpixels

In Figure 3-9, there are SSAA examples of with an array of 4x4 Subpixels, for a total of 16 Subpixels. As can be seen, for thin vertical triangles, the number of Subpixels can jump from 0 to 4, when the triangle moves sideways (or thin horizontal triangles moving upward). This is a disadvantage of Subpixels organized in array form. On the other hand, square arrays of NxN Subpixels are well suited for AA filters when different weights are assigned to Subpixels, depending on their position relative to the center of the Pixel.

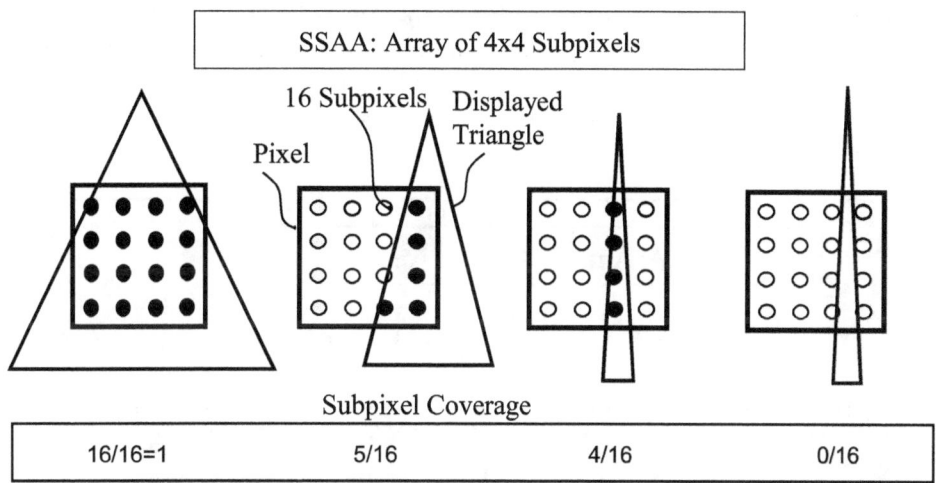

Figure 3-9 SSAA Examples of Triangles and 4x4 Subpixels

SSAA with array of 8x8 Subpixels

When using a larger array of Subpixels, such as 8x8=64 Subpixels, the problem with narrow triangles is reduced. Refer to Figure 3-10

There is a better solution using only 32 Subpixels, as shown in the next example.

Anti-Aliasing

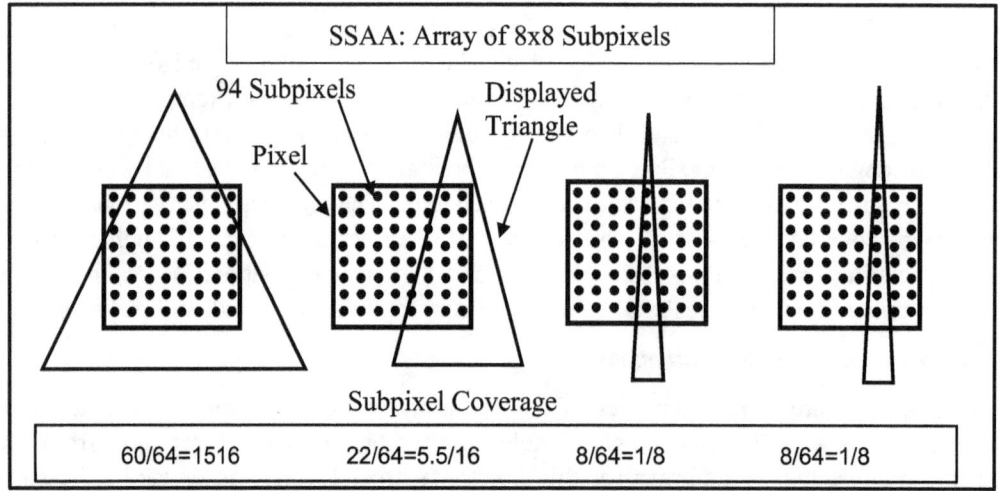

Figure 3-10 SSAA Examples of Triangles and 8x8 Subpixels

SSAA with array of 4x8 Subpixels

In Figure 3-11, there are SSAA examples with an array of 4x8 Subpixels, for a total of 32 Subpixels. The 4 rows of 4 Subpixels are repeated with an offset from their original position. This is an improvement over the array of 4x4 Subpixels, without using 8x8 Subpixels. For thin triangles, the number of covered Subpixels is more stable, when the triangle moves vertically or sideways.

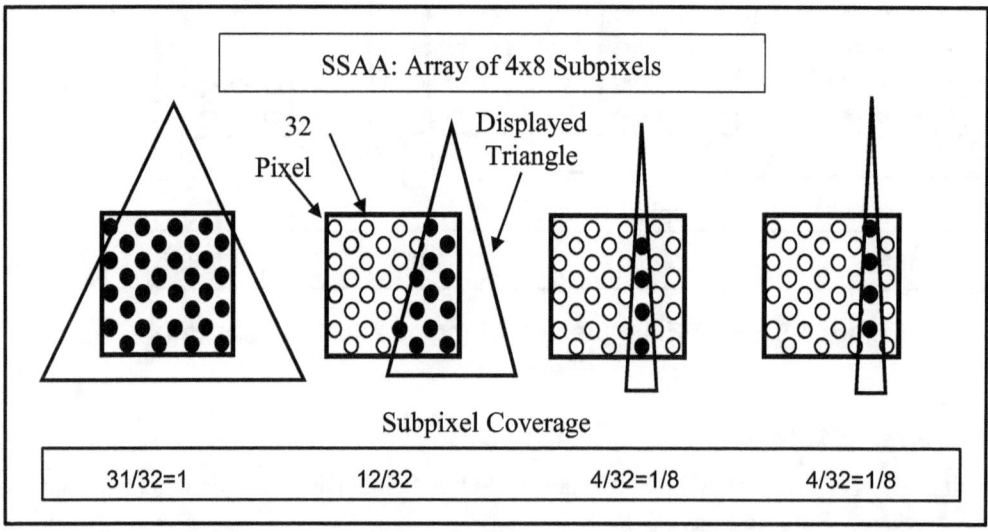

Figure 3-11 SSAA Examples of Triangles and 4x8 Subpixels

Anti-Aliasing

MSAA and BON with array of 8 sparse Subpixels

In Figure 3-12, the same triangle examples are shown with MSAA (or BON), using only 8 sparse Subpixels. Here, the Subpixels a positioned so that no more than two are aligned. This results into a more efficient use of Subpixels. But there is still a problem when some triangle edges are aligned with pairs of Subpixels. In this example, the number of Subpixels can jump from 0 to 2, when triangles move across the Pixel.

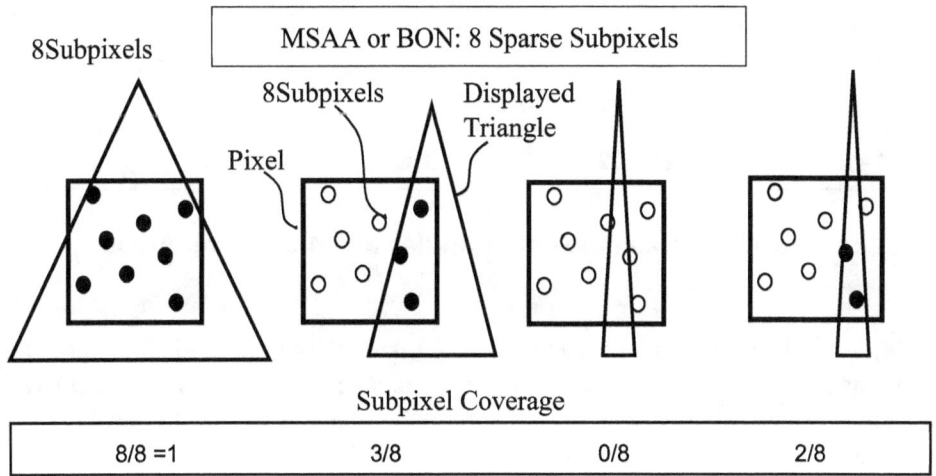

Figure 3-12 MSAA or BON: Examples of Triangles and 8 Sparse Subpixels

ABAA with array of 4 and 8 Subpixel Areas

While most methods are based on Point Sampling, in this book a new method that relies on Area Sampling is introduced. It is referred to as Area-Based Anti-Aliasing (ABAA). This method divides the Pixel into N Subpixel areas. It consists of computing the Pixel area that is covered by a polygon and assigning this area to N Subpixel areas. ABAA is much simpler and more accurate than MSAA and is less computation intensive.

In Figure 3-13, using the same triangle example, the 4 triangles intersect a Pixel divided into 4 Subpixel Areas of equal size, using the ABAA method.

Anti-Aliasing

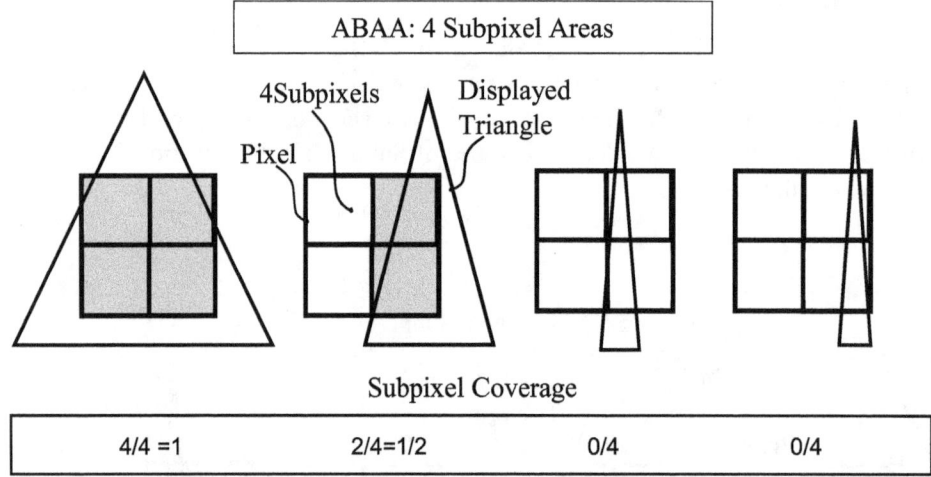

Figure 3-13 ABAA Examples of Triangles and 4 Subpixel Areas

In Figure 3-14, using the same triangle example, the 4 triangles intersect a Pixel divided into 8 Subpixel Areas of equal size When compared with the example of 8 Subpixels with MSAA, the Subpixel assignment with ABAA is more accurate and continuous. Also, the location of the covered Subpixel Area is close to the original covered area.

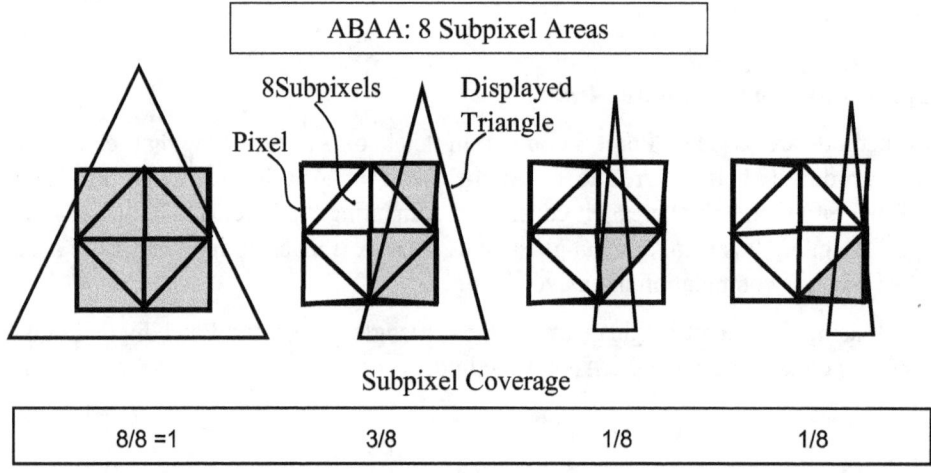

Figure 3-14 ABAA Examples of Triangles and 8 Subpixel Areas

3.5.1 Advantages of ABAA over MSAA

There are many advantages of ABAA over MSAA. As discussed previously, there are serious weaknesses of MSAA with N Subpixels. When a triangle edge is parallel to any segment connecting 2 Subpixels, there is an increment of *di=2/N* (instead of *1/N*) when the edge transitions from one side to the other side of that segment. With 8 Subpixels there are:

$1+2+3+4+5+6+7 = sum(1\ to\ 7) = 28$ cases of Subpixel pairs

that can be aligned with a polygon edge. When an edge is crossing one of these segments, the intensity will have an increment of *1/4,* instead of *1/8*. Implementations with more than 2 aligned Subpixels should be avoided. Implementations with 2 aligned Subpixels should be worst case.

Comparisons of Intensity Steps Between SSAA, MSAA and ABAA

One way to compare the AA methods described in this book is to count the intensity steps as edges move across Pixels. This is done for edge slopes that vary over a 90 degree angle. For this comparison, 2 group of edges are used in the comparison:
- Horizontal edges *(HE)*, when $|dx|>|dy|$: Slope HSlp
- Vertical edges *(VE)*, when $|dx|>=|dy|$: Slope VSlp

In a later chapter, 'ABAA with 8 Subpixel Areas', the performances of ABBA8 with MSAA8 are compared with a computer simulation. Inside of an 8x8 Pixel span, 8 thin triangles with a base of 1 Pixel and a height of 8 Pixels are organized as a fan. Part of the results for 0 to 90 degrees are reproduced in Figure 3-15, 'Number of Intensity steps for ABAA8 and MSAA8'.

In Table 3-2, the AA methods are compared when edges move accross a Pixel as vertical edge slopes *VSlp=dx/dy* or horizontal edge slopes *HSlp=dy/dx* vary between *0.0* and *1.0*.

For vertical and horizontal edges *(Slp=0.0)*, all of these methods produce 8 equal steps.

ABAA is the most consistant and most efficient approach. With ABAA, the number of steps is always 8, independently of edge slope, as the covered area changes linearly across pixels.

Note that for *Slp=1.0*, ABAA does not show 8 steps in all cases. This is due to the interaction of the left and right triangle edges in the fans. But, for each left and right triangle edges, there will be 8 transition steps (by definition).

The SSAA solution is the most expensive. For 0 degree *(Slp==0.0)* and 45 degrees angles *(|Slp|==1.0)*, the results are similar to MSAA. For other slope angles, the resolution increases with SSAA, while it decreases with MSAA.

With MSAA, the number of steps can vary between 4 and 8 for slopes between 0.0 (horizontal or vertical) and 1.0 (45 degrees).

In most cases, SSAA and MSAA provide a decent approximation of the Subpixel Areas. As edges move across the Pixel area, they provide a gradual increment of Subpixel count. With MSAA, the thin triangle examples with edge *HSlp* or *VSlp* around *0.5* show poor results. The subpixel increments jump back and forth (Ex: 0 2 1 6 4 6 6 8).

Anti-Aliasing

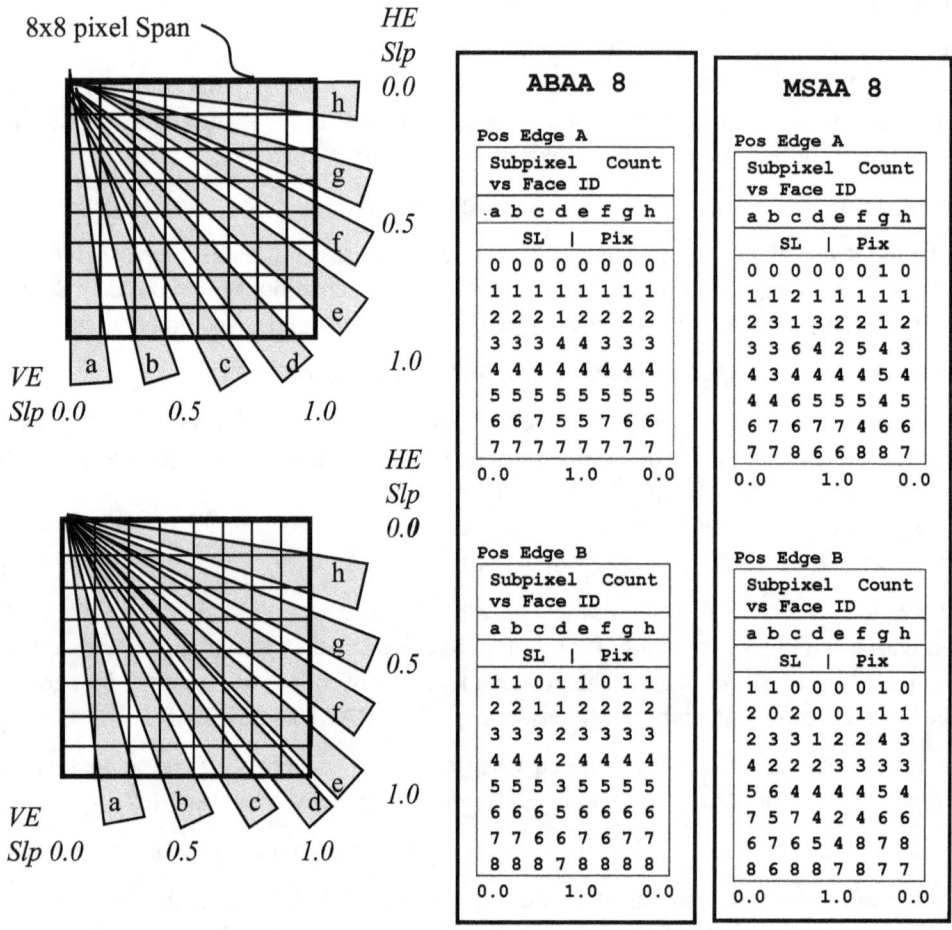

Figure 3-15 Number of Intensity steps for ABAA8 and MSAA8

#Steps vs Edge Slope	VSlp=0, HSlp=0 (Slp=0.0)	VSlp=1/8, HSlp=1/8 (Slp 0.125)	VSlp=1/4, HSlp=1/4 (Slp 0.25)	VSlp=1/2, HSlp=1/2 (Slp 0.5)	VSlp=1, HSlp=1 (Slp =1.0)
AA Method					
SSAA, 8x8	8	64	32	16	8
MSAA, 8 Queens	8	4 to 8	4 to 8	4 to 8	8
ABAA, N=8	8	8	8	8	8

Table 3-2 Comparison of Intensity Steps vs Edge Slopes

Chapter 4 Area of Trapezoid

In most cases, when an edge crosses a Pixel, it divides the Pixel area into 2 trapezoids. The areas of these trapezoids are easily computed and determine the covered areas. If the edge is a beginning edge, the area on the right side is the covered area. If it's an ending edge, the area on the left side is the covered area. In some cases, the trapezoid extends outside of the Pixel boundary. In these cases, the trapezoid area can also be used to determine the covered area. The efficiency of this operation depends on how polygon edges are processed.

Image rendering in CGI systems consists of many repetitive operations. Any improvement in the processing steps results in direct system performance. Processing edges requires many repetitive operations. In order to achieve optimum performances, an edge definition has been selected to achieve this goal.

4.1 Optimized Edge Definition for Area-Based Anti-Aliasing

Problem with Basic Edge Definition

There are disadvantages with the basic edge definition.

- Assume that the edge slope is: $ESlp = dx/dy$
- The slope size is unlimited and would reach infinity when the component $dy==0$
- Beside the slope, 2 coordinate components (x, y) are required to position an edge.

Optimized Edge Definition

The proposed edge definition requires only 2 components

- a slope with limited size $(|Slp| <=1)$,
- only one other intersection component $(x$ or $y)$ needed to position edges.

By limiting the elope size, this reduces the number of bits required for x, y and Slp for fixed point computations.

Two types of edges are defined to provide symmetry with respect to the X and Y screen coordinates: Vertical Edges (*VE*) and Horizontal Edges (*HE*).

This new edge definition optimizes the Tile-to-Tile and Pixel-to-Pixel traversing operations.

Note that this approach requires to define 2D square projection areas in the image, referred as tiles. The Pixel is the smallest Tile. In the general case all these square areas can be referred to as "Tiles".

About Symmetric Edge Definition

The problem of infinite slopes is solved by organizing edges into 2 edge types: *HE* and *VE*.

- *HE*, $HSlp = dx/dy$, when $|dy| > |dx|$
- *VE*, $VSlp = dy/dx$, when $|dy| < |dx|$
- *VE*, $VSlp = dy/dx$, when $|dy| == |dx|$

Area of Trapezoid

When $|dy| == |dx|$, the edge type is selected as *VE*, since edges are usually processed in images in top-down order.

The optimized edge definition provides many advantages over the basic edge definition, such as:

- Limit the slope size to no-greater than 1.0: $|ESlp|<=1$
- Provide symmetry in horizontal and vertical directions.
- Provide for efficient computation of Subpixel area computations
- Optimize the Tile-to-Tile and Pixel-to-Pixel traversing operations

About Rounding Fractions

Most of us have learned about Fraction Rounding in the 4th or 5th grade. We also have learned how to compute the area of triangles and trapezoids.

The problem with Fraction Rounding is that most of us never forget about it, as if it was the only solution for handling fractional numbers. We blindly apply rounding without thinking of the disastrous consequences. In my 1st book [6], I have described several cases with problems that would have been avoided early in 3D graphics by applying averaging instead of rounding. Averaging consists of replacing discarded fraction with 0.5. About this subject, I have come across patents that have been awarded for solving these ghost problems. Most of these problems deal with corner cases. By replacing rounding with averaging, there are no corner cases.

Area Computation for Trapezoids

On the other hand, most of us have forgotten about how to compute the area of triangles, parallelograms and trapezoids. It turned out that the area of trapezoids is key to my new solution for ABAA. The area of each trapezoid is equal to its Height multiplied by the average of its top and bottom Width [16].

4.2 Area of Trapezoid

ABAA relies on computing the areas of Pixels that are covered by the 3 edges of a triangle. The areas defined by each edge is first determined, then the triangle area is obtained by doing an AND function of the areas defined by these 3 edges.

There are 2 cases to be considered.

Edge Intersections with Pixel Boundaries Within 0.0 and 1.0

In the first case, it is assumed that the range of extended edge (EE) intersections with 2 opposite boundaries of Pixels is within *0.0* and *1.0*. The EE intersections with opposite Pixel boundaries divide the Pixel into **2 trapezoidal areas**. The area of each trapezoid is equal to its Height multiplied by the average of its top and bottom Width. For example, for *VEs*, the average of the Widths can be obtained on the Horizontal Midline at half distance between the top and bottom Pixel boundaries. The area of these 2 trapezoids is easily computed using the intersection of the **Midlines (*MidLn*)** with triangle edges that cross pixel boundaries.

Two types of Midlines have to be considered. Refer to Figure 4-1.

- For *VEs*, the Pixel height is *1.0*. The Horizontal Midlines (*H MidLn*) are at half distance between top and bottom boundaries of Pixels. The distance to the *H MidLn* is d. The area of the trapezoid is *1.0 *d = d*.
- For *HEs*, the Pixel width is *1.0*. The Vertical Midlines (*V MidLn*) are at half distance between left and right boundaries of Pixels. The distance to the *V MidLn* is d. The area of the trapezoid is *1.0 *d = d*.

Using the Midlines, the distance, *d*, from the left or top Pixel boundaries to the Midline intersection is obtained with only one measurement. From the distance on the Midlines, the covered area can be easily computed. In this example, the triangle edge is a beginning edge, with *BE=1*. The distance is obtained with only one measurement. In this case, with a resolution of *1/16*, the maximum error will be:

error = 1/16.

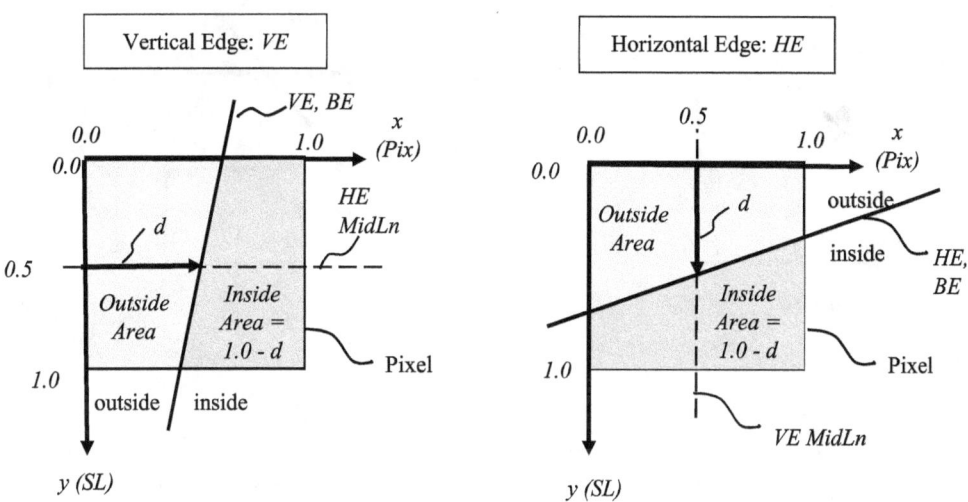

Figure 4-1 Area Measurements when Intersection within 0.0 and 1.0

Edge Intersection with Pixel Boundaries Not within 0.0 and 1.0

In the 2nd case, the EE intersections with opposite boundaries of Pixels is not within *0.0* and *1.0*. The EE intersections with opposite Pixel boundaries divide the Pixel into 2 trapezoidal areas, that extend outside of the Pixels. The area of the extended trapezoid is also easily computed by measuring the distance on Midlines.

Two types of extended areas have to be considered. These two cases are similar for *VE* and *HE*.

For *VE*, refer to Figure 4-2.

For *HE*, refer to Figure 4-3.

Area of Trapezoid

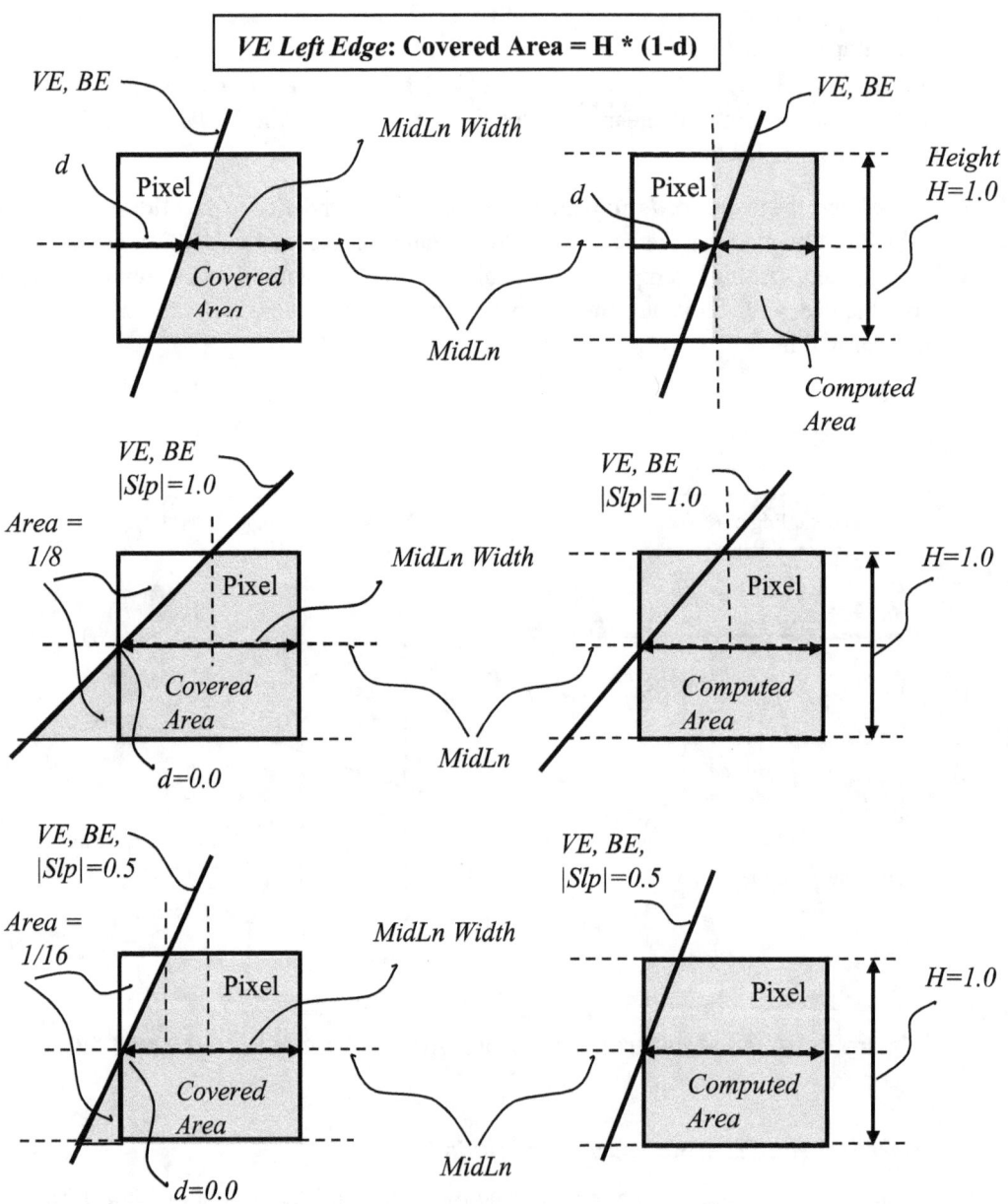

Figure 4-2 Pixel Covered Area Computation for *VE*

Area of Trapezoid

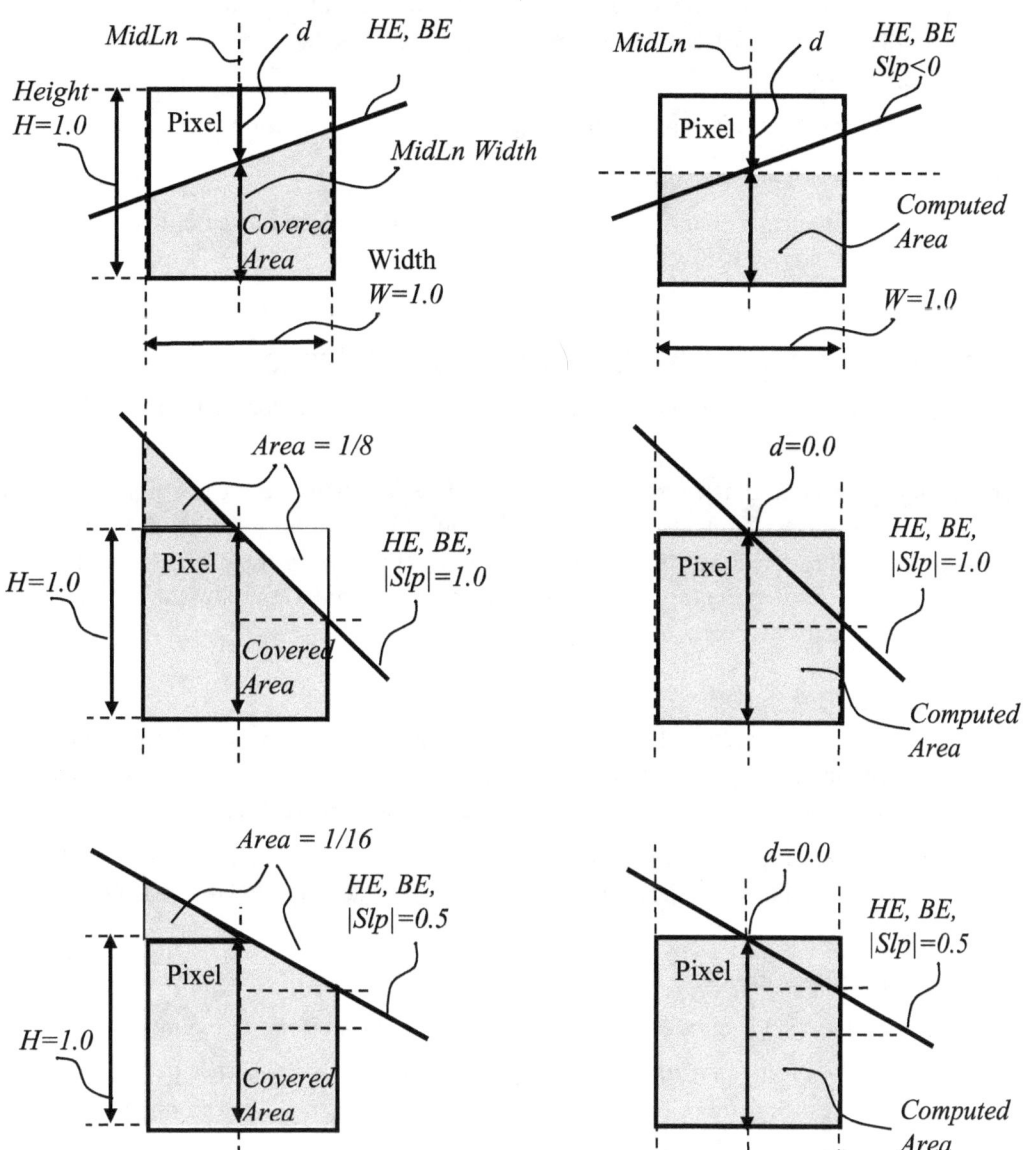

Figure 4-3 Pixel Covered Area Computation for *HE*

For EE with slope size up to 1.0, the maximum area outside of the Pixel is Pixel/8. When 4 Subpixel areas are used, the error is < 1/2 Subpixel. So, it can be ignored.

When 8 Subpixels are used, 2 case have to be considered, identified with the *S* flag.

Area of Trapezoid

S0 (Flag S=0), when the slope size is between *0.0* and *0.5*. The max extended area is <1/16.
In this case, 15/16 of Pixel area is covered when the edge enters the Pixel.

S1 (Flag S=1), when the slope size is between *0.5* and *1.0*. The max extended area is <1/8.
In this case, 7/8 of Pixel area is covered when the edge enters the Pixel.

When the distance *d* is zero, the trapeze area outside of the Pixel is compensated by the area inside of the Pixel, so the area error is zero. Same thing when *d==1.0*, the inside area is *1.0*.

Accuracy of Area computation with ABAA

With ABAA, the distance is obtained with only one measurement. In this case, with a resolution of *1/16*, the maximum error will be:

error = 1/16

4.3 Implementation of ABAA with Subpixel Areas

When I was developing my implementation of a new algorithms for antialiasing, I wrote a simulation program in C++.

After describing how *VE* and *HE* edges traverse the Tiles on the screen, came time to simulate how to handle intersected Pixels. For *VEs*, I had the top and bottom intersection available. While making some sketches I realized that the *VE* divided the Pixels into trapezoidal area. I quickly remembered that by adding the top and bottom intersections and dividing by 2, I had the area of the covered portions of the Pixel.

4.3.1 ABAA with 4 Subpixel Areas

Most implementations of Subpixel sampling for good AA use 8 Subpixel samples. So, I was looking for an implementation with 8 Subpixel areas. I did not even consider an implementation with 4 Subpixels. I was trying to convert the Pixel area into 8 Subpixel area.

It was not until year 2021, when I started to write this book that I found out how simple the 4 Subpixels implementation is. So, here I introduce the solution with 4 Subpixel areas first, because it is so simple.

Converting Trapezoidal Area into 4 Subpixel Areas

In this approach, the Pixel is divided into 4 square Subpixel areas. Refer to Figure 4-4.

Edges consist of 2 types, *VE* and *BE*. Also, the sign of the edge slope is to decide the order of Subpixels. In Figure 4-5, there is a representation of a beginning edge (*BE*) crossing 4 Subpixel Areas for the 4 Edge cases. There are 4 edge cases:
- *HE* and *Slp>0*
- *HE* and *Slp<0*
- *VE* and *Slp>0*
- *VE* and *Slp<0*

For *VE* and *HE*, the cases transition from one case to another when the slopes reach zero. For zero slopes, the decision is arbitratry.

Using this 4 Subpixels implementation, I was able to improve my 8 Subpixels implementation, as shown later on in this document.

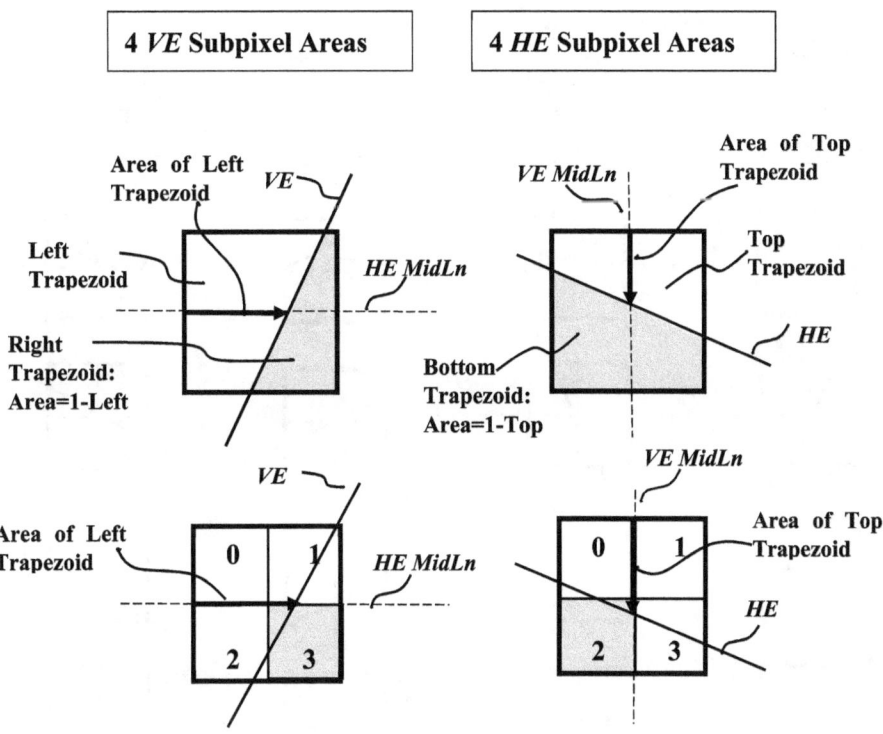

Figure 4-4 Four Subpixel Areas Intersected by *VE(BE)* and *HE(BE)*

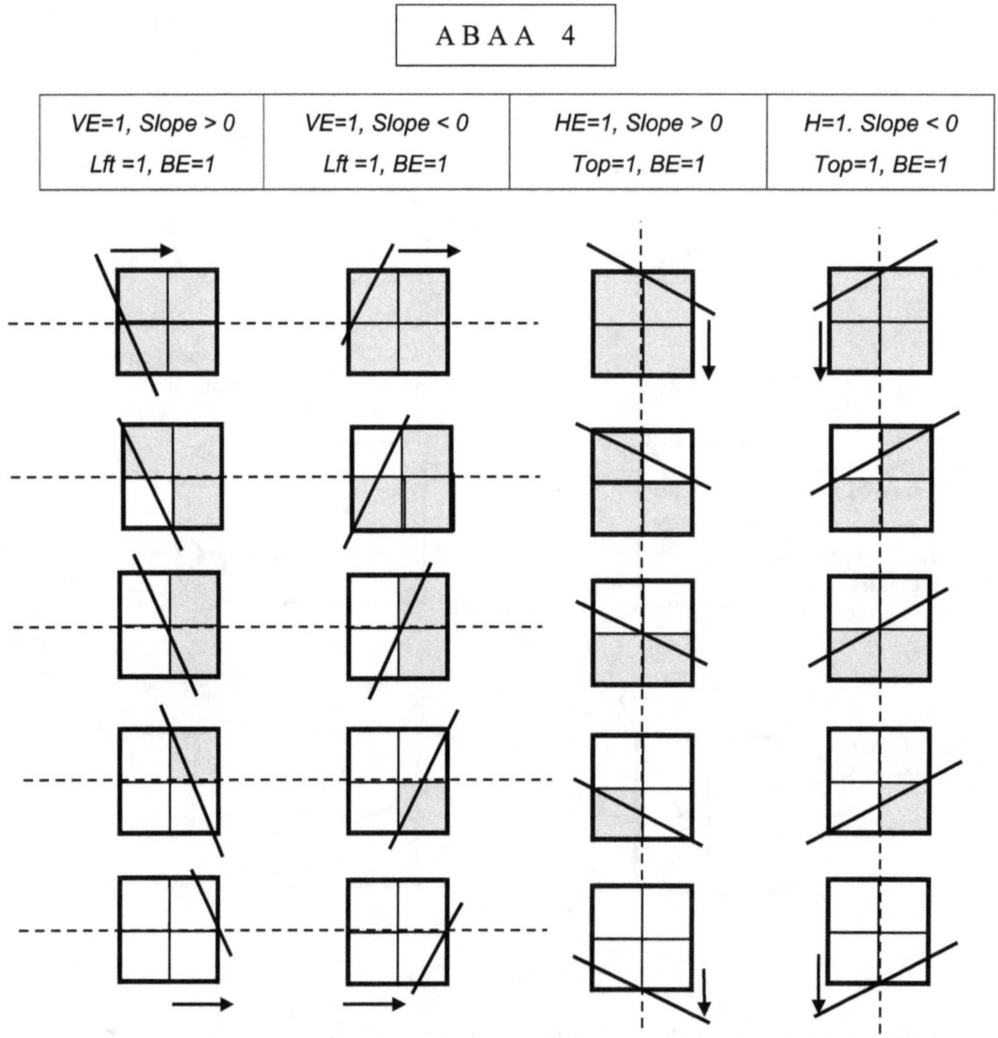

Area of Trapezoid

ABAA 4			
VE=1, Slope > 0 Lft =1, BE=1	VE=1, Slope < 0 Lft =1, BE=1	HE=1, Slope > 0 Top=1, BE=1	H=1. Slope < 0 Top=1, BE=1

Figure 4-5 Four Cases of Edge Crossing 4 Subpixel Areas

4.3.2 ABAA with 8 Subpixel Areas

As mentioned, when I started to write this book, I found out how simple the 4 Subpixels implementation is. I also found out that the 8 Subpixel implementation can be derived from the 4 Subpixel implementation by dividing the squares into 2 triangles. Also, this implementation should be symmetrical in x & y. Refer to Figure 4-6.

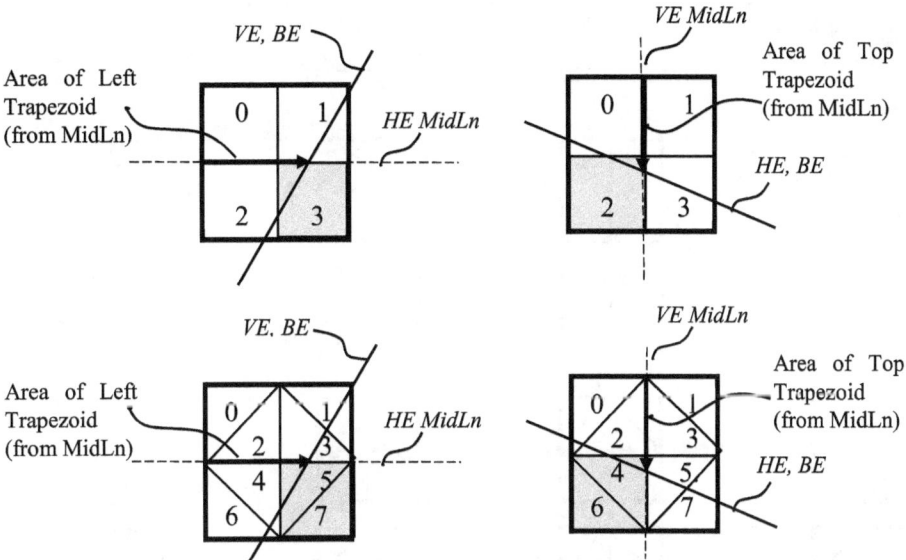

Figure 4-6 Expanding 4 Subpixels to 8 Subpixels

In this figure, the area covered by a beginning edge (*BE*) is shown as:
- Area covered by *VE, BE* is: 1- (Area of Left Trapezoid)
- Area covered by *HE, BE* is: 1- (Area of Top Trapezoid)

For ending edges (*!BE*), the area would be:
- Area covered by *VE, !BE* is: Area of Left Trapezoid
- Area covered by *HE, !BE* is: Area of Top Trapezoid

Depending on the edge slope ($|Slp| < 0.5$ or $|Slp| > 0.5$), the subpixel sequence will vary.

Example of ABAA with 8 Subpixel Areas

Using this assignment of 8 subpixel areas, it can be shown that when an edge moves across a Pixel, it results in 8 equal steps.

In Figure 4-7, there are 4 examples of a *BE* edges with $|Slp| < 0.5$. Edges are moving across the Pixel in 9 steps. For VEs, they move from left to right and the covered area is determined on the horizontal midline of the right trapezoid. For *HEs*, they move from top to bottom and the covered area is determined on the vertical midline of the bottom trapezoid. That is:

  HE: Covered_Area = 1- Area_of_Top_Trapezoid
  VE: Covered_Area = 1- Area_of_Left_Trapezoid

For $|Slp| > 0.5$, the sequence will be slightly different.

Area of Trapezoid

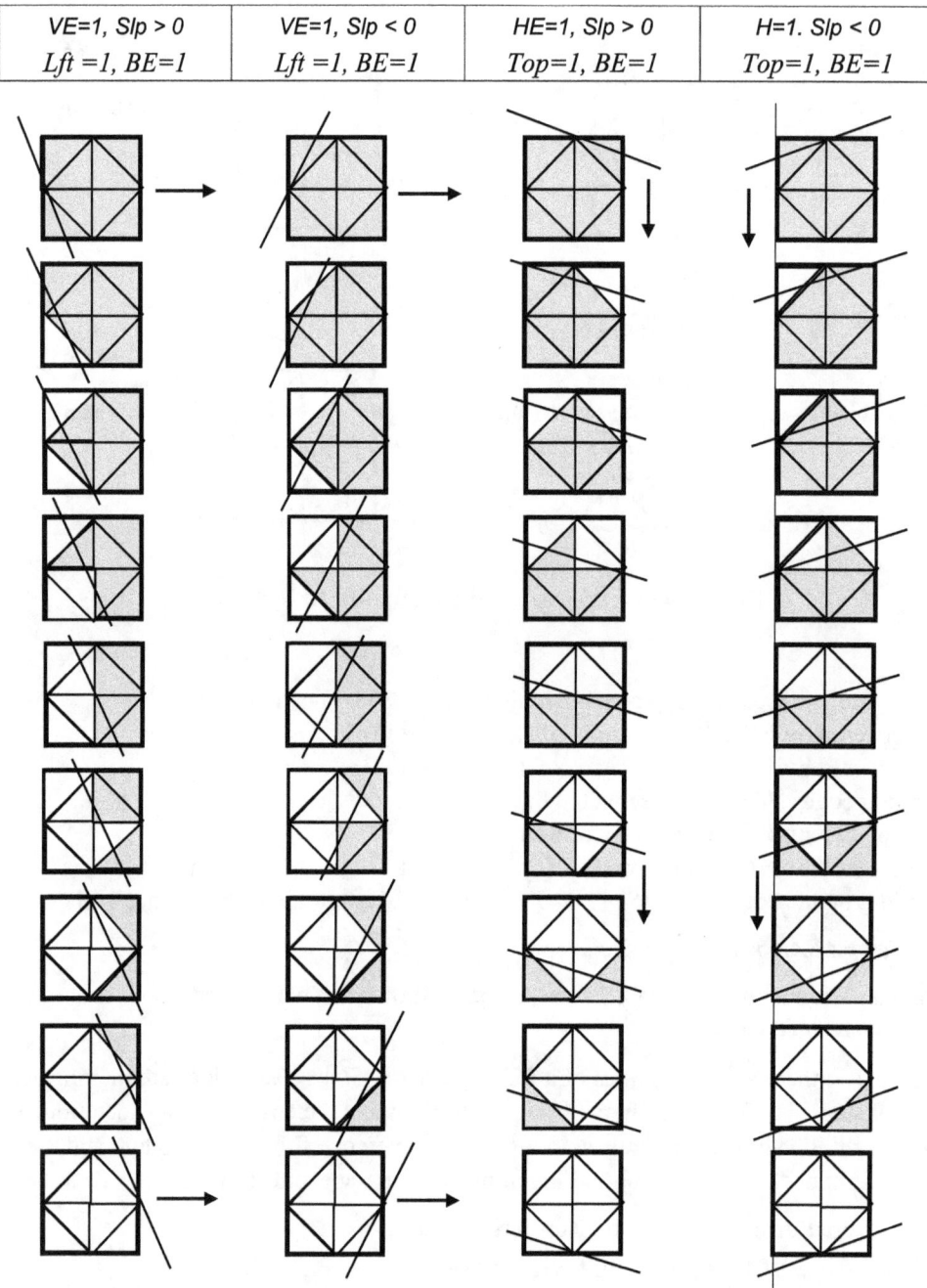

Figure 4-7 ABBA 8: 4 Cases of *BE* Edges Moving Across Pixels (|*Slp*|<0.5)

Chapter 5 Rendering Polygons and Triangles

In the last stages of rendering in 3D graphics, processing deals mainly with triangles. Before rendering, polygons and bicubic patches are always converted into a group of triangles using tessellation. For this reason, triangles rendering is described in this section.

Several examples in this chapter require some knowledge of binary numbers. One of the last chapters in this book provides useful information about binary numbers vs decimal numbers.

A simple and effective method for rendering triangles is introduced. Several characteristics of triangle edges are identified and used to simplify the rendering operations. Edge slope and edge type help on determining the Pixel area covered by triangles. But first, the image coordinate system has to be introduced.

5.1 Image Coordinates

In 2D descriptive geometry, the (X, Y) orthogonal coordinate system is defined by 2 coordinate axes.

- X axis points toward the right side of the image.
- Y axis points toward the top of the image.

But in graphics display (Xi, Yi) coordinate system, the Yi axis points downward on the image. Refer to Figure 5-1.

- Xi axis points toward the right side of the image.
- Yi axis points toward the bottom of the image.

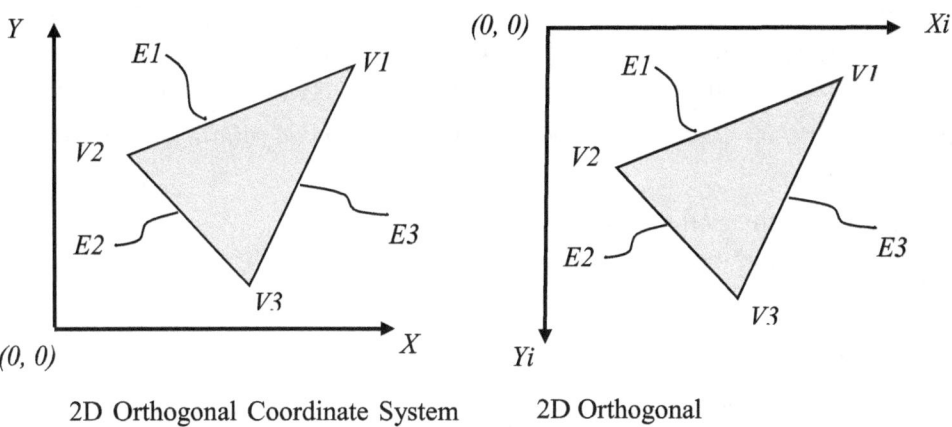

Figure 5-1 2D Orthogonal Coordinate Systems

I can guess why the 2D graphics displays use this coordinate system. This has to do with the evolution from text to 2D computer graphics. The earlier computer graphics were displaying text using the older CRT display monitors. Graphics images were developed later. Nowadays, the LCD and LED display monitors have been replacing CRT monitors. The earlier CRT displays were displaying text before 2D images. And, since text (English for example) starts on the top left of the display, the top left of the screen is the origin of the coordinate system for displaying characters and images imbedded inside of text. If you want to scroll text, you scroll down, no up. I think that if the pioneers of computer graphics used languages other than English, where you read from right to left for example, the coordinate graphics system might be different from the current standard for TV.

When 3D graphics objects are projected into a 2D image plane, the projected XY coordinates consist of fixed-point or floating-point values. The next step is to map that image onto an array of integer Pixels (Pix) and Scanlines (SL). Since the display area is described with binary numbers, a square area of size 2**N x 2**N is used as a drawing canvas.

5.1.1 Fixed-Point and Floating-Point Image Coordinates

The projected image is defined within a square area. The *Xi* and *Yi* limits of the image are described within a square canvas.

Refer to Figure 5-2.

The image coordinates are defined by two axes with *Xi* and *Yi* coordinates, as follows.

In the figure, the image is represented as a two-dimensional array of Pixels of integer size: *PixMax * SLMax*

- As can be seen in these figures, there are 2 coordinates units on each axis:
- - integer (*Pix* or *SL*) coordinates and
  - fixed-point (*xi* or *yi*) coordinates
- In the Image Display system, the image is retrieved from the Frame Buffer using an 'integer' memory address specified by (*Pix, SL*) coordinates and converted from digital to analog. The image it then displayed on Video Monitors or other image display systems

Depending on the context, the values on the coordinate axes can be defined with fixed point or with integer numbers.

- Horizontal axis from left to right, using:
  - integer Pixel (*Pix*) coordinate (between *0* and *PixMax*) or
  - fixed-point *xi* coordinate (between *0.0* and *1.0*).
- Vertical axis from top to bottom, using:
  - integer Scanline (*SL*) coordinate (between 0 and *SLMax*) or
  - fixed-point *yi* coordinate (between *0.0* and *1.0*).

Rendering Polygons and Triangles

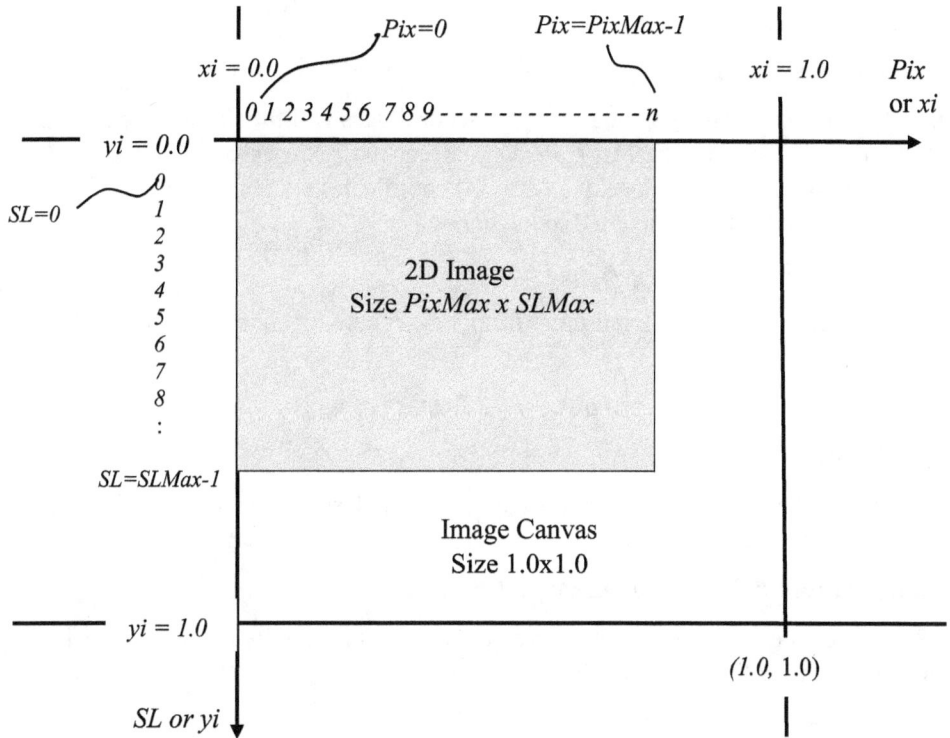

Figure 5-2 (Pix, SL) and (xi, yi) Image Coordinates inside Square Canvas

Integer (Pix or SL) coordinate

Pix and *SL* are integer numbers that define Pixel positions in the 2D image.
The horizontal integer coordinate *Pix* ranges from *0* to *PixMax-1*.
The vertical integer coordinate *SL* ranges from *0* to *SLMax-1*.
Pix and *SL* Coordinates are used to store and retrieve the Pixel data to/from an image buffer memory. The Pixel data is defined inside of the *Pix* and *SL* boundaries. The integer Pixel Coordinates are also used to access the memory locations inside that image buffer.

The range of *Pix* and *SL* variables depends on the horizontal and vertical range.

- For ranges up to *511*, it requires 9bit integers.
- For ranges up to *1023*, it requires 10bit integers.
- For ranges up to *2047*, it requires 11bit integers

Rendering Polygons and Triangles

Fixed-point (xi or yi) coordinate

The image coordinates *(xi, yi)* represent projection points in the image plane.

For example, for an *800x600* image, the fixed-point coordinates will fit within a *Pix* and *SL* range of *0* to *1023*. This corresponds to *1kx1k Pixels* and can be represented with 10bit *(Pix, SL)* coordinates. For each point in the image, the *(Pix, SL)* coordinates are obtained by multiplying the *(xi, yi)* coordinates by *1024* then converted to integer values.

(Pix, SL) = (integer(1024*xi), integer(1024*yi)

For the *(xi, yi)* coordinates, a 16-bit fixed-point format is suitable for an image of *1kx1k Pixels* and an accuracy of *1/16Pixel*.

This 16-bit signed fixed-point format of image coordinates *(xi, yi)* is:

sb.bbbbbbbbbb'bbbb

where '*s*' represents the sign bit and '*b*' represent a bit. The last 4 characters '*bbbb*' represent a Pixel fraction with Subpixel resolution.

Conversion from Fixed Point (xi, yi) to Integer (Pix, SL)

The *(Pix, SL)* coordinates in binary notation are obtained by shifting the point position 10 places to the right and truncating the 4 bits of fraction.

The values of *x* and *y* fixed point numbers can be defined in a range from *-1.0* to *+2.0*. This range covers a *3.0x3.0* image area.

The projected image has to fit within the *1.0x1.0* square Canvas area. That means that the *(xi, yi)* image coordinates are within *0.0* and *1.0*. The extended area is used for intermediate computations. The values outside of the image are used for interpolation. The portions of triangles that reside outside of the displayed image need to be clipped. Refer to Clipping patents [105][132].

5.2 Projected Triangles into Image Coordinates

In the 2D image, triangles can be defined by 3 vertices or 3 edges. Each triangle edge divides the image area into an inside area and an outside area. The triangle area is defined by an AND function of the 3 covered areas defined by the 3 triangle edges

5.2.1 Basic Triangle Edge Definition

The coordinate system for displaying computer generated images is aligned with the scan direction of TV and graphics display. That is:

- *Xi* coordinate is aligned with the Pixel display direction, that is from left to right.
- *Yi* coordinate is aligned with the Scanlines incremental direction, that is from top to bottom.

In Figure 5-3, there is a triangle defined within an *XiYi* coordinate system. It is defined by 3 vertices *V0*, *V1* and *V2*. The segments connecting the vertices define 3 edges *E0*, *E1*, and *E2*. So, the triangle can be defined in 2 ways:

- the triangle within the *XiYi* coordinate system is defined by 3 vertices as:
  triangle *(V1, V2, V3)*.
- the triangle can also be defined by the 3 edges as:
  triangle *(E1, E2, E3)*.

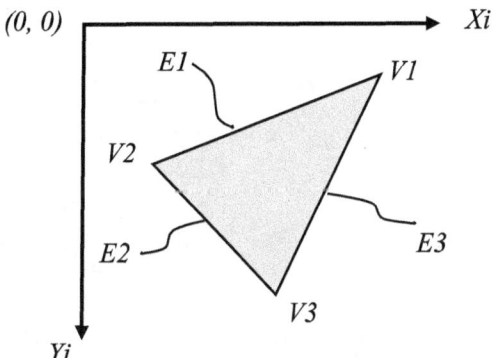

Figure 5-3 Triangle Consisting of 3 Vertices or 3 Edges

5.2.2 Edge Parameters Computation

An edge (E) can be represented by 2 vertices, or by a reference point (P) and a slope (S). This is the definition used when edges are first computed. The edge slope of a non-horizontal edge can be computed as:

$Slp = dx/dy$, when $dy != 0$.

In this definition, y is represented as the independent variable and x as the dependent variable. This is due to the fact that the image is processed in *SL*, or *Y*, order.

According to this definition, a true vertical edge has a zero slope. But there is a problem with this definition. Edges near the horizontal axis have a very large slope approaching infinity. In the worst case, the edge slope is infinity for true horizontal edges.

In general, a Polygon Edge is defined by 2 entities, where $i=1, 2$ or 3:

- Starting vertex: $Vi = (xi, yi))$
- Edge Slope: $Slpi = dxi/dyi$

With this definition, an edge is defined by 3 variables:

- xi
- yi
- $Slpi = dxi/dyi$, $dyi != 0$

The edge parameters are defined in Figure 5-4.

Rendering Polygons and Triangles

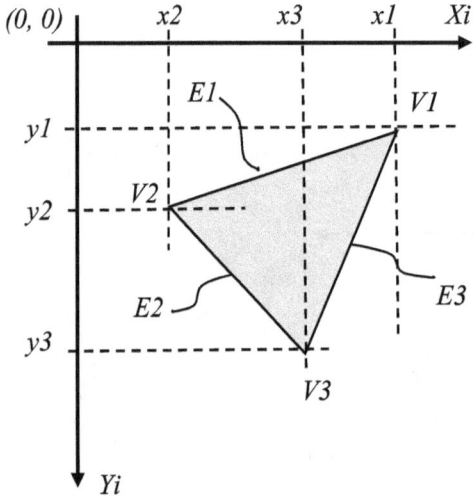

3 Triangle edges *(E1, E2, E3)* and 3 Slopes *(Slp01, Slp2, Slp3)*

Edge $E1 = (V1, V2)$, $Slp1 = (x2-x1)/(y2-y1) = dx1/dy1$

Edge $E2 = (V2, V3)$, $Slp2 = (x3-x2)/(y3-y2) = dx2/dy2$

Edge $E3 = (V3, V1)$, $Slp3 = (x1-x3)/(y1-y3) = dx3/dy3$

Figure 5-4 Triangle in 2D Image Coordinates

Note that this definition is suitable for a general description of the triangle. But, for computer graphics millions of triangles need to be processed and there are several problems/limitations with this definition.

First, floating point computations use more HW and memories and are slower than fixed point computations.

With floating point computations, the floating-point format could handle very large slope values. In the case of Horizontal Edges, a floating-point value near infinity could provide a good approximation. But, for fixed point implementation, this poses a problem. For fixed point computations a large number of digits are required for near horizontal edges. In the case of the DIGs that I worked on, the slopes had around 22 bits, while x and y were defined with only 14 bits. And with this limitation, the slope of horizontal edges could no represent the correct slope.

When polygons are rendered to generate a 2D image, the edge slope is iteratively used to compute edge intersections with Pixels and Scanlines. For Tile Traversing, the edge slope is iteratively used to jump from Tile to Tile. This type of operations is more efficiently accomplished with fixed point calculations.

Optimized Edge Format

In order to solve the problem of large slopes with fixed point representation, the edge format can be optimized to improve the efficiency of the traversing operation. One day, I realized that if there were two types of edges, vertical (*VE*) and horizontal (*HE* = !*VE*) edges, the maximum size of edge slopes could be limited to *1.0*. There would be complete symmetry in *Xi* and *Yi* coordinates. The number of bits required for edge slope, *ESlp,* would be similar to the number of bits for *xi* and *yi*.

In this approach, edges use a format similar to the *(xi, yi)* coordinates. A 16-bit fixed-point format for edge slopes *Slp* is suitable for an image of *1kx1k Pixels* and an accuracy of 1/16Pixel. This 16-bit signed fixed-point edge format for *xi, yi* and *Slp* is:

   sb.bbbbbbbbbb'bbbb

where '*s*' represents the sign bit and '*b*' represent a bit. The last 4 characters '*bbbb*' represent a Pixel fraction with Subpixel resolution.

5.2.3 Edge Definition for Triangle Rendering

When rendering polygons or more specifically triangles, edges are tested to determine the area that they cover. Basically, each edge divides the rendering area into two sides: the *inside* and the *outside*. On the *outside* of the edge, the area is not covered by the triangle. On the *inside* of the edge, the area is partially covered by the triangle. But, until all the edges are tested, the whole *inside* area is potentially covered by the triangle.

In this ABAA algorithm, edges are used to detect the Subpixel area coverage in two directions:

- For *VE*, the direction is left to right
- For *HE*, the direction is top to bottom

Also, edges have to be defined as beginning and ending edges. The edges are processed in counter clockwise direction. Depending on edge slope size, they are organized into 2 main types: *VE* and *HE*. More precisely, depending on their direction they can be referred as beginning (*BE=1*) or ending (*BE=0*) edges.

- *VE Lft (left), BE=1*, Direction down, with $dy>0$
- *VE Rgt (right), BE=0*, Direction top, with $dy<0$
- *HE Top (top), BE=1*, Direction left, with $dx<0$
- *HE Bot (bottom), BE=0*, Direction right, with $dx>0$

Refer to Figure 5-5.

Rendering Polygons and Triangles

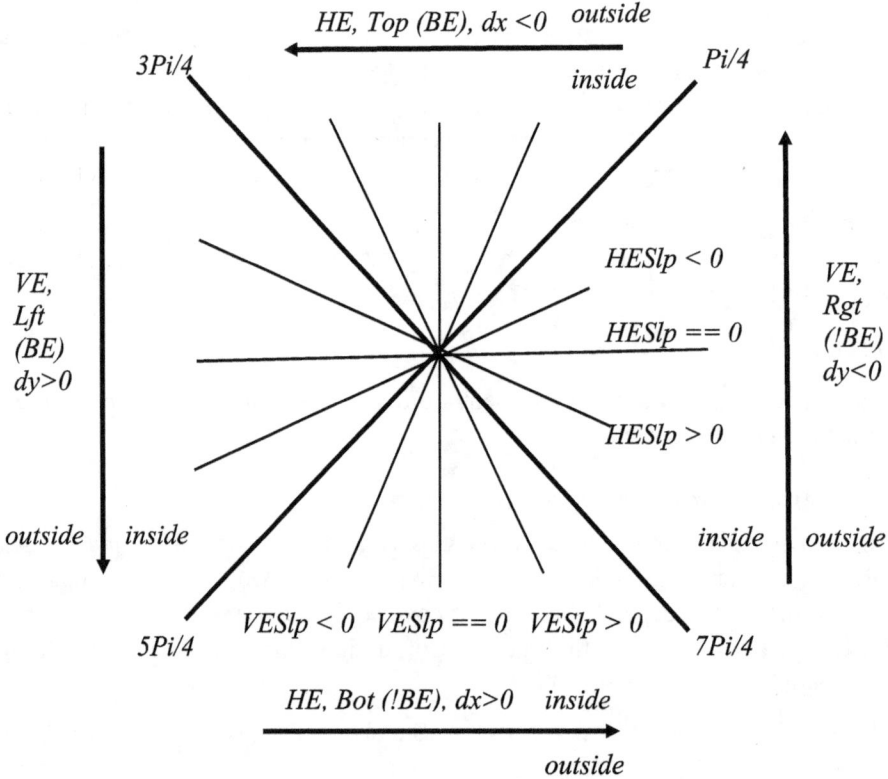

Figure 5-5 Beginning and Ending Edge Types

5.2.4 Definition of Edge Directions and Types

When a triangle is processed in the Geometric Processor, the order of triangle vertices has to be specified. The order can be clockwise like the movement of the hands on a clock, or counter-clockwise like the angle degrees in a circle.

In this document, the order of triangle vertices in 3D objects is counter-clockwise for the visible side of surfaces. For the back side of faces (not visible), the order is clockwise.

Edge Parameter Decoding is described in the flowchart of Figure 5-6.

The slope flags *S0* and *S1* are derived from the 3 most significant bits (*MSBs*) of the slope.

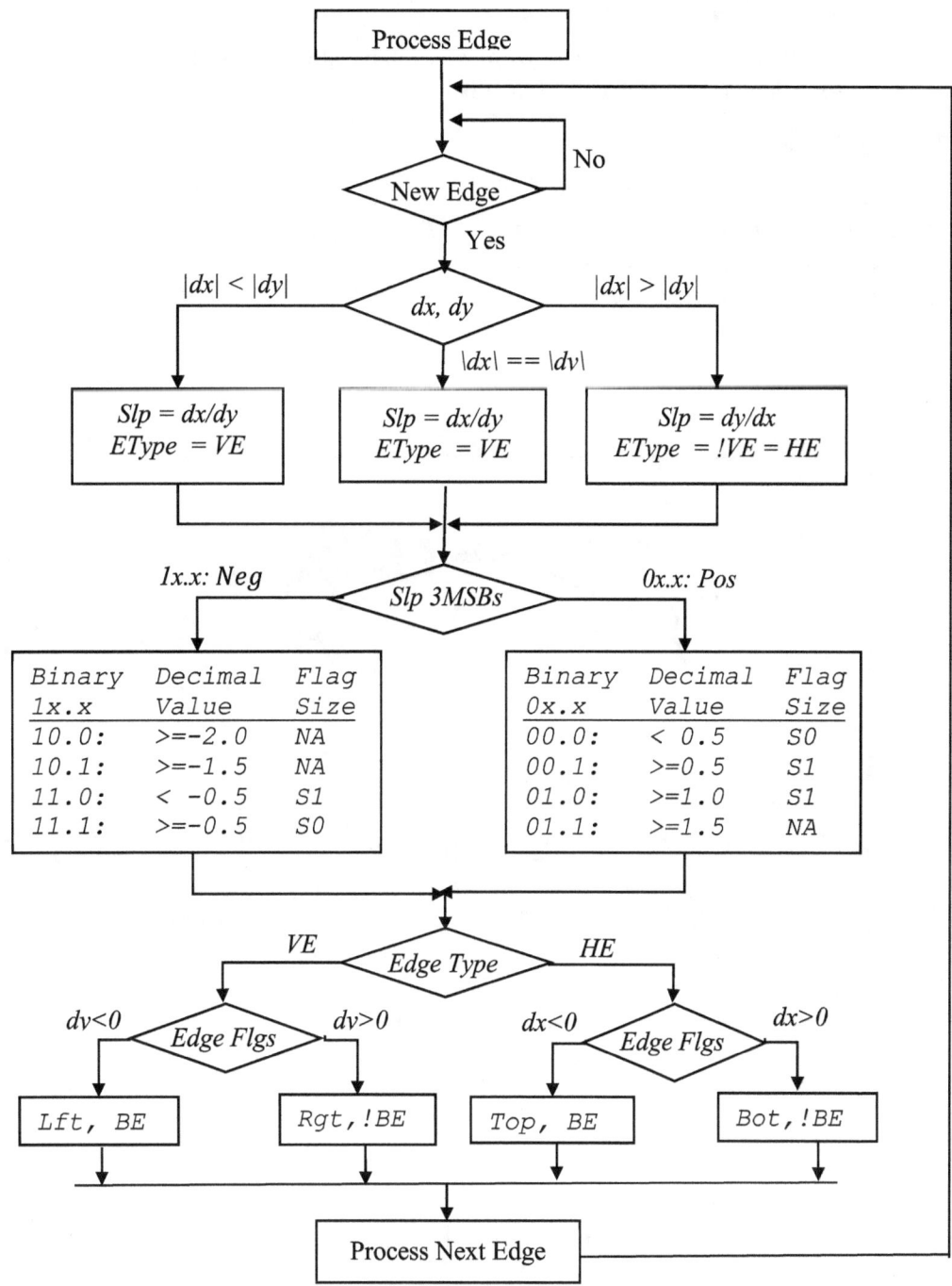

Figure 5-6 Edge Parameters Decoding

Rendering Polygons and Triangles

Process Angles in Counter-Clockwise Order

In this document, the triangle vertices are processed in counter-clockwise order This definition is important for determining which side of the Pixel is covered when an Edge crosses a Pixel.

8 Main Edge Types

Also, depending on their direction, edges can be Beginning *(BE)* or Ending *(!BE)* Edges.

There can be 8 edge types, depending on edge-angle, edge-direction and slope sign.
Refer to Figure 5-7, "Eight Cases of Edge Types".
The 4 side types are: *VE Left/Right (Lft/Rgt)* and *HE Top/Bottom (Top/Bot)*
Then, each side type can have a *positive* or a *negative* slope.

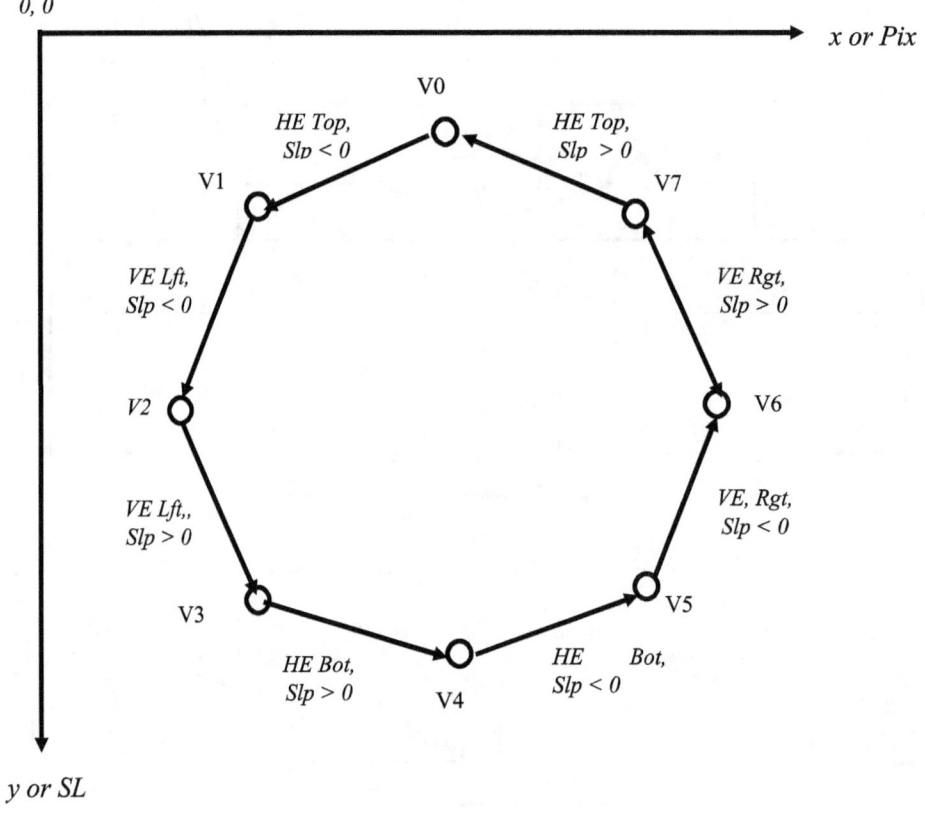

Figure 5-7 Eight Cases of Edge Types

5.2.5 Rendering a Triangle Inside of Spans

In Figure 5-8, a triangle inside of a Span is rendered according to info from the 3 edges

In this example, the Span area is defined by an array of 8x8 Pixels. Each Pixel area is divided into N Subpixels. So, the Span area consists of is 64*N Subpixels.

The Span area covered by the triangle is derived in 3 steps.

Step1:
Identify the parameters of the 3 triangle edges.
In this example the 3 edges have the following flags: '*HE Top*', '*VE Lft*' and '*VE Rgt*'.

Step2:
For each edge, evaluate the Span covered area. Set the covered Subpixel state to '*1*'.
Refer to *Area0*, *Area1* and *Area2*.
For each edge, all the covered Subpixels are set to '*1*' and the remaining Subpixels are set to '*0*'.

Step3:
The area '*TriArea*' covered by the triangle is obtained by doing the AND function of the 3 covered areas defined by edges. This AND operation (&) on the 3 covered areas is performed bitwise on all 64*N Subpixels.

After Step 3, the area, '*TriArea*', inside of the Span that is covered by the triangle is defined by the Subpixels that are set to '1'.

Rendering Polygons and Triangles

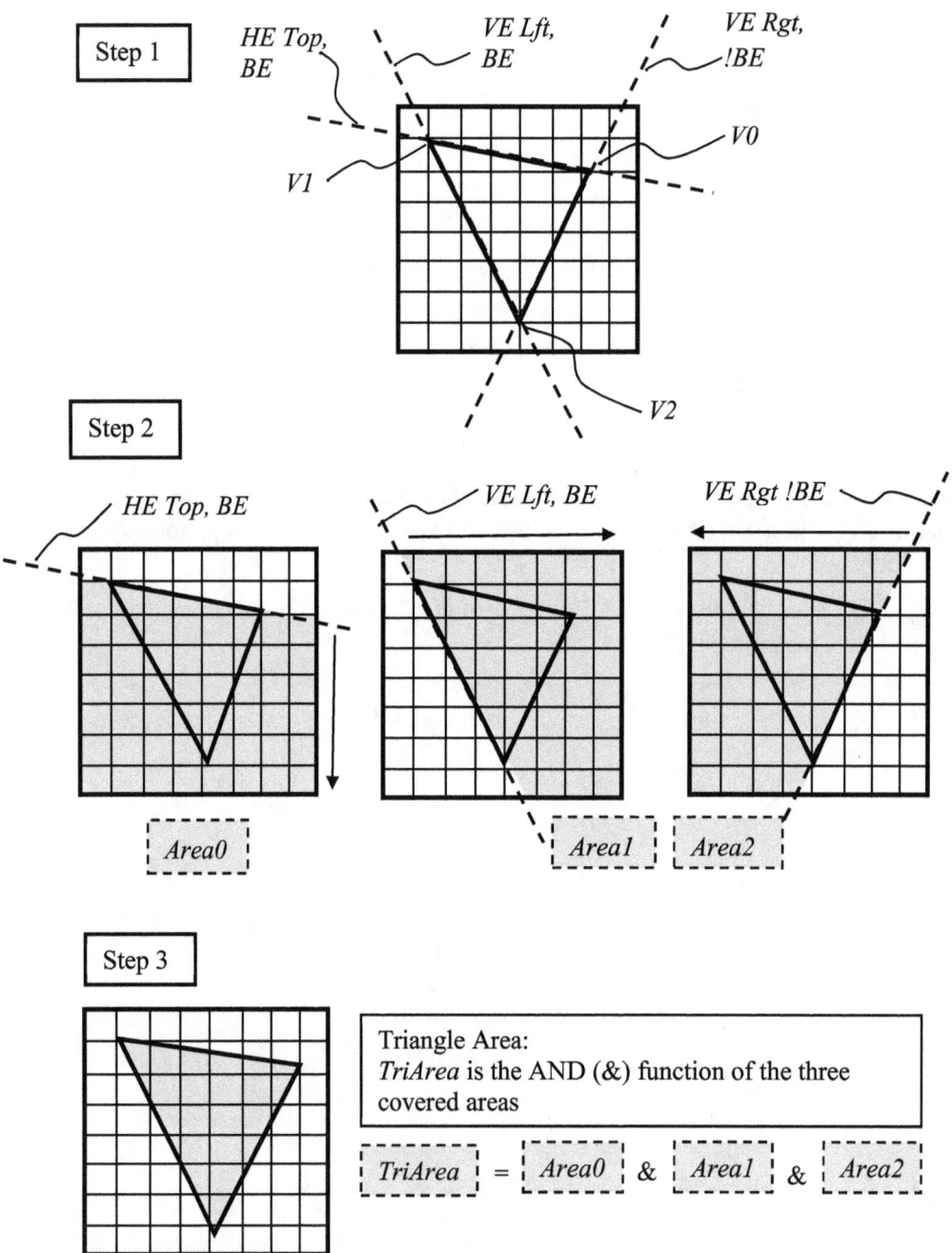

Figure 5-8 Triangle Rendering According to Edge Info

5.2.6 Edges Traversing Spans for Triangle Rendering

When the whole image is considered, the intersected Spans can be identified by rectangular areas defined by *Min* and *Max* values of the 3 vertices of the triangle to render.

In order to render triangles, the triangle edges are used to traverse Spans. The covered area of Spans is limited by the *Min/Max* dimensions of the triangle such as:

- *PixMin* and *PixMax*
- *SLMin* and *SLMax*.

As example, a triangle is inside of an area of 4x3 Spans intersects 9 Spans. The Pixel covered areas are obtained by using the 3 edges to traverse these Span areas.

Refer to In Figure 5-9, "Span Traversing with 3 triangle Edges".

Note that in this example, the triangle bottom edge is an *HE* with slope<0. In this case, there are 2 solutions: The selected approach depends on the algorithm implementation.

- Traverse the Spans from top to bottom. In this case the starting intersection point will be on the right side of the Rendering Area. This is approach used in this example.
- Traverse the Spans from left to right. In this case the starting intersection point will be on the top side of the Rendering Area.

Rendering Polygons and Triangles

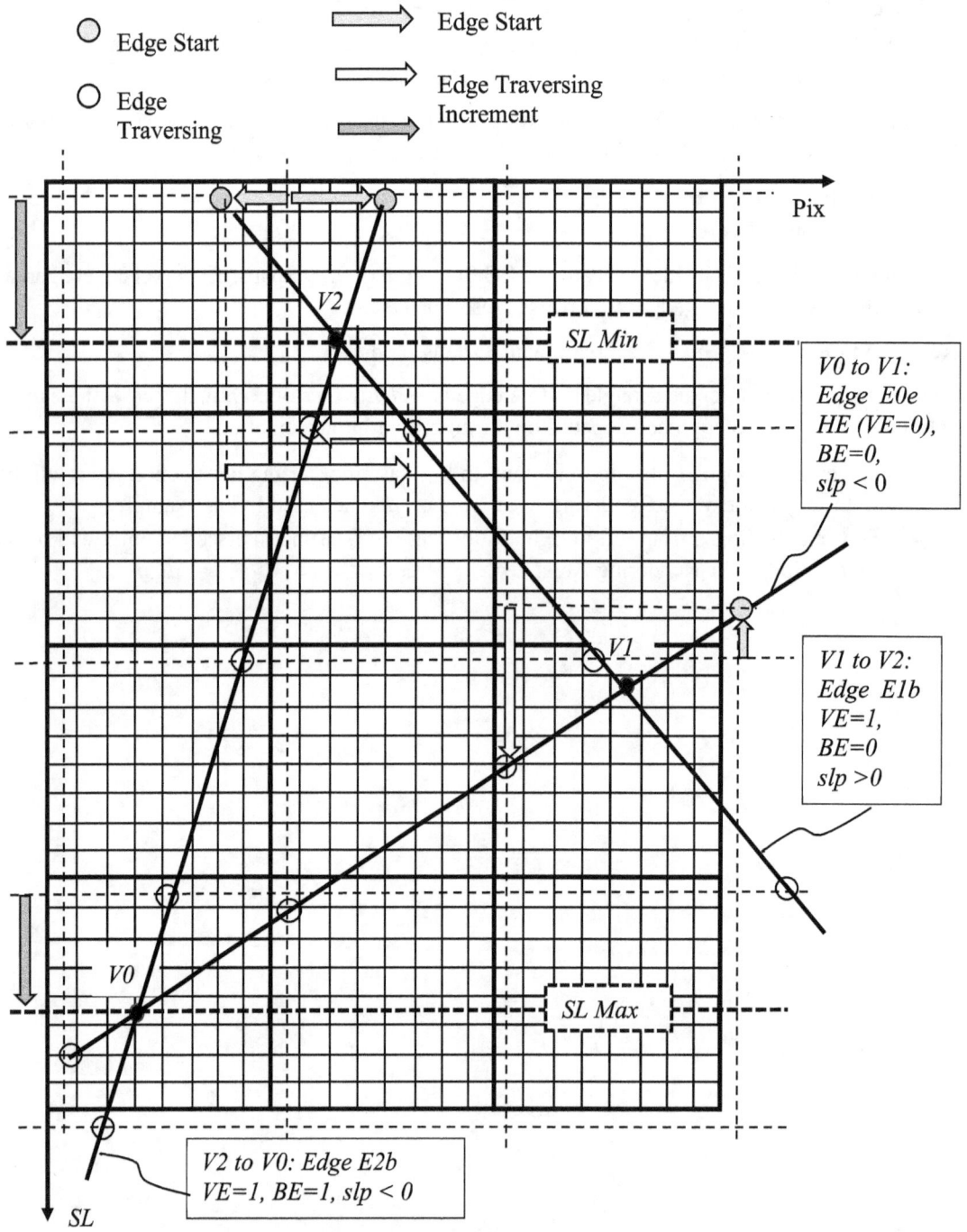

Figure 5-9 Span Traversing with 3 Triangle Edges

The images in these examples have been generated by a C-program. Since there are 8x8 Pixels in a Span, and up to 8 Subpixels in a Pixel, there are advantages to use octal binary numbers in the simulation. The edge coordinates and slopes are defined with octal numbers. The program input consists of edges defined as 'octal-char' input using numbers in 'octal ASCII' format.

In this example, the triangle is defined by 3 edges within an 8x8 Pixel Span.

No gray shade images

It is not practical to show images with gray shades. When printed, the images can be easier to evaluate at first. But, because of the limitation of the printing process, it would be difficult to evaluate the number of covered Subpixels between 0 and 8 inside of each Pixel with gray shades. The results would have been inconclusive.

Show results with a character Printer

By showing the covered Subpixels with an '*' or an ID number, the covered Subpixel are easily identified. By showing the covered Subpixel count inside of Pixels instead gray shade, it is easier to evaluate and compare the ABAA vs MSAA approaches. Also, by showing a number for the covered Subpixels, it helps identify the face to which the Subpixel belong. When there is only one face, the covered Subpixels are indicated with an '*'.

Figure 5-10 and 5-11 show the result from processing the 3 triangle edges and the final triangle, using ABAA 4. The final triangle is obtained by ANDing the results of the 3 triangle edges.

Rendering Polygons and Triangles

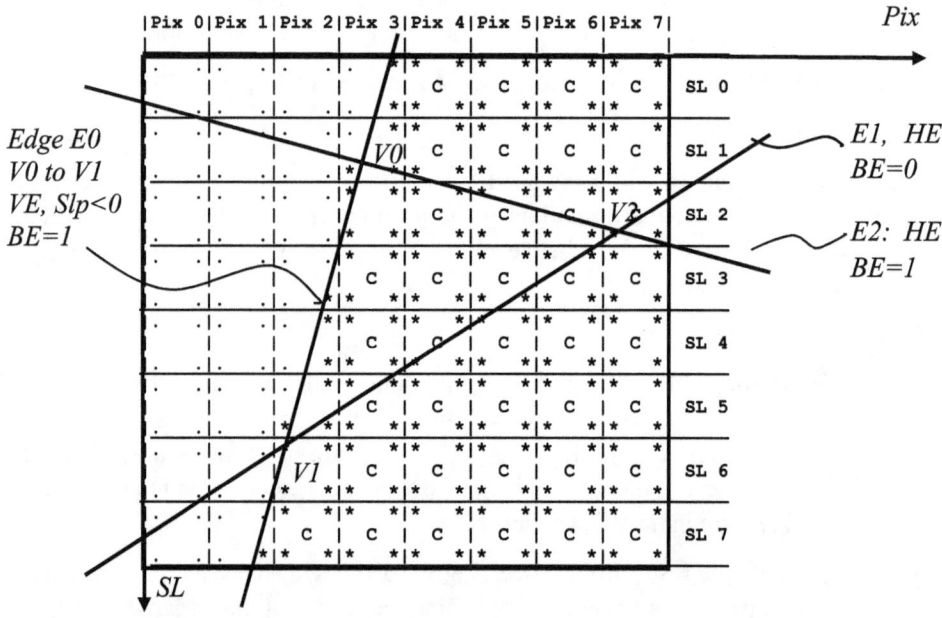

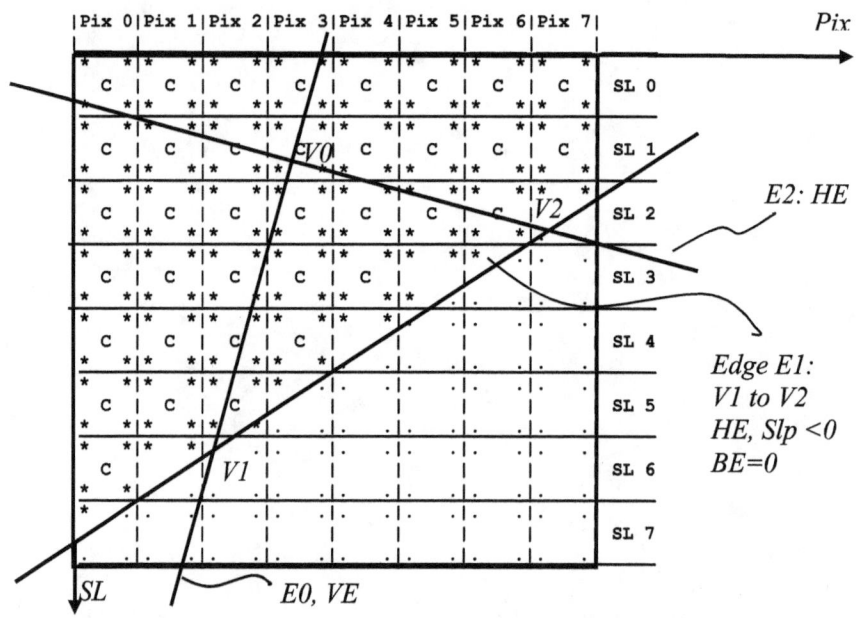

Figure 5-10 Processing of Edges E0 and E1

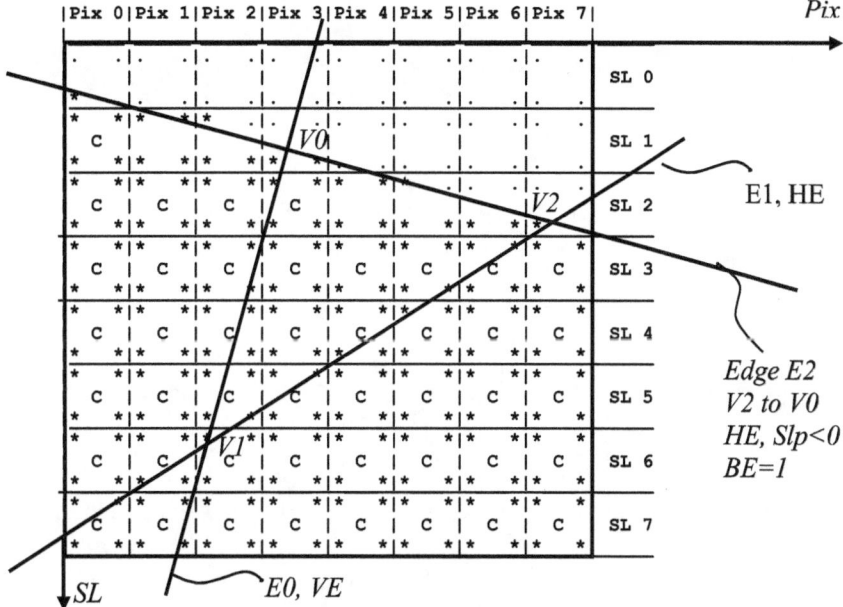

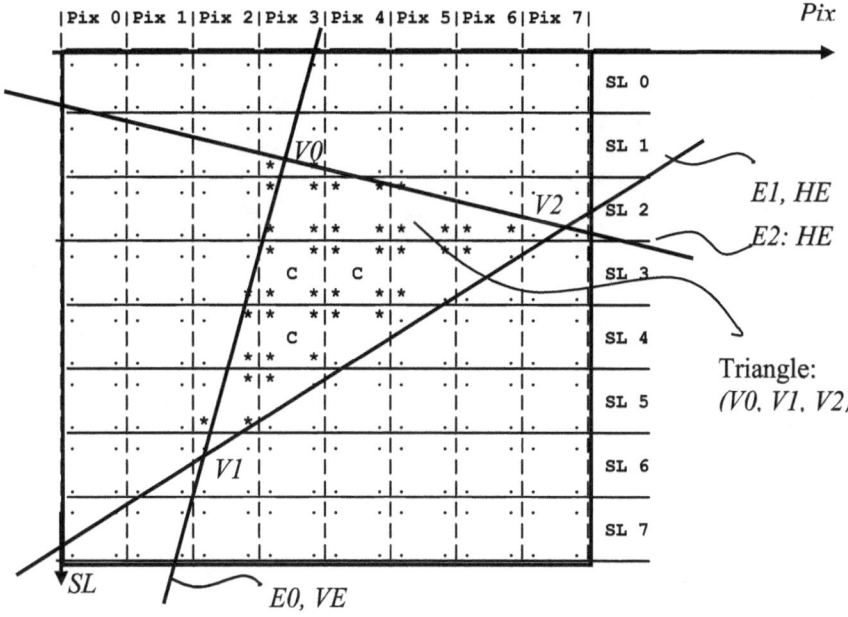

Figure 5-11 Processing of Edge E2 and Final Triangle

Chapter 6 ABAA with 4 Subpixel Areas

In this section, a solution for 4 subpixels assignment is presented, followed by a simulation comparing ABAA with MSAA.

6.1 Solution with 4 Square Subpixel Areas

The Pixel covered area is determined by the edge distance, d, on the Pixel *MidLn*. The distance is obtained with only one measurement. Using 4 fractional bits resolution, the maximum error will be: $e = 1/16$

In Figure 6-1, there are 2 cases for a negative *VE*, according to distance: $d>0.0$ and $d==0.0$. In both cases, the Computed Area is equal to the Covered Area.

- In the first case, it is assumed that the range of extended edge (EE) intersections with 2 opposite boundaries of Pixels is within 0.0 and 1.0. The EE intersections with opposite Pixel boundaries divide the Pixel into **2 trapezoidal areas**. Here the distance is $d>0.0$.
- In the 2nd case, the distance $d==0.0$, the slope is $|Slp|=|-1|=1.0$. This is the worst case. On the left boundary of the Pixel, the covered area on the left side is 1/8. It is equal to the uncovered are on the right side.

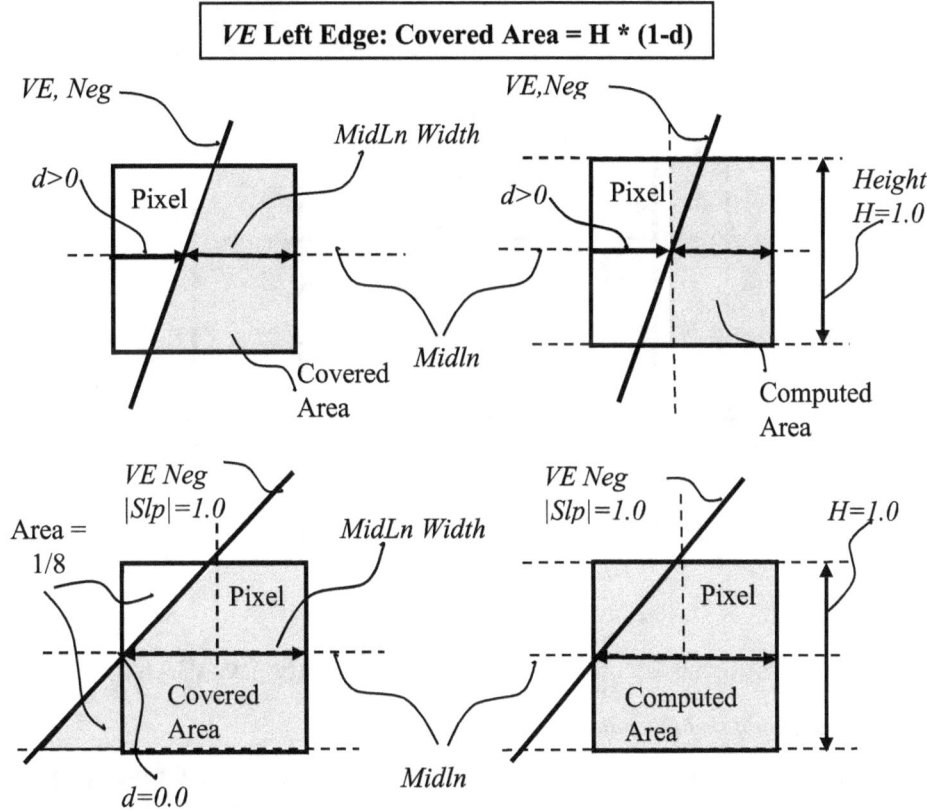

Figure 6-1 Pixel Covered Area Computation for Negative VE

ABAA with 4 Subpixel Areas

The 4 Subpixel transitions are identified according to 3 edge Flags.
- Edge orientation Flag: *VE vs HE*
- Edge Polarity Flag: *Pos vs Neg*
- Esge beginning or ending flag: *BE* vs *!BE*.

Pixel-Map for 4 Subpixels

In Figure 6-2, the 4 Subpixel solution is represented in a Pixel-Map. This Map describes the 4 edge cases with their corresponding Subpixel sequences.

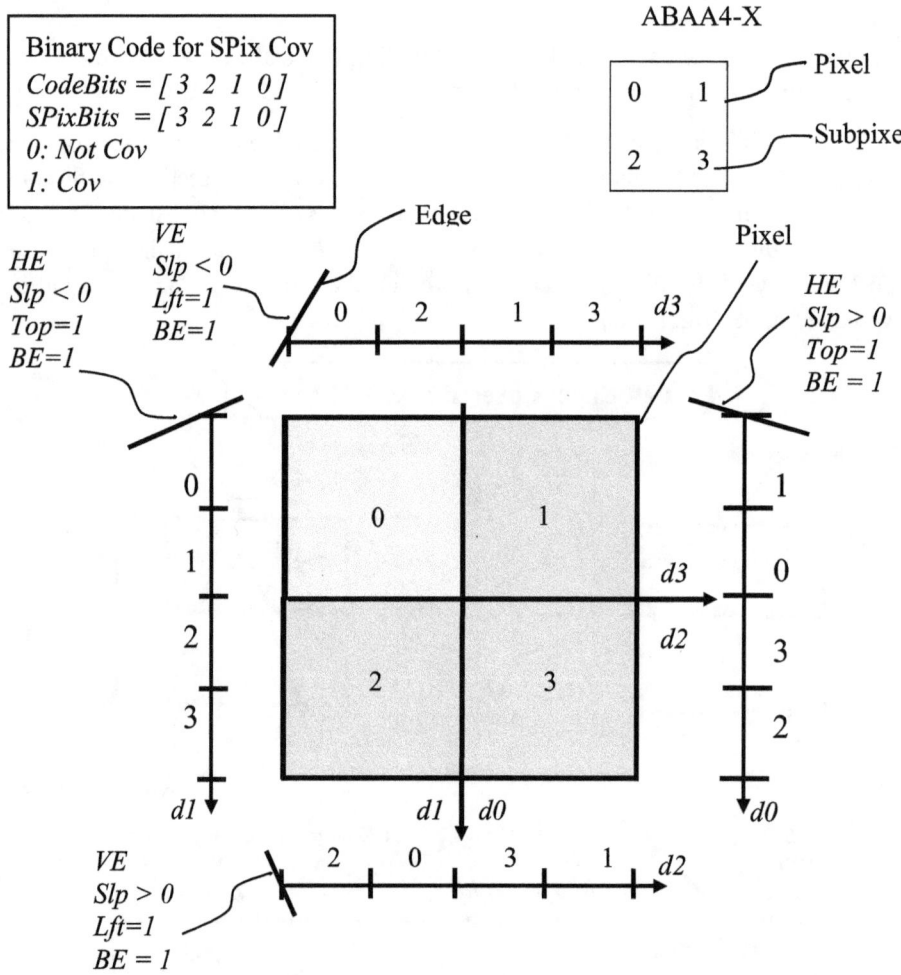

Figure 6-2 Pixel Map with 4 Edge Cases for ABAA4-X

Flowchart for 4 Subpixel Decoding

The same information can be represented in a flowchart. The decoding for the Subpixel sequence is described in the flowchart of Figure 6-3.

The Subpixel sequences can be stored in a table in local memory or other storage.
This figure shows the sequences when the Subpixels are turned on for beginning edges (*BE=1*).
For ending edges (*BE=0*) the sequences indicate when the Subpixels are turned off.

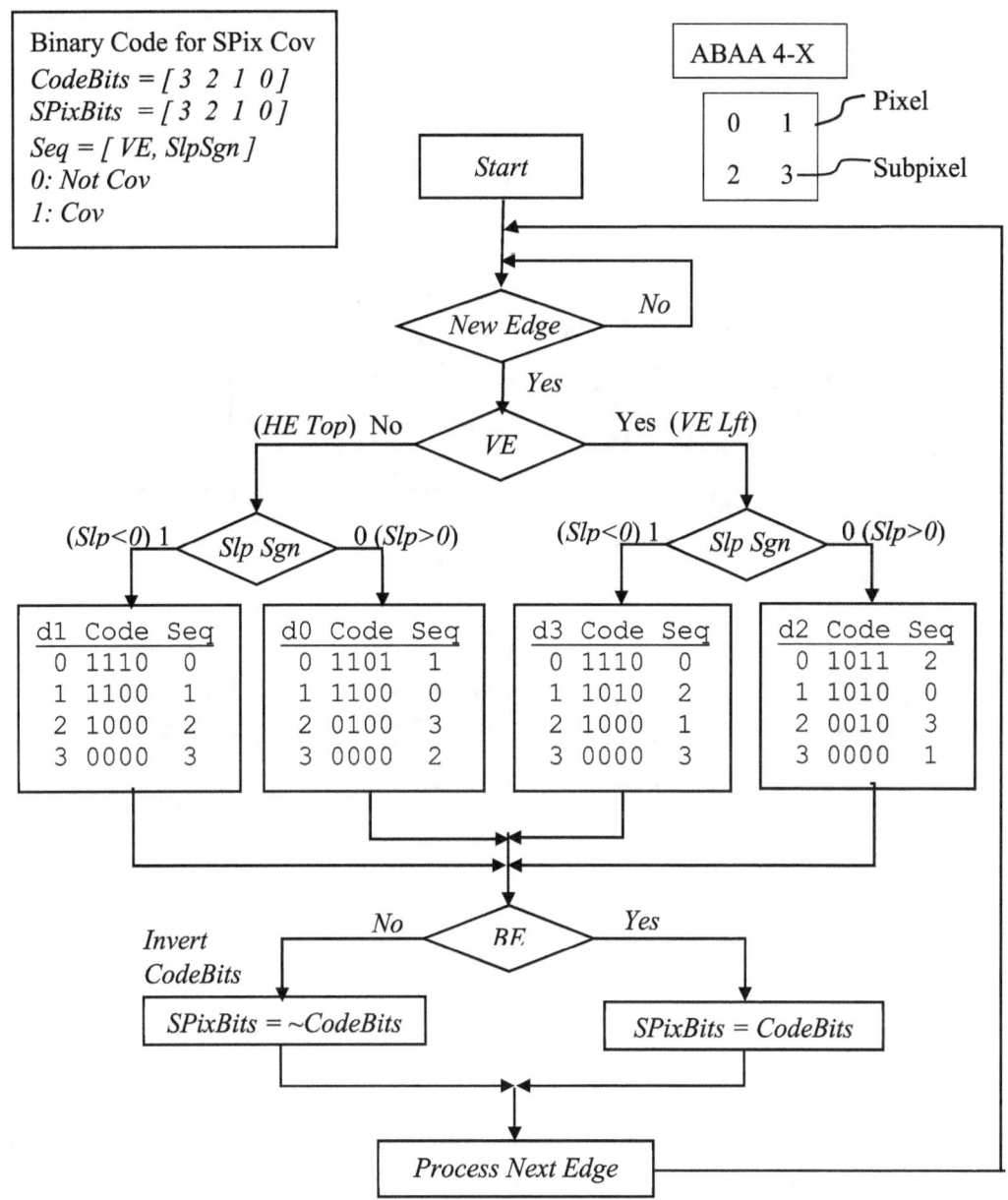

Figure 6-3 Flowchart to Decode Subpixel Mapping for ABAA4-X

ABAA with 4 Subpixel Areas

Example with 4 Subpixels

In Figure 6-4, there is a representation of an edge crossing 4 Subpixel Areas for the 4 Edge cases.

Each group of 4 edges that intersects the MidLn in the same quarter of distance d covers the same number of Subpixels.

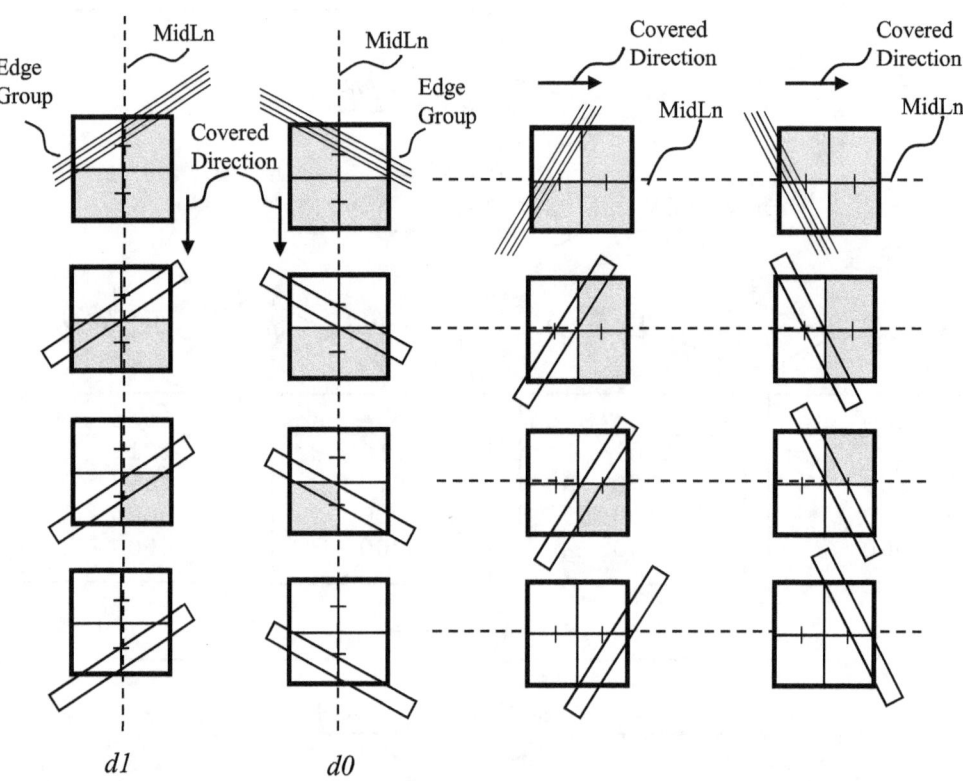

Figure 6-4 ABAA4-X: Four Cases of Edge Crossing 4 Subpixel Areas

6.1.1 ABAA vs MSAA Examples with 4 Subpixels

In Figure 6-5, there is a comparison of ABAA vs MSAA, for an edge movig across 4 Subpixels.

With ABAA, as the edge moves from left to right across the Pixel, there are 4 equal intensity transitions. With MSAA, when an edge crosses a pair of Subpixels that are aligned with that edge, there can be double intensity transitions.

ABAA with 4 Subpixel Areas

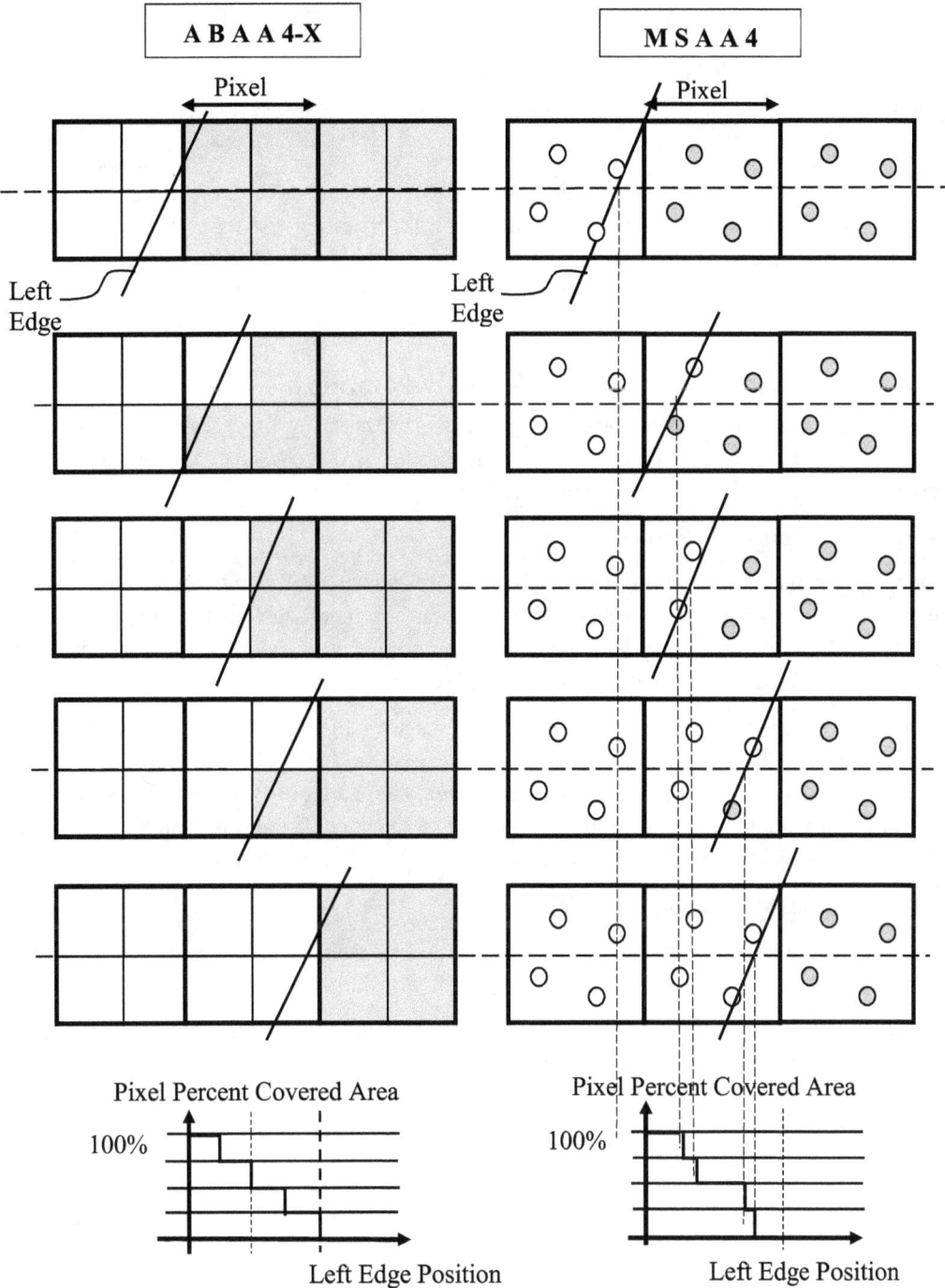

Figure 6-5 ABAA4-X vs MSAA4: Moving edge across 4 Subpixels

6.2 Example of ABAA4-X with Fans of Thin Triangles

These examples have been generated by a C-program.

In each figure there is a fan of 8 thin triangles. Each triangle is defined by 3 edges within an 8x8 Pixel Span.

It is not practical to show images with gray shades. When printed, the images can be easier to evaluate at first. But, because of the limitation of the printing process, the results can be inconclusive. Instead, the covered Subpixels are identified with a '*' character, or a face number, instead gray shades. This makes it is easier to evaluate and compare the ABAA vs MSAA approaches.

6.2.1 Comparison of ABAA vs MSAA with 4 Subpixels

The algorithms used for Subpixel processing can be evaluated by using thin triangles, of size approximately 8 Pixels long and 1 Pixel wide at the base. The test uses groups of 8 such triangles organize into fans spreading over an angle of Pi/2 (90 degrees).

Test Cases Consisting of 8 Narrow Triangle Fans

For the comparison of ABAA with MSAA, the test cases consist of 8 thin triangles organized as a fan displayed across a Span of size 8x8 Pixels. In each fan, there are four triangles (a, b, c & d) with vertical edges eight SL long (*VE*) and four triangles (e, f, g & h) with horizontal edges eight Pixel long (*HE*). The triangle bases are roughly 1 Pixel wide.

Since the triangle tops are 0 Pixel wide and the bottoms are 1 Pixel wide, the number of Subpixel increments per Pixel from top to bottom of triangle is expected to be 1/8 Pixels. In the case of 4 Subpixels, there should be 8 increments of ½ Subpixel. There are only 4 incremental steps of size 1/4 within a Pixel. Each number of Subpixels should be repeated so that the triangle width is near 0 at the top and near 4 Subpixels at the base, after 7 half Subpixel increments.

Four Test Cases with 8 Narrow Triangle Fans

Four cases of 8 thin triangle fans have been selected. They cover a wide range of cases: Even (A) and Odd (B) triangles. The cases are also mirrored into Pos and Neg edges.

Since there are gaps between the 8 triangles, the tests are organized into 2 sets A and B. In set A, there are 8 thin triangles with edges ranging from 0 to 90 degrees. In set B, there are also 8 thin triangles consisting of the gaps between the triangles of set A. Also, there are cases for Pos and Neg Edges. Although there are 4 examples, only the detailed result of the 1st example is shown in:

Figure 6-6, Fan example for ABAA 4 vs MSAA 4 for Pos Edges A

All the results from the 4 test cases with 4 Subpixels are combined into a single figure, as shown in Figure 6-7:
ABAA 4 vs MSAA 4 for Pos Edges A, ABAA 4 vs MSAA 4 for Pos Edges B,
ABAA 4 vs MSAA 4 for Neg Edges A, ABAA 4 vs MSAA 4 for Neg Edges B

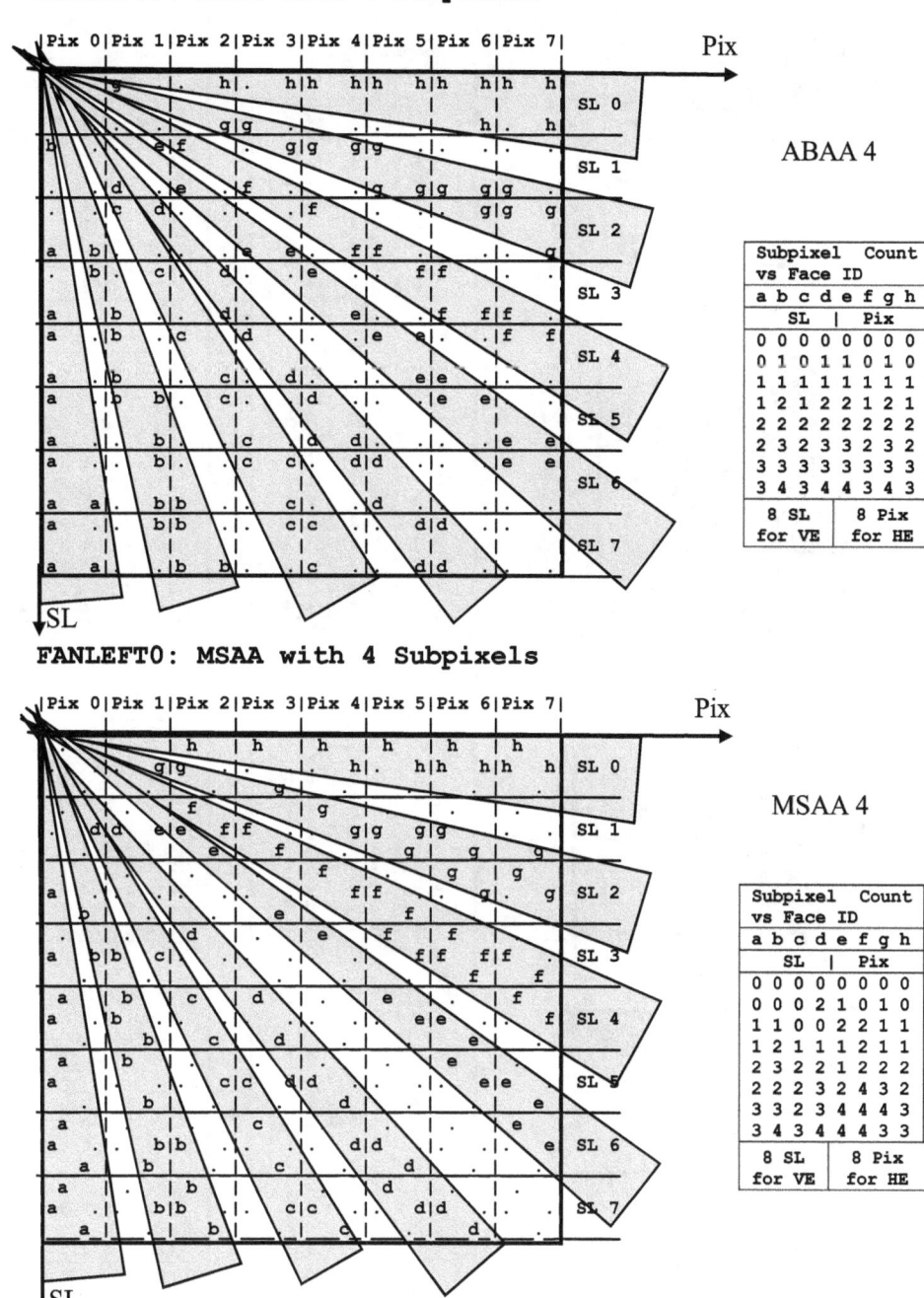

Figure 6-6 ABAA 4 vs MSAA 4 for Pos Edges A

ABAA with 4 Subpixel Areas

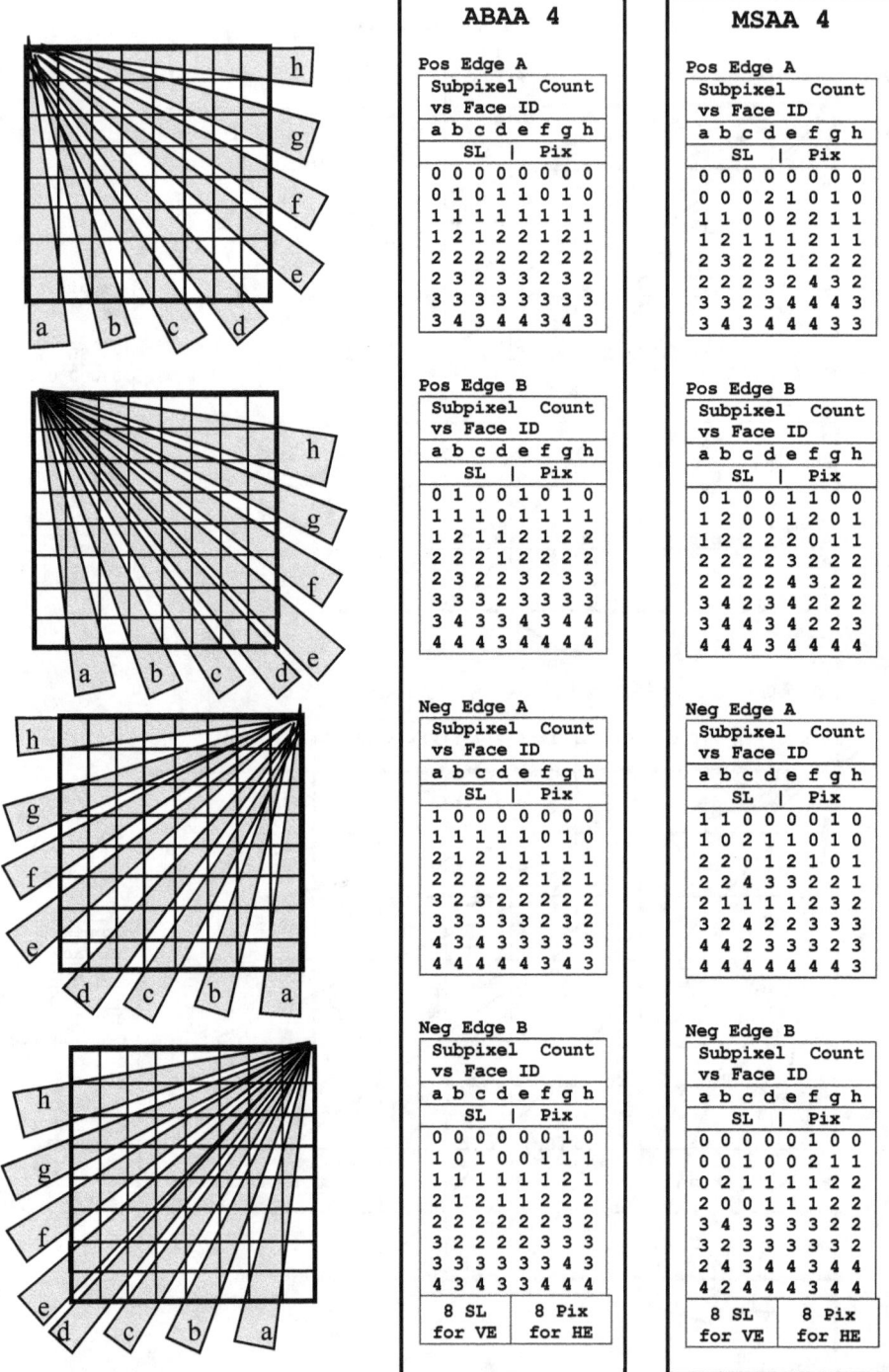

Figure 6-7 Summary of Results for 4 Examples with 4 Subpixels

Results for ABAA

In most cases, with ABAA, the increments are:
0, 0, 1, 1, 2, 2, 3, 3, or
0, 1, 1, 2, 2, 3, 3, 4, or
1, 1, 2, 2, 3, 3, 4, 4

Results for MSAA

For MSAA, some triangles are smoothly rendered, other are not, depending on the orientation.

Some Good: For MSAA, the increments are similar to ABAA, when the triangles edges are near Vertical (face a) or near Horizontal (face h). This is because the Subpixels are positioned according to the 4 Queen algorithm.

Some Bad: For other edge orientations, the increments are not constants. There are many increments of 2. There is also 'hesitation', when there are some steps with decrements (reverse count).

The results of Subpixel count per Pixel are shown in 4 sets of figures, for the 4 test cases. Beside the fan figures there are small tables showing the number of Subpixel per increments. The simulation results for ABAA and MSAA are shown and compared.

Counting the Subpixels

When estimating the number of Subpixels per Pixel, there are 2 cases:

For *VE* (figures a to d), the Subpixels are counted for each SL.

For *HE* (figures e to h), the Subpixels are counted for each Pix.

Results of Simulation Displayed with ASCII Characters

In order to make the computer output easy to read and to display, the 8x8 Pixels Span-Grids and the Subpixels are displayed using ASCII text characters. This provides an easy way to display the results and include valuable information into this document.

Summary of Results

Four Cases of Thin Triangle Fans' inside of an 8x8 Pixel Span have been presented. The results are summarized in 8 tables, 4 for ABAA and 4 for MSAA.

By comparing the ABAA 4 and MSAA 4 columns, is should be clear that ABAA 4 is vastly superior to MSAA 4.

Chapter 7 ABAA with 8 Subpixel Areas

The implementation of ABAA with 8 Subpixel Areas is a little more involved than the 4 Subpixel solution. It is derived from the 4 Subpixel solution by dividing the subpixels square areas by 2 along the 2 Pixel diagonals. In order to handle the additional cases, the slope size is used to create 2 Subpixel sequences. A slope flag, *S1* (and *S0 = !S1*), is introduced to indicate when the slope size is greater than *0.5*.

Note, that it is not necessary to indicate greater or equal (>=), since the slopes are truncated fixed point numbers, where the truncated portion is unknown. For this reason, the '>' symbol will be used to indicate '>='.

The binary format for the slope inside of a Pixel is: *Slp* = (s)s.bbbb.
Slp can be expressed in decimal or binary notation.
Decimal notation: -1.0 < S1 < -0.5   < S0 <   0.0   < S0 < 0.5   < S1 <   1.0
Binary notation: (1)1.0000 < S1 < 1.1000 < S0 < 0.0000 < S0 < 0.1000 < S1 < (0)1.0000

7.1 ABAA8-X Solution with 8 Half-Square Subpixel Areas

The Pixel covered area is determined by the edge distance, *d*, on the Pixel *MidLn*. The distance is obtained with only one measurement. Using 4 fractional bits resolution, the maximum error will be: *e = 1/16*

Refer to Example in Figure 7-1, for a Negative *VE*.

The 8 Subpixel transitions are identified according to 3 edge Flags.
- Edge Slope Flag: *S0*, when |*Slp*| <0.5; *S1*, when |*Slp*| > 0.5
- Edge orientation Flag: *VE vs HE*
- Edge Polarity Flag: *Pos vs Neg*
- Edge beginning/ending flag: *BE vs !BE*

The *BE* flag is used to invert the Subpixel active flags when *BE==0*.

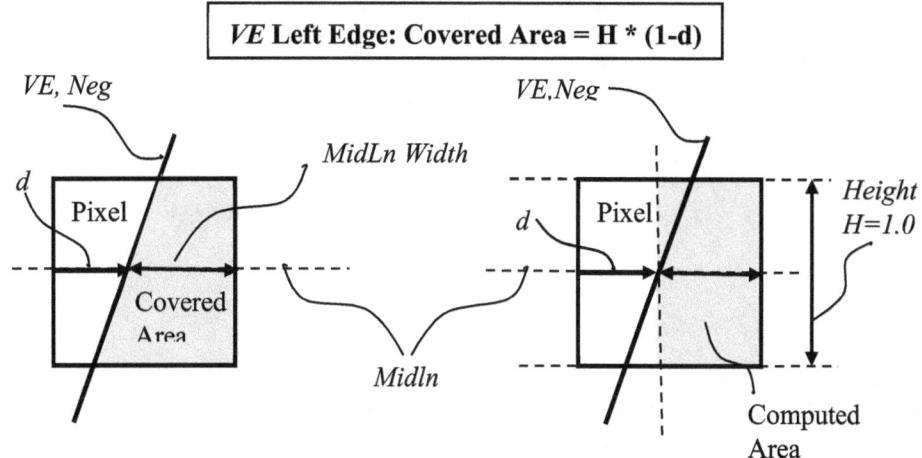

Figure 7-1 Example of Pixel Covered Area Computation for Negative VE

ABAA with 8 Subpixel Areas

Pixel Map for 8 Subpixels

In Figure 7-2, the 8 Subpixel solution is represented in a Pixel-Map. This Map describes the 8 edge cases with their corresponding Subpixel sequences.

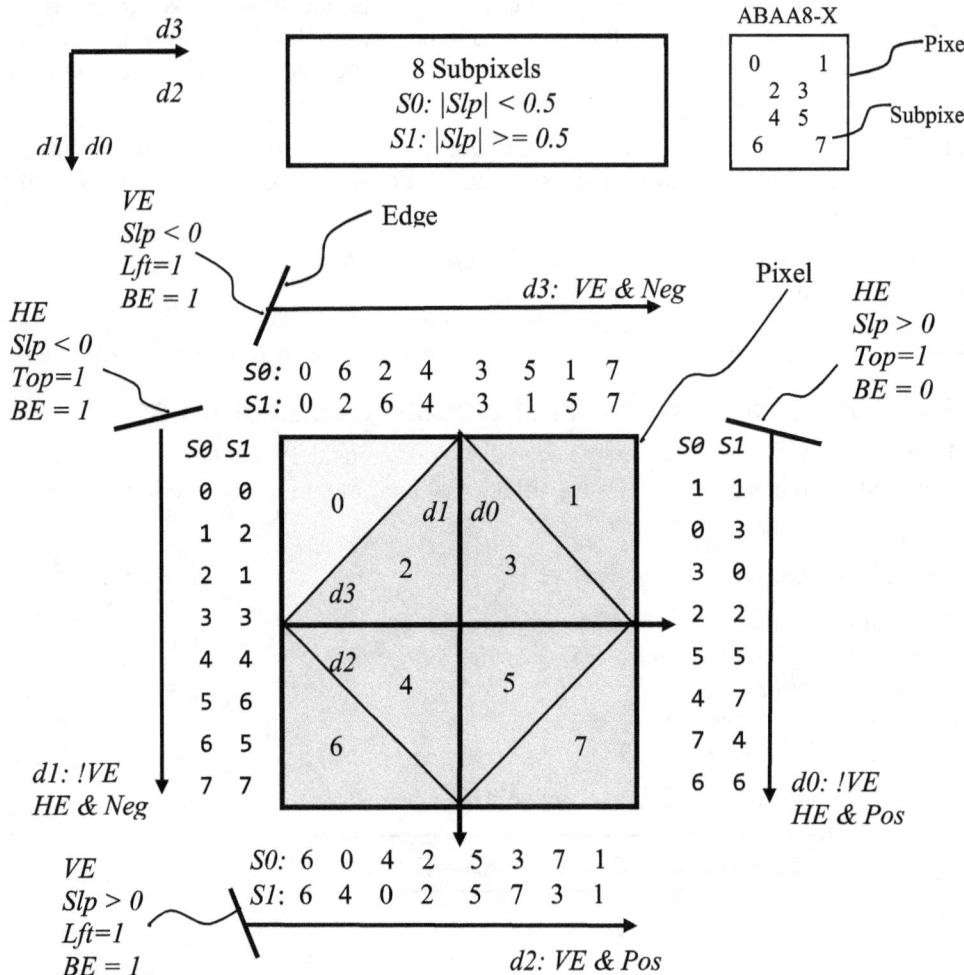

Figure 7-2 Pixel-Map with 8 Edge Cases for ABAA8-X

Flowchart for 8 Subpixel Decoding

The decoding for the Subpixel sequence is described in the flowchart in Figure 7-3. The Subpixel sequences can be stored in a table located in memory or other storage.

ABAA with 8 Subpixel Areas

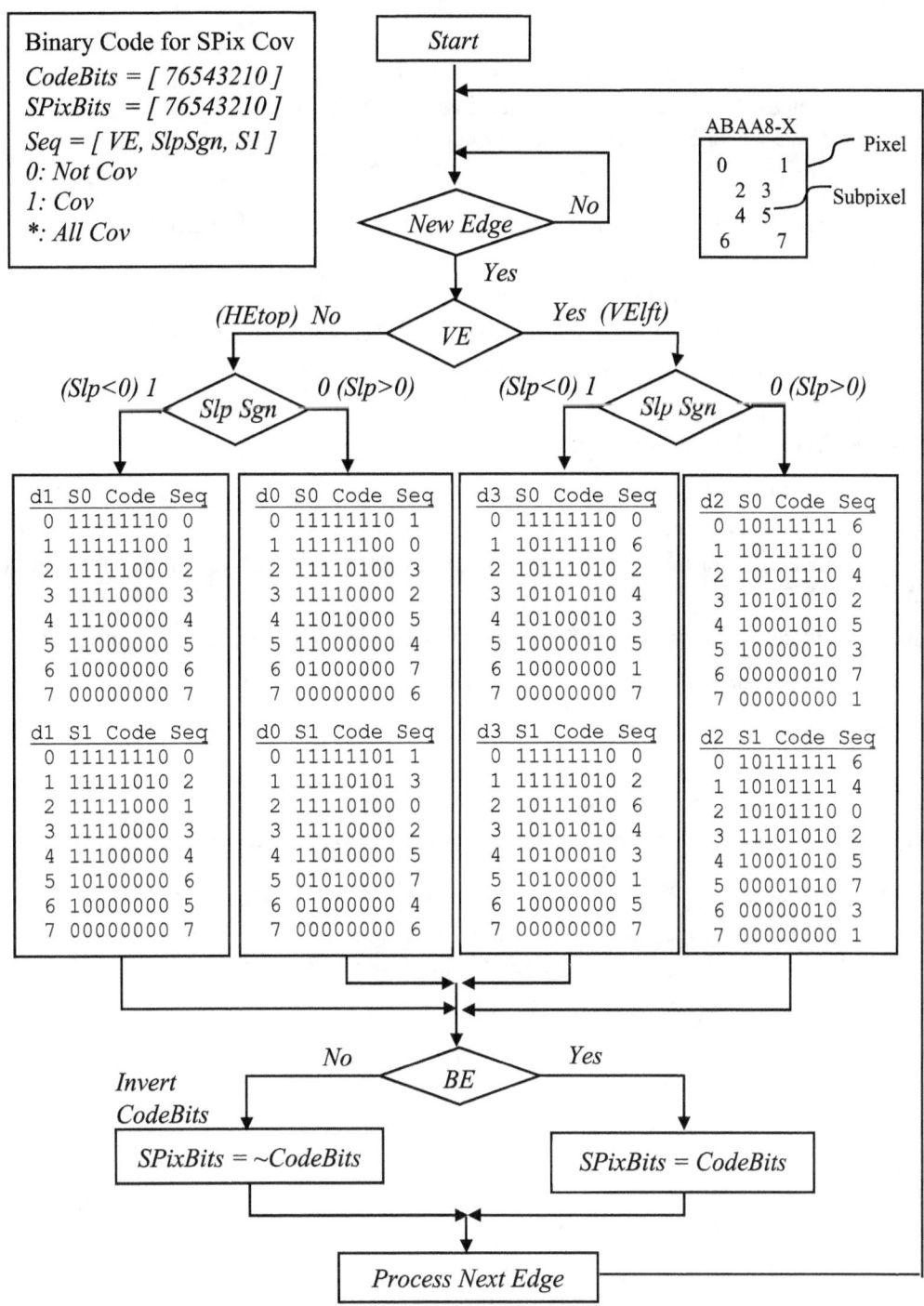

Figure 7-3 Subpixel Coverage Decoder for ABAA8-X

ABAA with 8 Subpixel Areas

This flowchart describes the processing of triangle edges for ABAA8-X. For each edge, the Subpixel sequence of active Subpixels is detected according to 3 Edge Flags. The 8 Subpixel sequences indicate which Subpixel areas are turned on according to these flags.

The first tested flag is *VE* vs *HE*.

The next tested Flag is the edge polarity according to the slope sign (Slp Sgn): *Slp<0* vs *Slp > 0*.

The 3rd flag is the slope size flag, *S1* vs *S0*. One Subpixel sequence is selected according to the slope size flag (*S0 or S1*) and the edge distances (*d0, d1, d2 and d3*) inside the Pixel boundaries along the *MidLn*. The edge distances are selected according to 2 flags: *VE, Slp Sgn*.

The Subpixel sequences are presented for beginning edges, that is *BE == 1*.

The fourth tested flag is the beginning edge flag *(BE* vs *!BE)*. For ending edges, the Subpixel active flags (*CodeBits*) in the table have to be inverted.

Esge Slope Size S1 vs S0

The 2 cases of Slope Size flags, *S0* vs *S1*, are illustrated in 2 examples. This Slope Size flag is needed to compensate for the 1/8 Pixel area portion outside of the left/top side of the trapezoid, when *|Slp|>0.5*.

In Figure 7-4 there are 2 examples of Slope transition at *|Slp|=0.5* and *|Slp|=1.0*, with *d=0.0*.

The case of *|Slp|==1.0* is the transition case when edges transition between *VE* and *HE* types.

ABAA Examples with 8 Subpixels

There are 2 similar figures that illustrate the 8 steps of *BE* edges moving across 8 Subpixels within a Pixel: one with *|Slp|<0.5 (Flag S0)*, one with *|Slp|>0.5 (Flag S1)*.

In Figure 7-5 ABAA: 4 Cases of Edge Moving Across 8 Subpixels *(S0: |Slp|<0.5)*

In Figure 7-6 ABAA: 4 Cases of Edge Moving Across 8 Subpixels *(S1: |Slp|>0.5)*

In these examples, the edges are shown with a rectangle. For each edge case, the rectangle represents the range of edge positions that define the same Subpixel area.

Detect "Inside" and 'Outside" Areas Defined by Edges

In the flowchart used for determining Subpixel areas sequences, the *BE* flag is tested to detect if the processed edge is a starting or an ending edge.

When *BE==1*, it is a starting edge and the Subpixel bit sequence indicates which Subpixels are turned on.

When *BE==0*, it is an ending edge and the Subpixel bit sequence indicates which Subpixels are turned off. The Subpixel sequence has to be inverted.

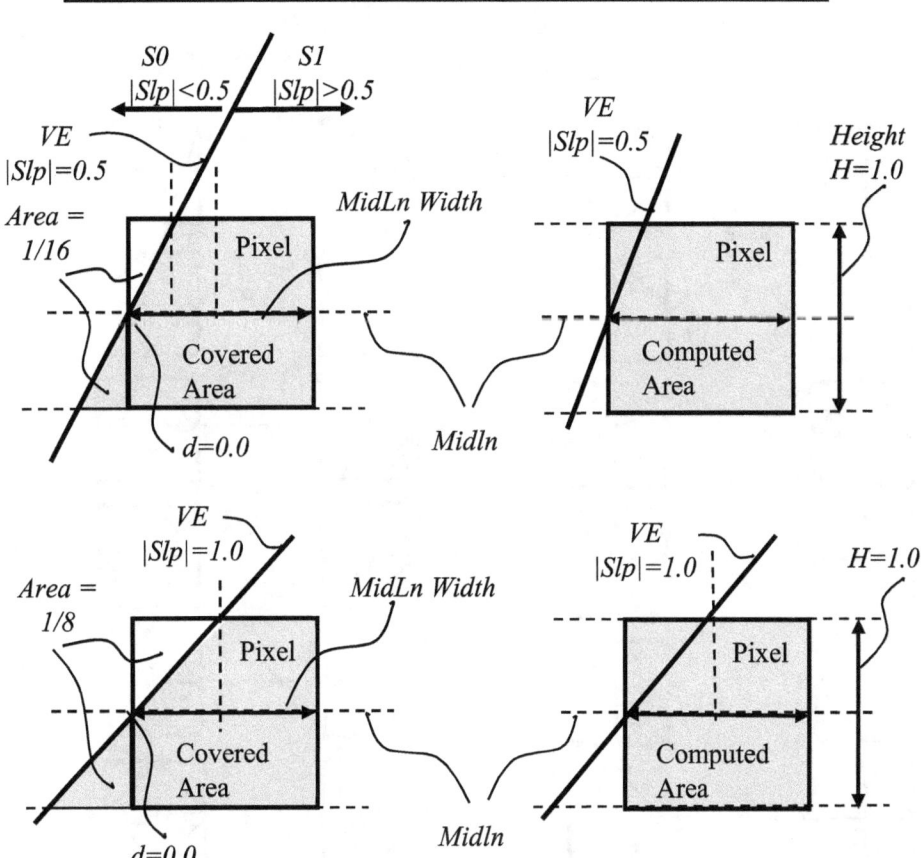

Figure 7-4 Example of Slope Transition from S0 to S1 for d=0.0

ABAA with 8 Subpixel Areas

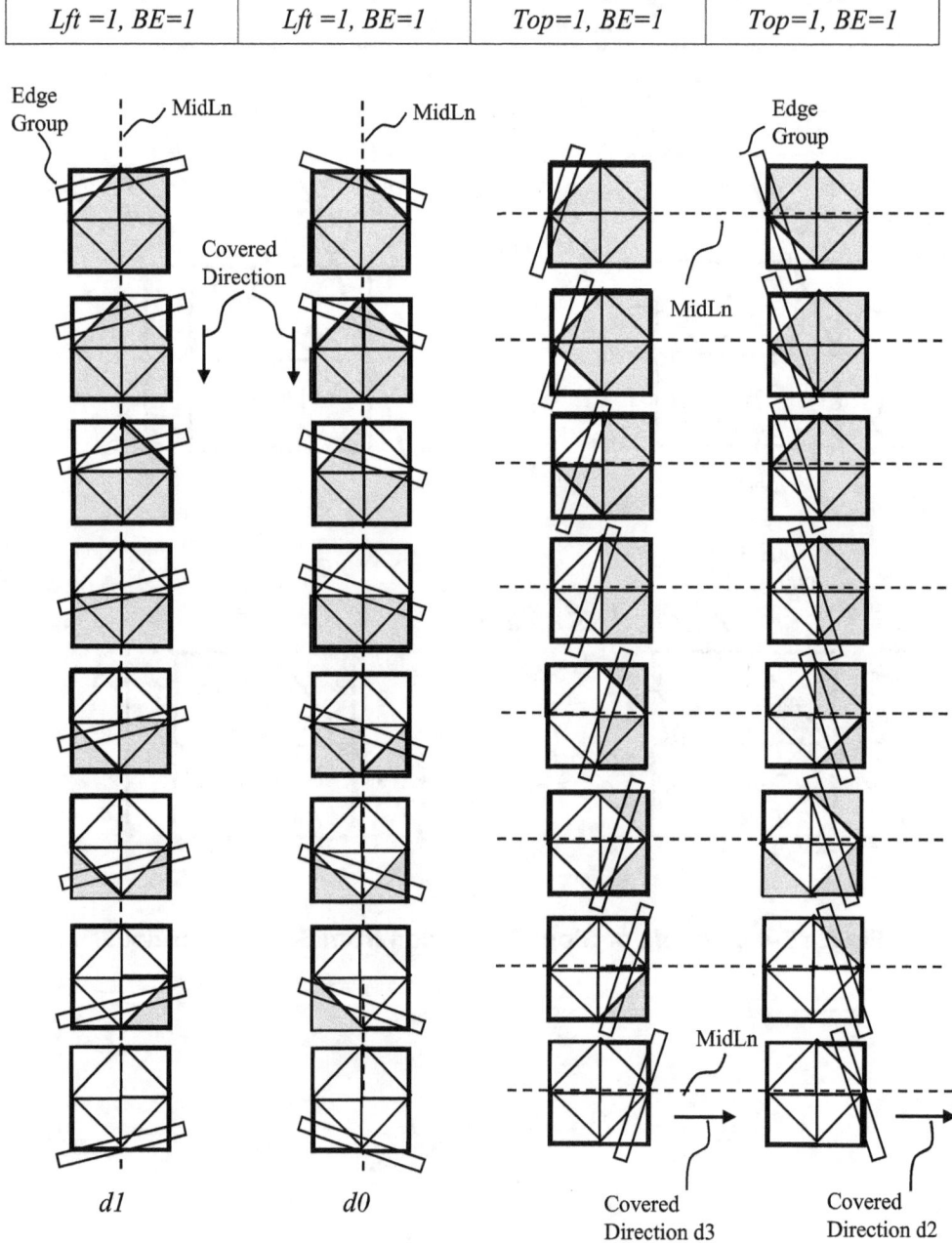

Figure 7-5 ABAA8-X: 4 Cases of Edge Moving Across 8 Subpixels (S0: |Slp|<0.5)

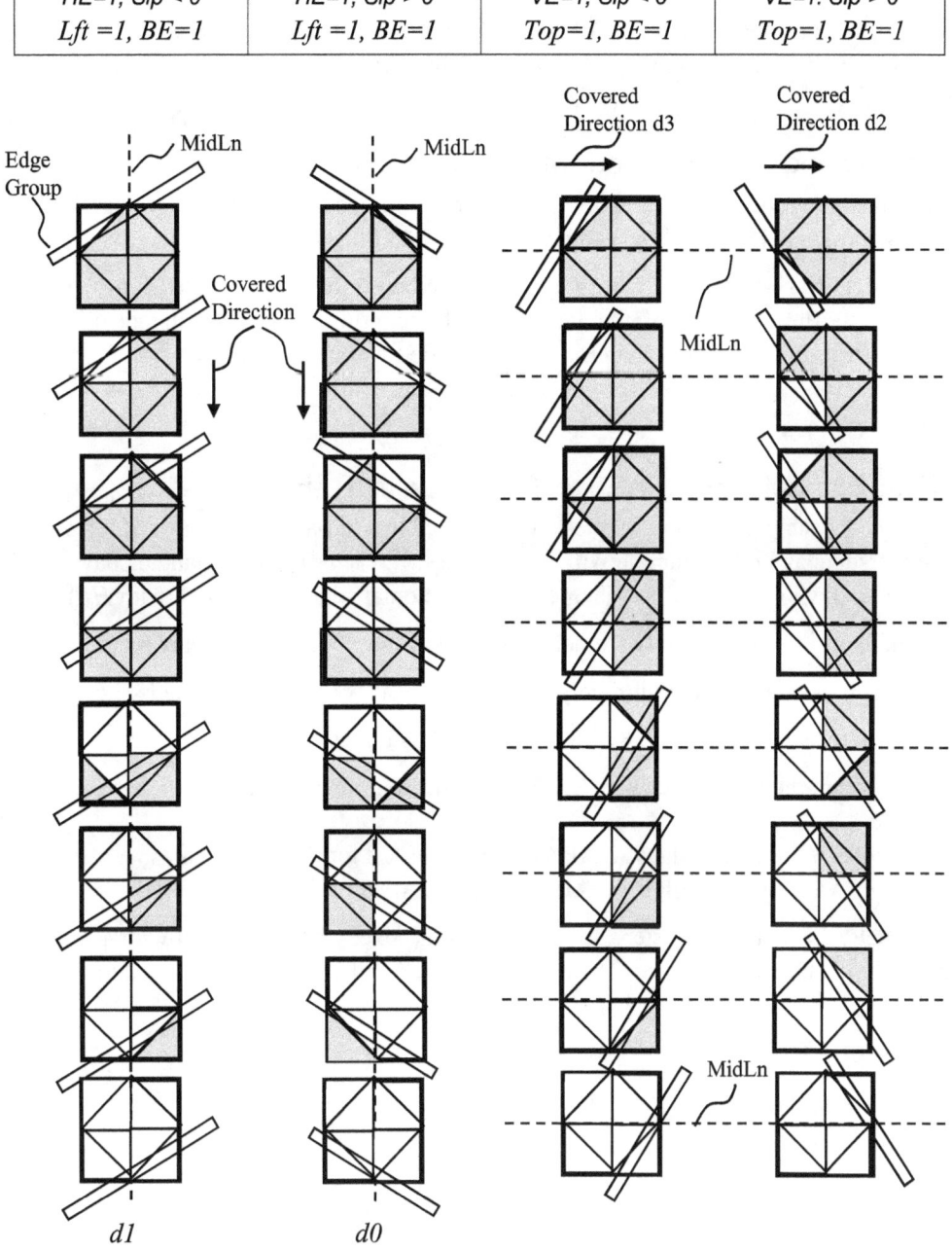

Figure 7-6 ABAA8-X: 4 Cases of Edge Moving Across 8 Subpixels (S1: |Slp|>0.5)

7.2 Comparison of ABAA8 vs MSAA8

For the comparison of ABAA with MSAA, using 8 Subpixels, the same approach as was used for 4 Subpixels is used here. The examples consist of the same test cases with 4 fans with 8 thin triangles each.

7.2.1 Thin Triangles Processed with 8 Subpixels

These examples have been generated by a C-program. In each figure there is a fan of 8 thin triangles. Each triangle is defined by 3 edges within an 8x8 Pixel Span.

It is not practical to show images with gray shades. When printed, the images can be easier to evaluate at first. But, because of the limitation of the printing process, the results can be inconclusive. Instead, the covered Subpixels are identified with a '*' character, or a face number, instead gray shades. This makes it is easier to evaluate and compare the ABAA vs MSAA approaches.

7.2.2 Four Examples of ABAA8 vs MSAA8 with Tri-Fans

For each of the 4 examples, 8 thin triangles are organized in a fan-array. The pairs of left and right edges are the same as in the example with 4 Subpixels. In each fan, four triangles have vertical edges (a, b, c & d with *VE*) and four triangles have horizontal edges (e, f, g & h with *HE*).

Although there are 4 examples, only the detailed result of the 1st example is shown in:

Figure Although there are 4 examples, only the detailed result of the 1st example is shown in:

Figure 7-7, Fan example for ABAA 8 vs MSAA 8 for Pos Edges A

All the results from the 4 test cases with 8 Subpixels are combined into a single figure, as shown in Figure 7-8:
ABAA 8 vs MSAA 8 for Pos Edges A, ABAA 8 vs MSAA 8 for Pos Edges B,
ABAA 8 vs MSAA 8 for Neg Edges A, ABAA 8 vs MSAA 8 for Neg Edges B

For 8 Subpixels, the incremental steps should be half the size, when compared with 4 Subpixels. The 8 steps should be 1/8 Pixel each. The results here are similar to the results in examples with 4 Subpixels.

Results for ABAA

For ABAA, in most cases, the increments are:
0, 1, 2, 3, 4, 5, 6, 7, or
1, 2, 3, 4, 5, 6, 7, 8

Results for MSAA

Some Good: For MSAA, the increments are similar to ABAA when the triangles edges are near Vertical (face a) or near Horizontal (face h). This is because the Subpixels are positioned according to the 4 Queen algorithm.

Some Bad: For other orientations, the increments are not constant, with many increments of 2. There is also 'hesitation', when there are some steps with decrements

ABAA with 8 Subpixel Areas

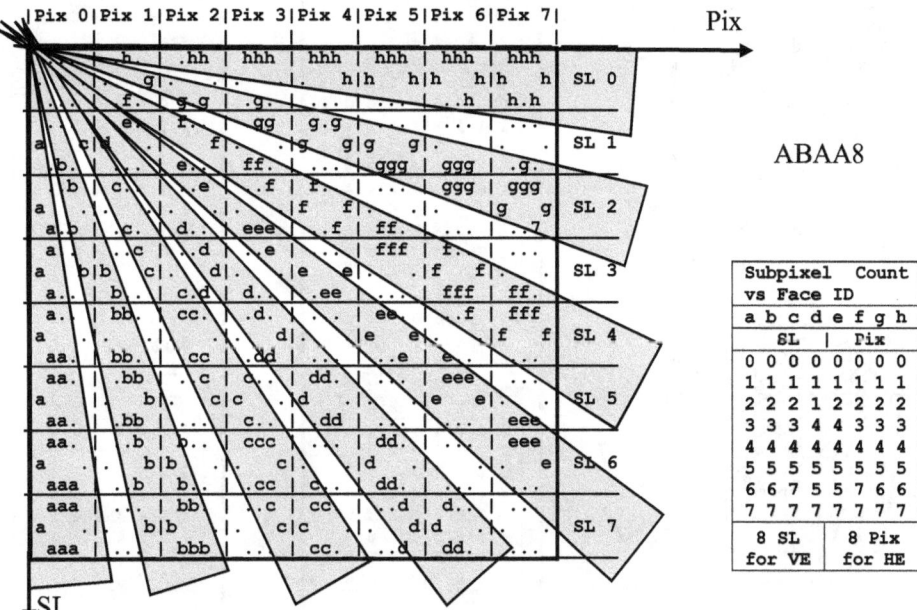

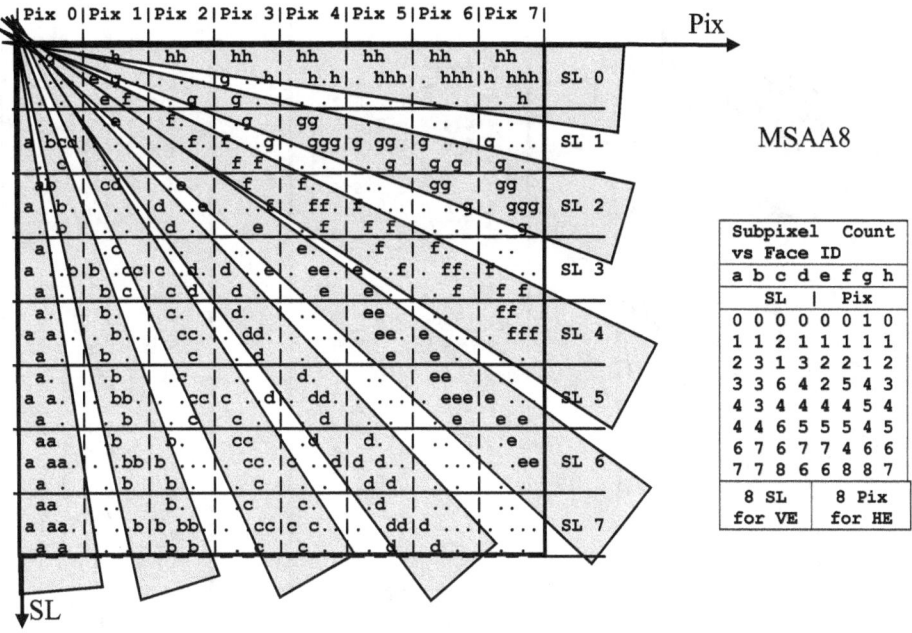

Figure 7-7 ABAA8 vs MSAA8 for Pos Edges A

ABAA with 8 Subpixel Areas

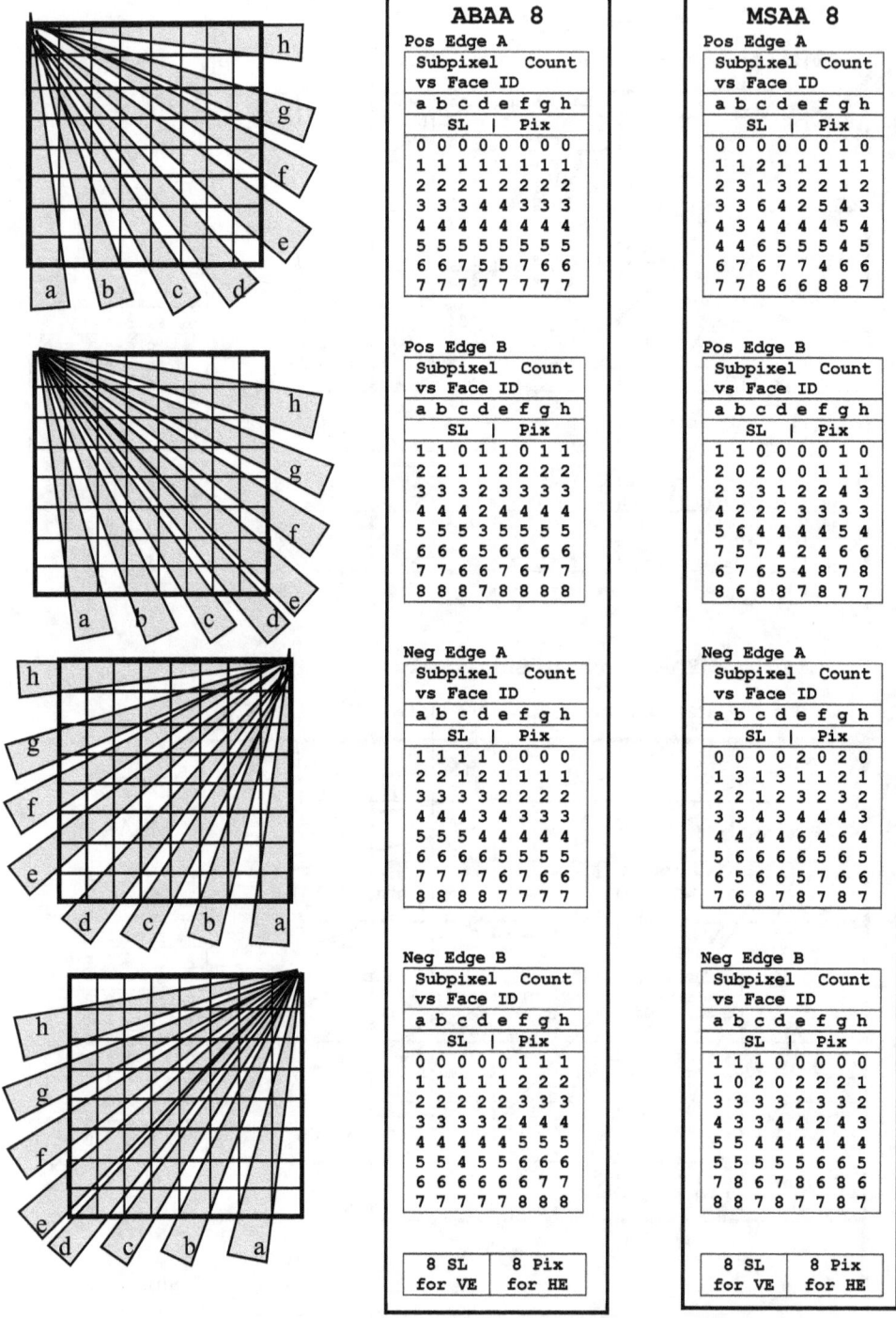

Figure 7-8 Four Cases of Thin Triangles with 8 Subpixels

Chapter 8 Inside the Binary World

Some of the concepts described in this chapter might seem simple and obvious to some readers. If the reader has a good understanding of designs with binary logic, this should be helpful. On the other hand, other readers might need some time to understand. For this reason, I have provided several references to Wikipedia, the free encyclopedia on the Web. These references should provide the necessary information to bring the reader up to date.

In this chapter, I provide several examples with binary numbers and also the related 'octal' and 'hexadecimal' notations.

8.1 Programmer and Computer Interaction

Most of the modern computers are based on PCs, with Intel processors, the Apple Mac, or families of ARM processors [74]. Data and operations are entered in high level language using *decimal* numbers. Then, the compiler converts the decimal numbers into *binary* numbers and all the operation are executed in *binary* arithmetic.

8.1.1 Fixed Point vs Floating Point

One nice thing about Floating Point (FloatPt) over Fixed Point (FixedPt) is that they have an almost infinite range of number values. In most applications, there is no need to worry about overflow during computations. The binary FloatPt format is described by the IEEE 754 Standard [18]. Another nice thing about FloatPt numbers is that they are implemented with *signed magnitude binary* numbers. This means that FloatPt numbers are symmetrical with respect to the *integer zero*. They have a *positive zero* that is slightly larger than the *integer zero*. They have a *negative zero* that is slightly smaller than the *integer zero*.

But, FloatPt numbers cannot accurately represent the values of integer 0. This is because the FloatPt numbers have a limited number of fraction bits. After the limited number of fraction bits, the truncated fraction of FloatPt numbers is *unknown*. For this reason, "*integer zero* cannot be represented with a FloatPt *zero*". The smallest FloatPt number has an *exponent 0* minus an offset of *-126,* corresponding to 2^{-126}. It has a fraction made of *23 zero bits*. But who knows what comes after these *23 zero bits*? There are an infinity number of bits, that have been truncated and ignored on the right side of these *23 zero bits*.

When implementing AA in Real-Time, the image processing has to be really fast, since the computations are performed on image Pixels. The number of Pixels on displayed images is roughly 1 million Pixels, or 1 Mega Pixel. AA computations have to be performed on all the Pixels that are intersected by triangle edges. The best approach is to implement the computation HW and also programs with FixedPt integers or binary numbers. FixedPt integers in the computers and also digital integrated circuits consist of integer binary numbers, where a point position is "assumed" by the context and the programmer.

For simulation purpose, computations could be performed with FloatPt, although FloatPt numbers are not well suited for the AA implementations. FloatPt HW is efficient for multiplications. But for addition and subtraction FloatPt HW is inefficient and requires more circuitry. Also, AA computations require logic and math operations that can be easily implemented with integer numbers.

8.1.2 Inside each Computer there is a Binary World

From the outside, a computer is programmed by writing code using decimal numbers and decimal arithmetic. Then the compiler converts these decimal numbers into binary numbers for the program execution. When the results need to be printed on paper or displayed on a terminal, the printer driver converts these binary numbers into decimal numbers.

Most SW programmers are not aware of what's happening inside of the computer HW. The interaction between programmers and computers HW is hidden by the operating system. Inside of the computer, "Binary is the Law". There are millions of bits inside of the computer fighting for computing time and memory space. So, unless you are involved with the operations inside computers, you are not aware that 'Inside each Computer there is a Binary World'.

Refer to Figure 8-1, "Interaction between Programmer and Computer".

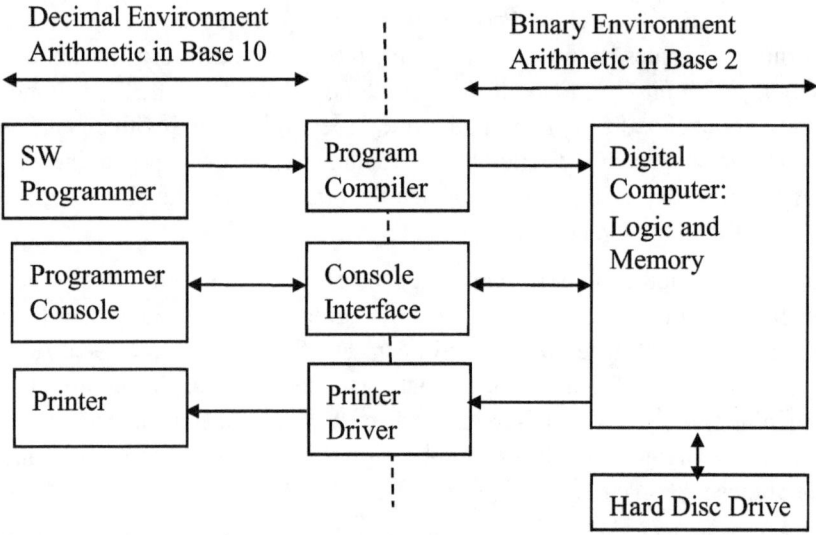

Figure 8-1 Interaction between Programmer and Computer

While the math functions can be described with *decimal* integers, FixedPt or FloatPt numbers, the operations inside of the computer are always performed with *binary* numbers. For *binary* integer numbers in computer HW, the notion of FixedPt and Point Position does not exist. It exists in our "head" as we keep track of the point position during the operations. This similar to doing operation on paper and pencil with fractions of decimal numbers. Regardless of the point position, the operations with FixedPt *binary* numbers remain the same.

8.1.3 Pixel Colors and ARGB Color Components

The output of CGI systems consists of rectangular images made of arrays of *PixMax* x *SLMax* color Pixels, displayed at 60 frames per sec. The image size is on average 1k x 1k Pixels.

Because the color output can be defined by a number of bits such as 16, 24 or 32 bits, the Pixel color is computed with binary number calculations.

Since the purpose of designing a CGI system is to produce color images, the reader should be familiar of the CGI system output format.

Each Pixel if of size 1x1 and has a uniform color defined by 3 or 4 components (*Alpha, Red, Green, Blue*). The (*A, R, G, B*) components can be defined with:

- 32 bits with *(A[8], R[8], G[8], B[8])*, where *A* is the alpha transparency.
- 24 bits *(R[8], G[8], B[8])*
- 16 bits *(R[5], G[6], B[5])*

For 32-bit color, the components are defined by 8-bit integer values ranging from *0* to *255*.

```
31      28      24      20      16      12      8       4       0
+-------+-------+-------+-------+-------+-------+-------+-------+
|       A[8]    |       R[8]    |       G[8]    |       B[8]    |
+-------+-------+-------+-------+-------+-------+-------+-------+
```

For the 16-bit format, *R[5]* and *B[5]* range from 0 to 31. *G[6]* ranges from 0 to 63.

```
15      12      8       4       0
+-------+-+-----+-----+-+-------+
|  R[5] |   G[6]  |  B[5]  |
+-------+-+-----+-----+-+-------+
```

8.2 Decimal vs Binary Number

Since I am trying to be clear in presenting my ideas, I have to be cautious and may over explain some of the concepts. Some readers might not agree with my selections for describing the AA operations with a mix of Decimal and Binary numbers. I will use the number base that make the most sense.

In computer memories, the memory addressing is organized in memory blocks. For practical reasons, the memory blocks are also organized in power of 2. This way, the base or starting addresses of memory block use incremental blocks sizes with lower bits being *0*. For example, for incremental block addresses of 1kB, the lower bits will consist of 10 zero bits. For incremental block addresses of 1MB, the lower bits will consist of 20 zero bits.

When writing a computer program, the SW programmer has the freedom to assign large memory blocks of any size. For example, a memory block of size 1 Million (decimal 1 M) locations can be specified. This makes sense.

But, when a HW designer has to allocate a large memory block for its local data base, he has no other choice than selecting a power of 2, such as binary 1M=1'048'576=0x100000 (in hexadecimal) locations. This makes sense.

Inside the Binary World

The AA computation are performed near the end of the 3D image computations. They consist of simple and quick operations with binary numbers of size between 8 and 16 bits.

8.2.1 Decimal Digit vs Binary Digit

While most of the computations in every day's life deal with decimal numbers, in modern computers all operations are done with binary numbers.

Decimal numbers are defined as numbers base 10. They are made up of 10 decimal digits. Each digit can have one of the following values:

0, 1, 2, 3, 4, 5, 6, 7, 8, 9.

Logic Design [19] deals with defining circuit using Boolean expressions and binary arithmetic.

Binary numbers are defined as numbers base 2. They are expressed with bits binary digits, or that have only 2 states. Each "binary digit" can have one of the following values: *0* and *1*.

A "binary digit" is referenced to as a "bit".

Just like digital numbers, the binary numbers are defined by a sequence of binary digits. They can be signed and unsigned. For signed numbers, the most significant bit (*MSB*) is *0* for positive numbers and *1* for negative numbers.

Binary numbers use 3 to 4 times more digits than decimal numbers to represent the same value. Refer to example in table 8-1

Integer Number	Decimal: 3 decimal digits	Binary: 9 or 10 bits	Hexadecimal: 2 or 3 hex digits
unsigned	255	0 1111 1111	0x0ff
unsigned	255	1 0000 0000	0x100
signed	+256	01 0000 0000	0x 100
signed	-256	11 0000 0000	0x f00 = - 0x100

Table 8-1 Comparison between Decimal and Binary Numbers

The space between digits is used to facilitate reading.

A special case of binary number is the Boolean variable, which is a single digit with 2 values: *True (==1)* and *False (==0)*.

When comparing numbers or comparing alpha-numeric expressions (i.e. sentences), the result is expressed as "*True*" or "*False*".

Note that the symbol "==" (double =) indicates "equal" when expressions are "compared".

In order to make the binary numbers more readable, the bits in binary numbers can be organized in group of 3 to form "*octal*" numbers or in group of 4 to form "*hexadecimal*" numbers.

Inside the Binary World

Octal numbers are defined as numbers base 8. They are made up of 8 octal digits. Each octal digit can have the following values:

octal (0, 1, 2, 3, 4, 5, 6, 7) corresponding to *binary (000, 001, 010, 011, 100, 101, 110, 111)*.

Hexadecimal numbers, or simply "hex numbers", are defined as numbers base 16. They are made up of 16 hexadecimal digits, or simply "hex digit". Each hex digit can have the following values:

0, 1, 2, 3, 4, 5, 6, 7, 8, 9. a, b, c, d, e, f.

Or:

0, 1, 2, 3, 4, 5, 6, 7, 8, 9. A, B, C, D, E, F.

Each hexadecimal digit, from 0 to f, corresponds to a group of 4 bits, as follows: *0000, 0001, 0010, 0011, 0100, 0101, 0110, 0111, 1000, 1001, 1010, 1011, 1100, 1101, 1110, 1111*

A summary of numbers and Bases is shown in Table 8-2.

As example, the integer number 321 is used.

Digits	Base	Single Digits	Zero	Number Example
decimal	10	0, 1, 2, 3, 4, 5, 6, 7, 8, 9	0	321
Boolean (single bit)	2	False, True	False	True (non-zero)
Binary (bit or bits)	2	0, 1	0	1 0100 0001 (decimal 321 = 256 + 64 +1)
octal (group of 3 bits)	8	0, 1, 2, 3, 4, 5, 6, 7	o0	o501 (binary 101 000 001 = decimal 320+0+1)
hexadecimal or hex (group of 4 bits)	16	0, 1, 2, 3, 4, 5, 6, 7, 8, 9. a, b, c, d, e, f	0x0	0x141 (binary 1 0100 0001 = decimal 256+64+1)

Table 8-2 Numbers and Bases

Decimal 1k vs Binary 1k

What is not commonly known is that there is a difference between Decimal 1k and Binary 1k.

When we buy 1kg of bread, we get 1000 grams of bread.

When we buy 1 kbit of memory, we get 1024 bits.

When we buy a 100 Megabyte of Hard Disk Drive, it can be either 100'000 bytes of HDD, or 102,400 bytes of HDD

In Table 8-3, "Decimal 1k vs Binary 1k", some decimal and binary numbers are selected to show the difference between the definition of Decimal 1k and Binary 1k.

Inside the Binary World

Decimal	Binary (3bits)	Octal	Binary (4bits)	Hexadecimal
1	1	o1	1	0x1
2	10	o2	10	0x 2
4	100	o4	100	0x 4
8	1'000	o10	1000	0x 8
10	1'010	o12	1010	0x a
16	10'000	o20	1'0000	0x10
32	100'000	o40	10'0000	0x20
64	1'000'000	o100	100'0000	0x40
100	1'100'100	o144	110'0100	0x64
128	10'000'000	o200	1000'0000	0x 80
256	100'000'000	o400	1'0000'0000	0x100
512	1'000'000'000	o1000	10'0000'0000	0x200
1000 = dec 1k	1'111'101'000	o1750	11'1110'1000	0x3e8
1024 = dec 2**10	10'000'000'000 = bin 1k (kilo)	o2000	100'0000'0000 = bin 1k	0x400
1'000'000 = dec 1M (Mega) = dec 1k*1k				0x0f4240 = dec 1M
1'048'576 = dec 2**20	bin 1M (Mega) = bin 1k*1k	o4000000	bin 1M = bin 1k*1k	0x100000

Table 8-3 Decimal 1k vs Binary 1k

8.3 Binary Numbers

There are several references about binary numbers, logic design, integrated circuits, register transfer logic (RTL) and Verilog [19].

8.3.1 Operations with Binary numbers

The arithmetic computations with binary and decimal numbers consist mainly of 4 basic operations: addition *(+)*, subtraction *(-)*, multiplication *(*)* and division *(/)*. The exponent operation is represented here by *(**)* in C programs, or by *(^)* in Excel spreadsheets. For example, "*x to the power 4*" is represented by "*x**4*", or "x^4".

Beside these four basic operations, the binary numbers can also be combined with Boolean operations.
Refer to Table 8-4 for Operations with Decimal and Binary Numbers.

In the case of Expression comparisons, the expression

   z = (x == y);

Can be rewritten in Verilog language as:

if (x == y)
  z = TRUE; // or z = 1'b1;
else
  z = FALSE; // or z = 1'b0;

The symbol // is used to insert comments in Verilog and C program code.

There are 2 types of symbols for the operators *AND, OR, Invert* and *EXOR*.

The bitwise operators *(&, |, ~, ^))* apply to operations on bits of same weight in a group of binary numbers with same number of bits.

The single bit operators *(&&, ||, !, ⊕))* apply to a binary variables with value *True* or *False*.

Type	Operations	Symbol	Examples	Result
Arithmetic (any base)	Addition subtraction multiplication division exponent	+ - * / **	z = x + y z = x - y z = x * y z = x / y z = x**4 = x * x * x * x	any base: (binary or decimal)
binary: bitwise operator	AND OR Invert EXOR	& | ~ ^	C = A & B C = A | B B = ~A C = A^B = (A & ~B) | (~A & B)	binary
bit shift or binary exponent	left shift right shift	<< >>	// 4 left shifts B = A << 4 = A * 2**4 // 4 right shifts B = A >> A = A * 2**(-4)	binary
Boolean: single bit operator	AND OR Invert EXOR	&& || ! ⊕	C = A && B C = A || B B = !A C = A ⊕ B = (A && !B) || (!A && B)	Boolean
Boolean Comparison (x and y can be of any base; z is Boolean)	equal not equal greater greater or equal smaller smaller or equal	== != > >= < <=	C = (x == y) C = (x != y) C = (x > y) C = (x >= y) C = (x < y) C = (x <= y)	Compare x and y (Integer or Floats) Result is Boolean C

Table 8-4 Operations with Decimal and Binary Numbers

8.3.2 Boolean Single-Bit Operator

In Figure 8-2, the four binary operations AND, NAND, OR and NOR are represented with their "Truth Tables" and "Gate" symbols. In these tables, the *1's* and *0's* could also be represented with their *True* and *False* states.

Note that in these examples, there are only 2 bits at the input of each symbol. In fact, each input can have more than 2 bits.

For example, for an AND gate with 3 inputs A, B and C, the output is D = A && B && C.

2 Input	AND Gate
Input A B	Output C = A && B
0 0	0
0 1	0
1 0	0
1 1	1

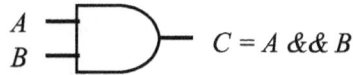

$C = A \,\&\&\, B$

2 Input	NAND Gate
Input A B	Output C = ! (A && B)
0 0	1
0 1	1
1 0	1
1 1	0

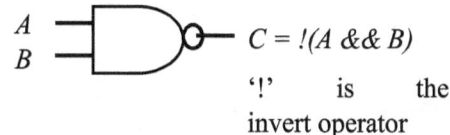

$C = !(A \,\&\&\, B)$

'!' is the invert operator

2 Input	OR Gate
Input A B	Output C = A || B
0 0	0
0 1	1
1 0	1
1 1	1

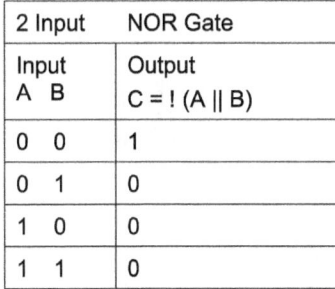

$C = A \,||\, B$

2 Input	NOR Gate
Input A B	Output C = ! (A || B)
0 0	1
0 1	0
1 0	0
1 1	0

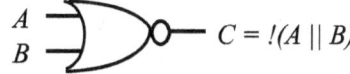

$C = !(A \,||\, B)$

Figure 8-2 AND, NAND, OR and NOR Truth Tables and Gate Symbols

Inside the Binary World

The single bit operators *(&&, ||, !, ⊕))* apply to a pair of binary numbers with values:

0 (= False) or *1 (= True)*

In Figure 8-3, the two binary operations exclusive OR (or EX-OR) and Exclusive NOR (or EX-NOR) are represented with their "Truth Tables" and "Gate" symbols.

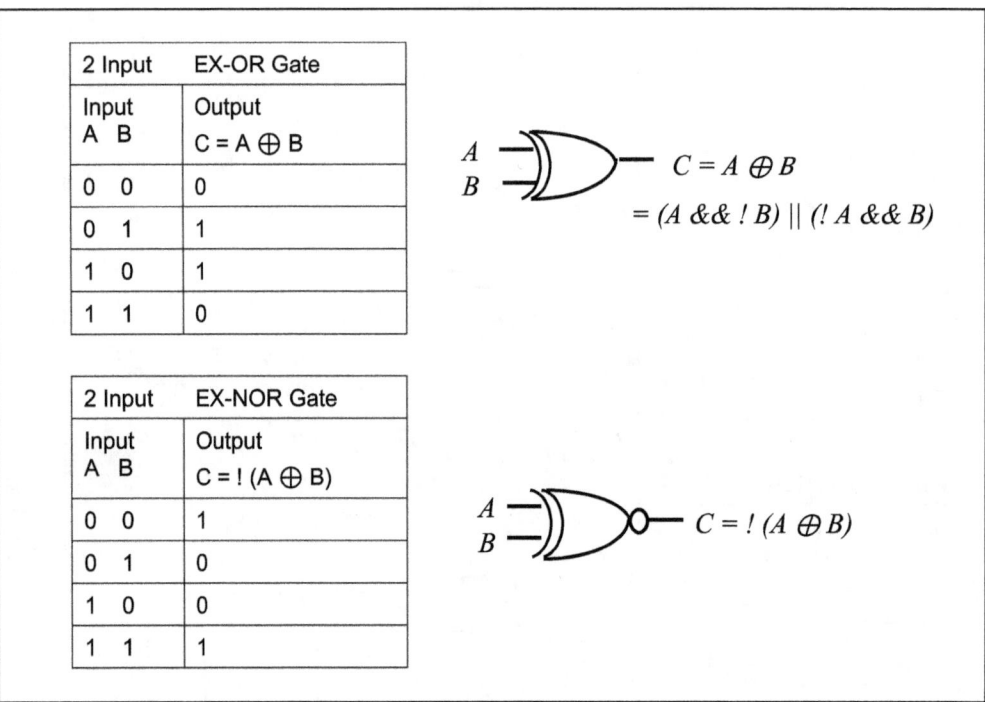

Figure 8-3 Exclusive OR and NOR Truth Tables and Gate Symbols

De Morgan's Theorem

The De Morgan's Theorem is a particularly powerful tool in digital design [19].
The theorem states that the complement *(boolean invert: !)*) of ANDed *(&&)* terms Is Equal To the ORed *(||)* complemented *(inverted: !)* terms .

For example:

   ! (A && B) = !A || !B

Likewise, the complement *(!)* of ORed *(||)* terms Is Equal to the ANDed *(&&)* complemented *(!)* terms.
For example:

   ! (A || B) = !A && !B

8.3.3 Integer Multiple-Bits Bitwise Operator

The bitwise operators *(&, |, ~, ^))* apply to operations on bits of same weight applied to groups of binary numbers with same number of bits. Refer to examples in Table 8-5

Examples of Bitwise Operations:			
Bitwise AND	Bitwise OR	Bitwise EX-OR	Invert Bits
1010 & 0101 = 0000;	1010 | 0101 = 1111;	1010 ^ 0101 = 1111;	~0101 = 1010;
1010 & 0010 = 0010;	1010 | 0010 = 1010;	1010 ^ 0010 = 1000;	~1010 = 0101;
0000 & 1111 = 0000;	0000 | 1111 = 1111;	0000 ^ 1111 = 1111;	~0000 = 1111;
1111 & 1111 = 1111;	1111 | 1111 = 1111;	1111 ^ 1111 = 0000;	~1111 = 0000;

Table 8-5 Examples of Bitwise AND, OR, EX-OR and Invert

8.3.4 Binary Coded Decimal Integers

For finance computations, the earlier computers used *base 10 binary numbers*, instead of the more familiar *binary* numbers *base 2*. The *number 10* is the product of two primary numbers: *2 and 5*. The computations were implemented with logic base ten using a *Binary Coded Decimal* numbering system (refer to IBM EBCDIC). The *Binary Coded Decimal* numbers in *base 10* consists of groups of *4 bits* that are a subset of the *binary hex* numbers *base 16*.

For *BCD* numbers, the maximum digit is *(decimal) 9*, or *(binary) 1001*. The next *BCD* increment is *(decimal) 10*, that is expressed as EBCDIC *10000*. The *binary* values of *decimal 10 to 19*, as represented by *BCD binary 10000 to 11001 (or BCDhex 0x10 to 0x19).*

Binary values *1010 to 1111 (or hex 0x0a to 0x0f)* are skipped. Refer to Table 8-6.

Decimal 0 to 9: 0, 1, 2, 3, 4, 5, 6, 7, 8, 9	Binary code in EBCDIC for decimal 0 to 9: 0 0000, 0 0001, 0 0010, 0 0011, 0 0100, 0 0101, 0 0110, 0 0111, 0 1000, 0 1001
	Binary values 01010, 0 1011, 0 1100, 0 1101, 0 1110, 0 1111 are skipped.
Decimal 10 to 19 10, 11, 12,1 3, 14, 15, 16, 17, 18, 19	Binary code in EBCDIC for decimal 10 to 19: 01 0000, 01 0001, 01 0010, 01 0011,0 1 '0100, 01 0101, 01 0110, 01 0111, 01 1000, 01 1001

Table 8-6 Decimal Numbers vs EBCDIC

While divisions in *base 2* will always complete when the divisor is a multiple of *2*, divisions in *base 10* will always complete when the divisor is either a multiple of *2* and/or *5*.

8.4 Comparison of Different Integer Types

I have many years working with logic and binary numbers. But, for many readers, this can be a new experience. For this reason, in this section there are tables of different integer types. These tables are provided here so that the reader can get familiar with the different formats provided for integer numbers like: decimal integer, binary integer, octal, hexadecimal and binary coded decimal (BCD).

8.4.1 Integer Tables

A comparison of different types of Integers is shown in the following tables. For positive integers, refer to Table 8-7. For negative integers, refer to Table 8-8.

Decimal Count	Binary Coded Decimal	Binary Count	Octal Count	Binary Octal Count	Hex Count	Binary Hex Count
0	0000 0000	00000 0	0 0 0	000 000 000	0x0000	0000 0000
1	0000 0001	00000 1	0 0 1	000 000 001	0x0001	0000 0001
2	0000 0010	00001 0	0 0 2	000 000 010	0x0002	0000 0010
3	0000 0011	00001 1	0 0 3	000 000 011	0x0003	0000 0011
4	0000 0100	00010 0	0 0 4	000 000 100	0x0004	0000 0100
5	0000 0101	00010 1	0 0 5	000 000 101	0x0005	0000 0101
6	0000 0110	00011 0	0 0 6	000 000 110	0x0006	0000 0110
7	0000 0111	00011 1	0 0 7	000 000 111	0x0007	0000 0111
8	0000 1000	00100 0	0 1 0	000 001 000	0x0008	0000 1000
9	0000 1001	00100 1	0 1 1	000 001 001	0x0009	0000 1001
10	0001 0000	00101 0	0 1 2	000 001 010	0x000a	0000 1010
11	0001 0001	00101 1	0 1 3	000 001 011	0x000b	0000 1011
12	0001 0010	00110 0	0 1 4	000 001 100	0x000c	0000 1100
13	0001 0011	00110 1	0 1 5	000 001 101	0x000d	0000 1101
14	0001 0100	00111 0	0 1 6	000 001 110	0x000e	0000 1110
15	0001 0101	00111 1	0 1 7	000 001 111	0x000f	0000 1111
16	0001 0110	01000 0	0 2 0	000 010 000	0x0010	0001 0000
17	0001 0111	01000 1	0 2 1	000 010 001	0x0011	0001 0001
18	0001 1000	01001 0	0 2 2	000 010 010	0x0012	0001 0010
19	0001 1001	01001 1	0 2 3	000 010 011	0x0013	0001 0011
20	0010 0000	01010 0	0 2 4	000 010 100	0x0014	0001 0100
21	0010 0001	01010 1	0 2 5	000 010 101	0x0015	0001 0101
22	0010 0010	01011 0	0 2 6	000 010 110	0x0016	0001 0110
23	0010 0011	01011 1	0 2 7	000 010 111	0x0017	0001 0111
24	0010 0100	01100 0	0 3 0	000 011 000	0x0018	0001 1000
25	0010 0101	01100 1	0 3 1	000 011 101	0x0019	0001 1001
26	0010 0110	01101 0	0 3 2	000 011 010	0x001a	0001 1010
27	0010 0111	01101 1	0 3 3	000 011 011	0x001b	0001 1011
28	0010 1000	01110 0	0 3 4	000 011 100	0x001c	0001 1100
29	0010 1001	01110 1	0 3 5	000 011 101	0x001d	0001 1101
30	0011 0000	01111 0	0 3 6	000 011 110	0x001e	0001 1110
31	0011 0001	01111 1	0 3 7	000 011 111	0x001f	0001 1111
32	0011 0010	010000 0	0 4 0	000 100 000	0x0020	0010 0000

Table 8-7 Decimal vs Binary Positive Integer Numbers

Inside the Binary World

Decimal Count	Binary Coded Decimal	Binary Count	Octal Count	Binary Octal Count	Hex Count	Binary Hex Count
-1	1 10011001	11111 1	1 777	111 111 111	0xffff	1111 1111
-2	1 10011000	11111 0	1 776	111 111 110	0xfffe	1111 1110
-3	1 1001 0111	11110 1	1 775	111 111 101	0xfffd	1111 1101
-4	1 1001 0110	11110 0	1 774	111 111 100	0xfffc	1111 1100
-5	1 1001 0101	11101 1	1 773	111 111 011	0xfffb	1111 1011
-6	1 1001 0100	11101 0	1 772	111 111 010	0xfffa	1111 1010
-7	1 1001 0011	11100 1	1 771	111 111 001	0xfff9	1111 1001
-8	1 1001 0010	11100 0	1 770	111 111 000	0xfff8	1111 1000
-9	1 1001 0001	11011 1	1 767	111 110 111	0xfff7	1111 0111
-10	1 1001 0000	11011 0	1 766	111 110 110	0xfff6	1111 0110
-11	1 1000 1001	11010 1	1 765	111 110 101	0xfff5	1111 0101
-12	1 1000 1000	11010 0	1 764	111 110 100	0xfff4	1111 0100
-13	1 1000 0111	11001 1	1 763	111 110 011	0xfff3	1111 0011
-14	1 1000 0110	11001 0	1 762	111 110 010	0xfff2	1111 0010
-15	1 1000 0101	11000 1	1 761	111 110 001	0xfff1	1111 0001
-16	1 1000 0100	11000 0	1 760	111 110 000	0xfff0	1111 0000
-17	1 1000 0011	10111 1	1 757	111 101 111	0xffef	1110 1111
-18	1 1000 0010	10111 0	1 756	111 101 110	0xffee	1110 1110
-19	1 1000 0001	10110 1	1 755	111 101 101	0xffed	1110 1101
-20	1 1000 0000	10110 0	1 754	111 101 100	0xffec	1110 1100
-21	1 0111 1001	10101 1	1 753	111 101 011	0xffeb	1110 1011
-22	1 0111 1000	10101 0	1 752	111 101 010	0xffea	1110 1010
-23	1 0111 0111	10100 1	1 751	111 101 001	0xffe9	1110 1001
-24	1 0111 0110	10100 0	1 750	111 101 000	0xffe8	1110 1000
-25	1 0111 0101	10011 1	1 747	111 100 111	0xffe7	1110 0111
-26	1 0111 0100	10011 0	1 746	111 100 110	0xffe6	1110 0110
-27	1 0111 0011	10010 1	1 745	111 100 101	0xffe5	1110 0101
-28	1 0111 0010	10010 0	1 744	111 100 100	0xffe4	1110 0100
-29	1 0111 0001	10001 1	1 743	111 100 011	0xffe3	1110 0011
-30	1 0111 0000	10001 0	1 742	111 100 010	0xffe2	1110 0010
-31	1 0110 1001	10000 1	1 741	111 100 001	0xffe1	1110 0001
-32	1 0110 1000	10000 0	1 740	111 100 000	0xffe0	1110 0000

Table 8-8 Decimal vs Binary Negative Integer Numbers

References

Books
[1] Schottky and Low-Power Schottky Data Book, from AMD Inc. 1977.
[2] Blinn, James F.: *Jim Blinn's Corner: A Trip Down The Graphics Pipeline*,
Morgan Kaufmann Publishers, Inc., 1996, ISBN 1-55860-387-5
Websites: http://www.jimblinn.com/
Wikipedia: https://en.wikipedia.org/wiki/Jim_Blinn
[3] Blinn, James F.: *Jim Blinn's Corner: Dirty Pixels*,
Morgan Kaufmann Publishers, Inc., 1998, ISBN 1-55860-455-3
Chapter 2: 'What We Need Around Here is More Aliasing'
Chapter 8: 'The Wonderful World of Video'
Chapter 3: 'Return of the Jaggy'
Chapter 13: ' NTSC: Nice Technology, Super Color'
[4] Blinn, James F.: *Jim Blinn's Corner: Notation, Notation, Notation*,
Morgan Kaufmann Publishers, Inc., 2003, ISBN 1-55860-860-5
[5] Franklin C. Crow:
'The Aliasing Problem in Computer-Generated Shaded Images,'
Comm. ACM, Vol. 20, No. 11, Nov. 1977, pp. 799-805.
Franklin C. Crow: 'A Comparison of Antialiasing Techniques', IEEE CG&A, 1981
[6] 'New Fixed-Point Math for Logic Design', Michel Rohner
Lulu.com, 2020.
[7] Video Demystified, Paperback, 5th Edition by Keith Jack

Websites URL
[8] Author's Website: Michel A Rohner
https://www.michelrohner.net
https://www.michelarohner.com
https://www.anti-aliasing.com
[9] Website of Michael A. Rohner Jr:
https://www.rohnerart.com
https://www.instagram.com/rohnerart

[10] Computer Graphics, Geometry and Other
[11] Computer Graphics Tutorial
https://www.tutorialspoint.com/computer_graphics/index.htm
[12] Bresenham's Line Drawing Algorithm
Wikipedia: https://en.wikipedia.org/wiki/Bresenham's_line_algorithm
[13] 'Bézier curves', 'Bicubic Patches' and 'B-Spline'
Bézier surfaces: https://en.wikipedia.org/wiki/B%C3%A9zier_surface
Bicubic Patches: http://www.inf.ed.ac.uk/teaching/courses/cg/d3/bezierPatch.html
B-Spline: https://www.sciencedirect.com/science/article/pii/S0010448520300488

References

    Paul de Casteljau: https://en.wikipedia.org/wiki/Paul_de_Casteljau
    De Casteljau's algorithm: https://en.wikipedia.org/wiki/De_Casteljau%27s_algorithm
[14] Wikipedia: Triangle, Strip and Fan
    Triangle: https://en.wikipedia.org/wiki/ Triangle
    Strip: https://en.wikipedia.org/wiki/Triangle_strip
    Fan: https://en.wikipedia.org/wiki/Triangle_fan
[15] Examples of 3D Representation with Polygons Mesh
    Polygon Mesh: https://en.wikipedia.org/wiki/Polygon_mesh
    https://graphicsjourney.wordpress.com/2015/12/09/3d-representation/
    https://www.blender.org/support/tutorials/
    https://conceptartempire.com/polygon-mesh/
    https://en.wikipedia.org/wiki/File:Mesh_we2.jpg
    https://en.wikipedia.org/wiki/File:Vertex-Vertex_Meshes_(VV).png
[16] Wikipedia: Area of Trapezoid and Parallelogram
    https://en.wikipedia.org/wiki/Trapezoid
    https://en.wikipedia.org/wiki/Parallelogram
[17] Engineering Notes – Home, by D. Rose: Coordinate, Interpolation & Quaternions
      http://danceswithcode.net/engineeringnotes/index.html
      http://danceswithcode.net/engineeringnotes/rotations_in_3d/rotations_in_3d_part2.html
[18] IEEE 754, Floating-point arithmetic, from Wikipedia, the free encyclopedia
    https://en.wikipedia.org/wiki/IEEE_754
    https://en.wikipedia.org/wiki/Floating-point_arithmetic#Addition_and_subtraction
[19] Logic Design, Digital Circuit Design, Register-Transfer Level (RTL) and Verilog
   Integrated Digital Circuit Design
    https://en.wikipedia.org/wiki/Integrated_circuit_design#Digital_design
   RTL Design and Verilog
    https://en.wikipedia.org/wiki/Register-transfer_level
    https://en.wikipedia.org/wiki/Verilog
   Logic and De Morgan Theorem
    https://www.sciencedirect.com/topics/computer-science/de-morgans-theorem

[20] Wikipedia: Coordinate System and Linear Algebra
    https://en.wikipedia.org/wiki/Coordinate_system
    https://en.wikipedia.org/wiki/Linear_algebra
[21] Wikipedia: Dot Product or Scalar Product (Result is a Scalar number)
    https://en.wikipedia.org/wiki/Dot_product
[22] Wikipedia: Cross Product or Vector Product (Result is a Perpendicular Vector)
    https://en.wikipedia.org/wiki/Cross_product
    https://en.wikipedia.org/wiki/Perpendicular
[23] Rotations in Three-Dimensions, Rotation Matrix
[24] Wikipedia: Rotation Matrix
    https://en.wikipedia.org/wiki/Rotation_matrix
[25] Wikipedia: Matrix Multiplication
    https://en.wikipedia.org/wiki/Matrix_multiplication_algorithm

References

[26] Wikipedia: Aircraft Principal axes Roll, Pitch and Yaw
https://en.wikipedia.org/wiki/Aircraft_principal_axes

[27] Wikipedia: Euler Angles and 'Roll, Pitch and Yaw'
https://en.wikipedia.org/wiki/Euler_angles#Tait%E2%80%93Bryan_angles

[28] Yaw, pitch, and roll rotations
https://hallaweb.jlab.org/experiment/g2p/survey/Yaw_Pitch_Roll_Rotations.pdf

[29] Swedish pop group ABBA,1974 to 1983
https://en.wikipedia.org/wiki/ABBA

[30] Coordinates, Texture Mapping and Occulting

[31] Wikipedia: Bari Centric Coordinates.
https://en.wikipedia.org/wiki/Barycentric_coordinate_system

[32] Wikipedia: Texture Mapping
https://en.wikipedia.org/wiki/Texture_mapping
Wikipedia: Texture Mipmap
https://en.wikipedia.org/wiki/Mipmap
Wikipedia: Texture Anisotropic Filtering
https://en.wikipedia.org/wiki/Anisotropic_filtering

[33] Occulting and Hidden Surface Removal
Wikipedia Hidden-Surface Determination
https://en.wikipedia.org/wiki/Hidden-surface_determination

[34] Warnock algorithm
Wikipedia: Hidden Surface Algorithm using Divide and Conquer
https://en.wikipedia.org/wiki/Warnock_algorithm

[35] Z-Buffer and Rasterization
https://en.wikipedia.org/wiki/Z-buffering

[36] A Characterization of Ten Hidden-Surface Algorithms
I. Sutherland, R. Sproull, R. Schumacker. Published 1974, ACM Computer Survey
https://dl.acm.org/doi/10.1145/356625.356626   or
https://web.archive.org/web/20160103063614/http://design.osu.edu/carlson/history/PDFs/ten-hidden-surface.pdf

[37] E. C. Catmull, 'A Hidden-Surface Algorithm with Anti-Aliasing',
Computer Graphics, Vol. 12, No.3, Aug. 1978, pp. 6-11. (From Siggraph '78 proceedings.)

[38] J. F. Blinn, 'Computer Display of Curved Surfaces',
Univ. of Utah PhD dissertation, Dec. 1978.

[40] TV Standards

[41] Standard-Definition Television
https://en.wikipedia.org/wiki/Standard-definition_television

[42] Graphics Displays
Graphics Display Resolution
https://en.wikipedia.org/wiki/Graphics_display_resolution
Refresh Rate
https://en.wikipedia.org/wiki/Refresh_rate
Interlaced Video
https://en.wikipedia.org/wiki/Interlaced_video

References

[43] Standard TV: STV
  ITU (International Telecommunication Union)
    https://en.wikipedia.org/wiki/International_Telecommunication_Union
  Comité Consultatif International pour la Radio, a forerunner of the ITU-R
    https://en.wikipedia.org/wiki/CCIR
  Recommendation BT.601 for TV digital encoding
    https://en.wikipedia.org/wiki/Rec._601
    https://www.itu.int/rec/R-REC-BT.601-6-200701-S/en
  Recommendation BT.656 for TV digital encoding
    https://en.wikipedia.org/wiki/ITU-R_BT.656
    https://www.itu.int/rec/R-REC-BT.656-5-200712-I/en
  Television ChannelFrequencies
    https://en.wikipedia.org/wiki/Television_channel_frequencies
[44] Video Compression and HDTV
  H.264, Advanced Video Coding (AVC):
    https://en.wikipedia.org/wiki/Advanced_Video_Coding
  H.265, High Efficiency Video Coding (HEVC):
    https://en.wikipedia.org/wiki/High_Efficiency_Video_Coding
  DCT Discrete Cosine Transform
    https://en.wikipedia.org/wiki/Discrete_cosine_transform
  Motion compensation:
    https://en.wikipedia.org/wiki/Motion_compensation
[45] Color Space and Color Conversion
  Color Space: https://en.wikipedia.org/wiki/Color_space
  Color Conversion: https://docs.opencv.org/4.5.0/de/d25/imgproc_color_conversions.html
  YCbCr: https://en.wikipedia.org/wiki/YCbCr
[46] sine and cosine function:
    https://en.wikipedia.org/wiki/Sine_and_cosine
[47] Wikipedia: Integrated Circuit (IC)
    https://en.wikipedia.org/wiki/Integrated_circuit
    https://en.wikipedia.org/wiki/Planar_process
    https://en.wikipedia.org/wiki/Jean_Hoerni
    https://en.wikipedia.org/wiki/Robert_Noyce
    https://en.wikipedia.org/wiki/Gordon_Moore
[50] Computer Generated Imagery (CGI)
[51] Wikipedia: Computer graphics 1950s, 60s, 70s, 80s, 90s, 2000s, 2010s
    https://en.wikipedia.org/wiki/Computer_graphics
[52] Wikipedia: Computer-generated imagery (CGI)
    https://en.wikipedia.org/wiki/Computer-generated_imagery
[53] David C. Evans and Ivan Sutherland (E&S)
    https://en.wikipedia.org/wiki/Evans_&_Sutherland
[54] Wikipedia: Real-time 3D computer graphics
    https://en.wikipedia.org/wiki/Real-time_computer_graphics

[55] TV and Graphics Display Resolution. Refresh Rate
Wikipedia: https://en.wikipedia.org/wiki/Standard-definition_television
Wikipedia: https://en.wikipedia.org/wiki/Broadcast_television_systems
Wikipedia: https://en.wikipedia.org/wiki/High-definition_television
Wikipedia: https://en.wikipedia.org/wiki/Graphics_display_resolution
Wikipedia: https://en.wikipedia.org/wiki/Refresh_rate (TV or CGI Refresh Rate)
Wikipedia: https://en.wikipedia.org/wiki/Interlaced_video

[60] Aliasing and Anti-Aliasing
Definition of Aliasing According to Mariam Webster Dictionary
https://www.merriam-webster.com/dictionary/aliasing

[61] Wikipedia: Aliasing, Jaggies, Moiré Pattern, Spatial Anti-Aliasing, Multi-Sample
Aliasing: https://en.wikipedia.org/wiki/Aliasing
Jaggies: https://en.wikipedia.org/wiki/Jaggies
Moiré Pattern: https://en.wikipedia.org/wiki/Moir%C3%A9_pattern
Spatial AA: https://en.wikipedia.org/wiki/Spatial_anti-aliasing
MSAA: https://en.wikipedia.org/wiki/Multisample_anti-aliasing
Solutions to 8 Queens Puzzle: https://en.wikipedia.org/wiki/Eight_queens_puzzle

[62] Wikipedia: Nyquist and sinc() function
Nyquist frequency: https://en.wikipedia.org/wiki/Nyquist_frequency
Nyquist Rate: https://en.wikipedia.org/wiki/Nyquist_rate
Nyquist–Shannon sampling theorem:
https://en.wikipedia.org/wiki/Nyquist%e2%80%93Shannon_sampling_theorem
Sampling Function sinc(): https://en.wikipedia.org/wiki/Sinc_function
Triangular, tent or Bartlett window: https://en.wikipedia.org/wiki/Triangular_function

[63] Wikipedia: Convolution Theorem and Fourier Window
Convolution Theorem: https://en.wikipedia.org/wiki/Convolution_theorem
Window Function: https://en.wikipedia.org/wiki/Window_function

[64] Subpixel Rendering and MSAA
https://www.gpumag.com/anti-aliasing/

[65] A Quick Overview of MSAA, Written by MJP, Oct 24 2012
https://mynameismjp.wordpress.com/2012/10/24/msaa-overview/

[66] Tutorial Multisampling Anti-Aliasing, A Closeup View (8 Pages)
May 22, 2003 / by aths / page 1 of 8 / translated by 3DCenter Translation Team
http://alt.3dcenter.org/artikel/multisampling_anti-aliasing/index_e.php

[67] Anti-Aliasing Analysis from Toms Hardware
Part 1: Settings and Surprises (8 pages), by Don Woligroski April 13, 2011
https://www.tomshardware.com/reviews/anti-aliasing-nvidia-geforce-amd-radeon,2868.html
https://www.tomshardware.com/author/don-woligroski
Part 2: Performance (19 Pages), by Don Woligroski, November 21, 2011
https://www.tomshardware.com/reviews/anti-aliasing-performance,3065.html

[68] Nvidia Presents Adaptive Temporal Anti-Aliasing Technology, by Zhiye Liu July 31, 2018
https://www.tomshardware.com/author/zhiye-liu
https://www.tomshardware.com/news/nvidia-adaptive-temporal-antialiasing,37534.html

References

[69] MSAA Example at flickr.com for 2x2, 3x3 and 4x4 Subpixel array:
   https://www.flickr.com/photos/dominicspics/3991177364/in/photostream/

[70] Computers Programming and 3D Graphics

[71] Assembly and High-Level Languages
   https://en.wikipedia.org/wiki/High-level_programming_language

[72] C-Programming Language
   https://en.wikipedia.org/wiki/C_%28programming_language%29

[73] Cray-1 Super Computer, 1976-77
   The first Cray-1 system was installed at Los Alamos National Laboratory in 1976
   https://en.wikipedia.org/wiki/Cray-1
   http://ed-thelen.org/comp-hist/CRAY-1-HardRefMan/CRAY-1-HRM.html
   https://www.cray.com/company/history

[74] Wikipedia: Apple II (1977) and IBM Personal Computer (1982)
   https://en.wikipedia.org/wiki/Apple_II
   https://en.wikipedia.org/wiki/IBM_Personal_Computer
   ARM processors:
   https://www.arm.com/products/silicon-ip-cpu

[75] Wikipedia: Microsoft Flight Simulator
   In 1982, Artwick's company licensed a version of *Flight Simulator* for the IBM PC to Microsoft,
   marketed as *Microsoft Flight Simulator 1.00*.
   https://en.wikipedia.org/wiki/Microsoft_Flight_Simulator

[76] Computer Graphics Interfaces: Wikipedia:
   Direct3D: https://en.wikipedia.org/wiki/Direct3D
   OpenGL: https://en.wikipedia.org/wiki/OpenGL

[77] Wikipedia; Video Cards
   https://en.wikipedia.org/wiki/Video_card
   Supported Hardware/Video Cards (OpenGL)
   https://reactos.org/wiki/Supported_Hardware/Video_cards

[78] Oak Technology Warp5, Wikipedia
   https://en.wikipedia.org/wiki/Oak_Technology
   http://fireeye.tripod.com/warp5.html
   http://fireeye.tripod.com/benchgr.html

[79] Counting Bits
   Hamming Weight:
     https://en.wikipedia.org/wiki/Hamming_weight
   Brian Kernighan's algorithm
     https://www.techiedelight.com/brian-kernighans-algorithm-count-set-bits-integer/
     https://graphics.stanford.edu/~seander/bithacks.html#CountBitsSetKernighan

[80] Flight Simulators and CGI

[81] Wikipedia: Flight Simulator
   https://en.wikipedia.org/wiki/Flight_simulator
   https://en.wikipedia.org/wiki/Flight_simulator#Vertical_Motion_Simulator_(VMS)_at_NASA/Ames

Wikipedia: Joystick
https://en.wikipedia.org/wiki/Joystick

[82] Report: 'Computer Generated Imagery (CGI) Current Technology',
US Army Material Development and Readiness Command, Orlando Florida, Sep 26 1980
https://apps.dtic.mil/dtic/tr/fulltext/u2/a091636.pdf

[83] Bruce J. Schachter
Publication: B. Schachter 'Computer Image Generation for Flight Simulation',
IEEE Computer Graphics and Applications (IEEE CG&A), October 1981.
Schachter 'Computer Image Generation', Book Hardcover
John Wiley and Sons; 1st Edition (January 1, 1983)
ISBN-10: 0471872873, ISBN-13: 978-0471872870

[84] Wikipedia: GPU
https://en.wikipedia.org/wiki/Graphics_processing_unit

[85] GPU Technology Conference 2014
GPU-Based Visualization for Flight Simulation,
Tim Woodard Director of Research and Development Diamond Visionics www.dvcsim.com
https://on-demand.gputechconf.com/gtc/2014/presentations/S4440-gpu-based-visualization-flight-simulations.pdf

[86] Evans & Sutherland (E&S) Wikipedia
https://en.wikipedia.org/wiki/Evans_%26_Sutherland
E&S History 2005:
https://www.youtube.com/watch?v=FHhYAUgY3S0
https://forum.beyond3d.com/threads/ct5-evans-sutherland-simulator-how-did-it-work.57664/
Utah inventions: The birth of computer graphics
https://www.ksl.com/article/36039333/utah-inventions-the-birth-of-computer-graphics

[87] E&S CT-5 Videos
CT-5 Flight Simulator, 1981
https://archive.org/details/CT5FlightSimulator
https://www.youtube.com/watch?v=6W-qb_jHRhA
Evans & Sutherland 'The Tactical Edge'
Part 1: https://www.youtube.com/watch?v=06mbwNg1Vw4
Part 2: https://www.youtube.com/watch?v=7e7_GiCc-HA

[88] E&S CT-5 CGI, 1981
a) Was Evans & Sutherland CT5 really created in 1981?
https://computergraphics.stackexchange.com/questions/5693/was-evans-sutherland-ct5-really-created-in-1981
b) CT5 Evans Sutherland Simulator - How did it work?
https://forum.beyond3d.com/threads/ct5-evans-sutherland-simulator-how-did-it-work.57664/#post-1914013

[89] GE CompuScene
The Simulator Revolution
https://www.airforcemag.com/article/1289simulator/

[90] Link Flight Simulators

[91] The Link trainer is a mechanical engineering historical landmark
http://web.mit.edu/digitalapollo/Documents/Chapter2/linktrainer.pdf
Wikipedia: Link Trainer
https://en.wikipedia.org/wiki/Link_Trainer

References

[92] Link Aviation History
   http://www.susandoreydesigns.com/genealogy/clirehugh/LinkAviationHistory.pdf
[93]   Life After Link
   http://lifeafterlink.org/index.shtml
   http://lifeafterlink.org/brochure.shtml
[94] Computers in Spaceflight: The NASA Experience (until 1975, before DIG-1):
  Making New Reality: Computers in Simulations and Image Processing:
    https://history.nasa.gov/computers/Ch9-1.html
  Crew-training simulators:
    https://history.nasa.gov/computers/Ch9-2.html
  NASA Contractor Report 182505, CONTRACT NASW-3714, March 1988.
   James E. Tomayko, Wichita State University, Wichita, Kansas)
      https://history.nasa.gov/computers/Compspace.html
  June 10, 2021, Space shuttle simulator returns to NASA to be restored for display
      https://history.nasa.gov/computers/contents.html
  Old SMS with Images from Camera Model and Mini Computers, before 1977
      https://www.facebook.com/pg/The.Shuttle.Mission.Simulator/posts/
[95] NASA *S*pace Shuttle Program, 1972–2011
  Wikipedia: Space Shuttle program
    https://en.wikipedia.org/wiki/Space_Shuttle_program
  Wikipedia: Space Shuttle retirement
    https://en.wikipedia.org/wiki/Space_Shuttle_retirement
  NASA's Space Shuttle Program Officially Ends After Final Celebration, 8/31/2011
    https://www.space.com/12804-nasa-space-shuttle-program-officially-ends.html
  Computers in Spaceflight: The NASA Experience
    https://history.nasa.gov/computers/Ch9-2.html
[96] NASA Houston, TX, SMS Visual systems from Link APO (1977):
  Selection and Training of Astronauts: 4 DIG-1 used in Shuttle Mission Simulator (SMS)
    https://science.ksc.nasa.gov/mirrors/msfc/crew/training.html
[97] NASA Ames Vertical Motion Simulator
   https://www.youtube.com/watch?v=0WaiAyU-3mU
   https://www.nasa.gov/simlabs/vms/technical-details
   DIG-1: Simulator Facility for Helicopter Air-to-Air Combat at NASA Ames
      https://apps.dtic.mil/sti/citations/ADA160693
      https://apps.dtic.mil/sti/pdfs/ADA160693.pdf
   NASA Ames Research Center (ARC):
      https://en.wikipedia.org/wiki/Ames_Research_Center
[98] Video Demo: Blue Box, The First Flight Simulator
   https://www.youtube.com/watch?v=PYTrjch_G64
[99] Link Flight Simulation Demo, Video
   DIG-2 Demo, 1984:
     https://www.youtube.com/watch?v=uy8sJ9AxvYI
[100] Patents Related to 3D Graphics and CGI Hardware

References

[101] Michel Rohner, all 6 Patents: 102 to 107
   https://patents.google.com/?inventor=Michel+Rohner

[102] High speed sorter
  US CA GB US4030077A Judit Katalin Florence, Michel Alexandre Rohner,
  The Singer Company
     https://patentimages.storage.googleapis.com/2b/61/eb/1fc2ba543dddb7/US4030077.pdf

[103] High speed sorter with concurrent access
  US CA GB US4031520A Michel Alexandre Rohner, The Singer Company
     https://patentimages.storage.googleapis.com/c4/a3/48/dbdecc345681b2/US4031520.pdf

[104] Clipping Polygon Faces through Polyhedron of Vision
  US US4208810A Michel A. Rohner, Judit Katalin Florence, The Singer Company
     https://patentimages.storage.googleapis.com/a0/f3/44/a90fdf19a95f4d/US4208810.pdf

[105] Resolvability Test and Projection Size Clipping of Polygon Face Display
  US US4291380A Michel Rohner, The Singer Company
     https://patentimages.storage.googleapis.com/05/4c/81/99f8b15eeb1883/US4291380.pdf

[106] Method and Apparatus for Generating Non-Homogenous Fog
  US US6064392A Michel A. Rohner, Oak Technology, Inc.
     https://patentimages.storage.googleapis.com/a8/3c/64/0e9ba707aeecd1/US6064392.pdf

[107] Method and apparatus for clamping image gradients
  US US6184887B1 Michel A. Rohner, Oak Technology, Inc.
     https://patentimages.storage.googleapis.com/fc/12/09/fa30d26af5f2ba/US6184887.pdf

[108] Patents from Robert W. Lotz, Link Flight Simulation
  Edge smoothing for real-time simulation of a polygon face object system as viewed by a moving observer
     https://patents.google.com/patent/US4208719A/en?inventor=Robert+W.+Lotz

[109] Video processor for real time operation without overload in a CGI system
     https://patents.google.com/patent/US4703439A/en?inventor=Robert+W.+Lotz

[110] Patents from Johnson K. Yan and Judit K. Florence, Link Flight Simulation
     https://patents.google.com/?inventor=Johnson+K.+Yan

[111] Modular digital image generator
  US US4570233A United States, Johnson K. Yan and Judit K. Florence
     https://patents.google.com/patent/US4570233A/en

[112] Method and apparatus for texture generation
  US US4615013A, Johnson K. Yan
     https://patents.google.com/patent/US4615013A/en?inventor=Johnson+K.+Yan

[113] Computer-generated image system to display translucent features with anti-aliasing
  US US4679040A, Johnson K. Yan
     https://patents.google.com/patent/US4679040A/en?inventor=Johnson+K.+Yan

[114] Method and apparatus for processing translucent objects
  US US4918625A, Johnson K. Yan
     https://patents.google.com/patent/US4918625A/en?inventor=Johnson+K.+Yan

[120] Other Patents from Rick Fadden at GE and ATI
     https://patents.google.com/?inventor=Richard+G+Fadden

References

[121] US4727365 Advanced Video Generator, General Electric Company, Syracuse, N.Y.
   https://patentimages.storage.googleapis.com/f9/a9/77/d6709f4495dbac/US4727365.pdf
[122] US4811245 Edge Smoothing
 Method of Edge Smoothing for a Computer Image Generation System
 William M. Bunker; Donald M. Merz; Richard G. Fadden, all of Ormond Beach, Fla.
 Assignee: General Electric Company, Syracuse, N.Y.
   https://patentimages.storage.googleapis.com/31/87/82/2c1dc6295665ef/US4811245.pdf
[123] US4905164 Modulating Color Texture, General Electric Company, Syracuse, N.Y.
   https://patentimages.storage.googleapis.com/ca/2c/35/44905db7758019/US4905164.pdf
[124] US4965745 YIQ Color Cell Texture General Electric Company, Syracuse, N.Y.
   https://patentimages.storage.googleapis.com/d2/df/35/1eb09fb7d6bfb9/US4965745.pdf
[125] US4974176 Micro Texture, General Electric Company, Syracuse, N.Y.
   https://patentimages.storage.googleapis.com/8e/79/0e/cac053ad4bbf38/US4974176.pdf
[126] US6002407 Cache Memory for Texture, Oak Technology, Inc., Sunnyvale, Calif.
   https://patentimages.storage.googleapis.com/98/76/08/873fe6f4564380/US6002407.pdf
[127] US6445392 Simplified Anti-Aliasing (Subpixel Generation), Ati International SRL
   https://patentimages.storage.googleapis.com/7b/1d/73/7b9778c52ca1d6/US6445392.pdf

[130] Clipping Patents from Evans and Sutherland:
[131] Wikipedia: Sutherland–Hodgman algorithm
 https://en.wikipedia.org/wiki/Sutherland%E2%80%93Hodgman_algorithm
[132] Reentrant polygon clipping
 I. Sutherland, G. W. Hodgman, Published 1974, Computer Science, Communication. ACM
 Patent: Computer graphics clipping system for polygons
   https://patents.google.com/patent/US3816726A/en?inventor=Sutherland+Hodgman
   https://patentimages.storage.googleapis.com/27/18/f3/578861e7cf22cf/US3816726.pdf
[133] US 3889107A System of polygon sorting by dissection, I. Sutherland
   https://patents.google.com/patent/US3889107A/en?inventor=Sutherland+Ivan&page=2
   https://patentimages.storage.googleapis.com/c0/5b/89/1050911af8995e/US3889107.pdf
[134] US3639736A Display windowing by clipping, I. Sutherland
   https://patents.google.com/patent/US3639736A/en?inventor=Sutherland+Ivan&page=3
   https://patentimages.storage.googleapis.com/fd/86/89/1881686afa716b/US3639736.pdf

About the Author

Michel Alexandre Rohner was born in Neuchatel, in the French part of Switzerland.

He graduated with a Matura in Math & Science from the Scientific Gymnasium in Neuchatel, Switzerland (in France, the equivalent of a Swiss Gymnasium is called a Lycée).

He earned his Diploma in EE at the ETH in Zurich, Switzerland

(Germ: Eidgenössische Technische Hochschule, Eng: Swiss Institute of Technology)

He earned his MSEE from Santa Clara University in CA.

He holds 6 important patents in the field of 3D computer graphics.

He is an ACM Member and IEEE Lifetime Member.

He is gifted at math, drawing and playing music instruments. He plays accordion, piano and electric bass. Before coming to the US, he played in a rock band, "The Sunshines", with his brothers and sister: *Jen-Jacques* (guitar), *Michel* (bass-guitar), *Anne-Lise* (keyboard) and *Mario* (drum). This band was popular in his home town of Neuchatel, Switzerland.

Michel worked many years at Link Flight Simulation, designing the fastest special purpose computers for 3D Real-Time Computer-Generated Imagery (RT CGI). He was a key designer and architect of the first Digital Image Generator (DIG) at Link flight Simulation. The DIG was a special purpose computer generating 3D scenes in real-time to be used in aircraft simulators. Four Link DIG systems were delivered to NASA Houston Space Center for the Space Shuttle Mission Simulator (SMS) [95][96]. At the time of delivery, the Link DIG had edge smoothing (anti-aliasing) and was the fastest RT CGI system in the world. It could produce out of the windows images made of 3400 projected triangles at a rate of 60 times per sec. With a price tag of more the $2M dollars, the DIG systems were not available to the general public. Michel continued working at Link, making significant improvements to the DIG, helping Link to win many simulator contracts.

First Job in the US

Soon after graduation from the ETH, Michel immigrated to the US and landed in the Bay Area in California. He was fortunate to get his first US job at the Advanced Product Operation (APO) of Link Flight Simulation in Sunnyvale, CA. Link had a long history designing simulator and trainers for the Army, Navy, Air Force and NASA [90].

As first assignment at Link APO, he designed a subsystem for the First Digital Radar Simulator in the DRLMS (Digital Radar Landmass Simulator) group at Link. This digital radar simulator was designed to train radar operators for the successful Air Force F4F Fighter and the E2C advanced warning plane (small AWAC). He designed the radar Equation Return Subsystem (ERS) of the DRLMS, that computed the signals returned from simulated radar electromagnetic pulses. This subsystem performed the many computations of the Radar Equation in log base 2 domain, using a rigid pipelined architecture.

About the Author

From Radar Simulator to Real-Time Computer-Generated Imagery

After completing the ERS design in the DRLMS system, Michel was fortunate again to be introduced to the team that was designing the first special purpose 3D RT CGI system from Link in Sunnyvale. The Link version of RT CGI systems was the 'Digital Image Generator' (DIG). The DIG was optimized for generating 3 or 4 Out The Window (OTW) 3D graphics scenes in real-time for training in aircraft flight simulators [90].

Michel designed several subsystems for the R&D DIG prototype. The R&D DIG prototype from Link had edge smoothing and a good image quality. It could produce images of around 500 triangles (1.5k triangle-edges) at the rate of 60 images per sec.

Designing the Fastest 3D RT CGI System

While waiting for the Space Shuttle contract award from NASA, he continued doing system testing and made significant improvements to the speed and image quality for the production DIG. He became familiar with all the subsystem implementations, and realized that by modifying some of the key subsystem processors, a speed improvement in the order of 5 to 10 times could be achieved, still using a single pipeline stream. He did the first speed improvement by optimizing the matrix and vector computations. After rotating the triangle vertices, the DIG has to perform Clipping to remove the portion of triangles that are outside of the field of view (FOV). While working on Clipping improvements, he invented and patented a faster Clipping algorithm [104]. After the Clipping operation, the triangles vertices are projected onto the image plane. For the projection, he implemented the divisions using log base 2 tables, so that each division could be executed in one cycle.

With these design improvements, Michel was awarded 6 important patents in the field of 3D RT CGI [100] to [107]. He became one of the lead engineers for the production DIGs from Link that could generate 4000 triangles (12000 edges) at the rate of 60 images per sec.

In the late 1970s, four Link DIG-1 systems were delivered to NASA Houston Space Center for the Space Shuttle Mission Simulator (SMS). At that time, there were only two other companies producing RT CGI systems at a cost above $1M, with a capability of generating 60 images per second, with around 1000 edges per image.

- Evans and Sutherland (E&S) in Salt Lake City, Utah
- General Electric Ground System Division (GE GSD) in Daytona Beach, Florida

At the same time, two other computers were announced:

- The Cray-1 super-computer [73] was announced and became the favorite platform for 3D graphics development, at a cost of $8M. It was used for general purpose non-RT CGI applications and algorithm development,
- The Apple II became available to the general public and could be used for playing simple 2D games, at a cost of less than $2k [74].

About the Author

NASA Requirement for Virtual Reality Virtual Reality Visual System

Back in 1968, NASA requested proposals for a Virtual Reality visual system to be used in the Shuttle Mission Simulators (SMS). Singer Link (later known as Link Flight Simulation) in Binghamton, NY, was the only company that responded.

Link Digital Image Generators Delivered to NASA for the SMS

There were two generations of visual systems from Singer Link that were delivered to NASA for the Shuttle Mission Simulators in Houston Space Center.

First, in the early 1970s, Singer Link in Binghamton delivered a computer system made of parallel mini computers (around 20) for the SMS visual system.

At the same time, Singer Link Advanced Product Operation (APO) in Sunnyvale, CA, began developing its Digital Image Generator (DIG) in R&D. The DIG was a special purpose digital computer, consisting of a single pipeline of optimized and dedicated subsystems. Each DIG could drive 3 or 4 display windows. Singer Link APO demonstrated the R&D DIG to NASA on time and was awarded the production contract for 4 DIGs. In 1977, the first production DIG-1 was delivered on schedule to NASA for the SMS in Houston Space Center, TX [96].

With the improved speed and image quality and edge smoothing, the DIG-1 was the best solution for the SMS program. No other system was available to prepare the Space Shuttle astronauts just in time for their first scheduled flights with Columbia on April 12, 1981. The four DIG-1s have been used to train all the Space Shuttle astronauts in Shuttle Mission Simulators (SMS), before they flew the actual Space Shuttles Missions into Space. There is a good description of the SMS DIG-1 in Reference [96].

At the time of delivery, the Link DIG was the fastest RT CGI system in the world. It could produce out of the windows images made of 4000 projected triangles (12,000 edges) at a rate of 60 images per sec (field rate). Overnight the standard for RT CGI performance moved from 1.5k triangle edges per image to 12k triangle edges.

After demonstrating the 10k edges/field capability to the military, Link got orders for 10 DIG-1 for the F-111 fighter simulators and one DIG-1 for the UH-60 Blackhawk helicopter simulator. The DIG was upgraded to DIG-2 in response to the Air-Force requirement of ¼ Subpixel resolution requirement. Also, the number of intersections per Scanline was increased from 256 to 512. The DIG-2 was used in the B-52 bomber simulator (12 simulators) and in 4 types of helicopter simulators (40 simulators), including the AH-64 Apache, UH-60 Blackhawk, AH-1 Cobra and CH-47 Chinook helicopters. Refer to the image on book back cover. With a price tag of more the $2M dollars, the DIG systems were not available to the general public. Within a period of 12 years, Link sold around 70 flight simulators, each with 3 or 4 window displays driven by DIG systems.

Michel worked many years at Link, making continuous improvement to the DIGs. He achieved the highest technical level of Senior Staff Scientist.

The Link DIG was the brainchild of *Judit Florence*. But, because of his many contributions to the DIG family, Michel was nicknamed '*the Swiss-Wiz*' (*wizard*) by the test engineers at Link.

About the Author

Designing 3D RT CGI Systems with Anti-Aliasing after Link

After leaving Link, Michel became a key contributor for the designs of two 3D graphics chips for the PC market and a line of Quad TV encoders and decoders chips.

He wanted to apply his knowledge of 3D RT CGI system to design the first PC graphics adapter for the PC Market. He got the opportunity while working in the 3D Graphics department at Oak Technology, in Sunnyvale. He was a key architect of the Warp5, the first PC graphics adapter with Non-Homogeneous Fog and Anti-Aliasing.

He also worked for few companies that were producing 3D graphics chips for the PC market. As a logic designer and system architect, he also spent several years doing real time logic designs [19] in FPGA and ASIC for TV circuits at MetaVideo, in Los Gatos, CA.

Currently, Michel has been working as a consultant for FPGA/ASIC/SOC design, verification and programming in C/C++, System Verilog and UVM.

Writing Books

Using its intensive experience with logic design [19] in 3D RT CGI and TV, Michel decided to write books to share his inventive designs and his novel approach to fixed point math.

In his first book, 'New Fixed-Point Math for Logic Design' [6], he introduces a new math approach for CGI computations. This approach solves several problems caused by 'rounding' results when implementing Fixed-Point Math in CGI applications. It uses 'averaging' instead of 'rounding' and was key in developing the ABAA solution for anti-aliasing.

In this new book, Michel has introduced a novel approach to AA, the Subpixel Area-Based Anti-Aliasing (ABAA). Because of his involvement in designing the fastest RT CGI systems and many years of experience dealing with AA, he has developed the ultimate approach to AA. Instead of sampling N fixed Subpixel points inside of a Pixel, ABAA accurately computes the Pixel area that is partially covered by polygons. This area is then allocated to N Subpixel areas. This approach and its implementation might appear simple. But it is the result of many years refinements using a deep understanding on how 3D RT CGI systems are implemented.

There are many advantages of ABAA.
• Better Image Quality, with less Subpixel samples when compared to MSAA.
• Proposed implementations can be scaled to 4 and 8 Subpixels, and even 16 and 32 subpixels.
• Simpler implementation and lower system cost.

Michel expects that this new approach will be widely accepted and result in improved quality and lower cost for future 3D graphics adapters and 3D RT CGI systems.

Michel's Son is a Popular Artist

Like his father, *Michael A. Rohner Jr* has a similar tendency for extreme attention to details. On the other hand, Michael Jr was not in particular fond of music and math, but was extremely gifted for drawing. So, instead of becoming an engineer like his father, he decided to become an artist. He has selected a challenging profession. It is difficult to be an independent producer of art and make a living of it. Luckily, he is popular in art shows in the Bay Area, New Mexico and Texas.

He has won several 'Best of Show' prizes. His attention to details is reflected in his drawings. He will spend hours adding details to his drawings until he is satisfied. Several of his creations are available and can be seen at his web site, *rohnerart.com* [9].

www.ingramcontent.com/pod-product-compliance
Lightning Source LLC
LaVergne TN
LVHW081450060526
838201LV00050BA/1756